Care or control?
Foster care for young
people on remand

Care or control?
Foster care for young people on remand

Jo Lipscombe

Published by British Association
for Adoption and Fostering
(BAAF)
Saffron House
3rd Floor, 6–10 Kirby Street
London EC1N 8TS
www.baaf.org.uk

Charity registration 275689

British Library Cataloguing in Publication Data
A catalogue record for this book is available
from the British Library

ISBN 1 905664 06 0

Editorial project management by Miranda Davies
Cover photos posed by models: main image,
Andrew Haig; further images by iD-Photography
Designed by Andrew Haig & Associates
Typeset by Avon DataSet, Bidford on Avon
Printed in Great Britain by Creative Print and
Design Ltd

BAAF is the leading UK-wide membership
organisation for all those concerned with
adoption, fostering and child care issues.

Acknowledgements

I am indebted to many people for making this research possible. First and foremost, my thanks go to the 18 young people who shared the stories of their lives with me, and to the eight remand foster carers who gave their time to talk about their experiences of caring for these and many other young people. My thanks also to the 13 women and men who discussed their role as youth court magistrates, and to the staff of the remand foster care scheme whose support was crucial to the success of this book. I am grateful for the co-operation and assistance of staff in a number of Young Offender Institutions and Youth Offending Teams, without which this research could not have been undertaken.

I would also like to thank the Home Office Research, Development and Statistics Directorate for their financial assistance with this research, and staff and students within the School for Policy Studies, University of Bristol, for their support and encouragement.

Finally, my thanks go to my family and to Clive for always being there.

About the author

Jo Lipscombe is an independent criminal justice consultant, with particular expertise with children and young people and youth justice. She is an honorary Research Fellow at the School for Policy Studies, University of Bristol, where she also completed her PhD. Previously, she was a Senior Consultant with a national crime reduction charity, and a Research Associate at the University of Bristol. She is co-author of *Fostering Adolescents*, with Elaine Farmer and Sue Moyers (2004).

Contents

Foreword
Andrew Rutherford

Preface

1   Introduction   **1**
Custodial remands   2
Remands to secure and non-secure accommodation   6
Community alternatives to custodial and residential remands   8
The extension of the boundaries of foster care   9
Remand foster care – an anomalous concept?   10
The research context   11

2   The theoretical and political background   **13**
The reductionist agenda   13
Public and political attitudes towards young offenders   16
The developmental approach   18

3   Remanding young people   **23**
Introduction   23
The history of custodial remands   24
Remanding children and young people   25
The court's decision   27
Summary   29

**4   Community alternatives: bail support and remand
foster care**   **30**
Introduction   30
Bail support   31
The history of remand foster care   33
Summary   42

5   **Research aims and methodology**   **43**
Introduction   43
Knowledge base and theoretical perspective   43
Research aims and objectives   45
Methodology   46
Case-file analysis   47
Interviews with young people   48
Interviews with foster carers   56
Interviews with magistrates   57
Payment   59
Discussions with other professionals   59
Analysis   59
Parameters of the research study   60
Summary   61

6   **Characteristics of the young people on remand**   **62**
Introduction   62
The 101 young people referred to the scheme   62
Who was and who was not placed with the scheme?   64
Factors influencing the decision to place a young person with
the scheme   67
The 13 young people not offered a placement by the scheme   71
The 46 young people accommodated by the scheme   73
The placements   75
The "success" of the placements   77
The wider benefits of remand foster care   79
Factors affecting breakdown   82
The interview participants   84
Summary   85

7   **Interviews with magistrates**   **86**
Introduction   86
The magistrates   87
Importance of the remand decision   87
Training, guidance and feedback   88
Remand provision   90
Remand decisions – criteria   99
Remand decisions – process   103
Other influential factors   106
Impact on sentencing   107
Summary   109

8 Young people's backgrounds and childhood experiences **111**

Introduction 111
Childhood experiences 111
Offending behaviour and experience of the justice system 123
Summary 130

9 Young people's experiences of remand foster care (Part 1) **131**

Introduction 131
Experiences of remand foster care 132
Impact of the placement on the young people and their offending behaviour 143
Summary 155

10 Young people's experiences of remand foster care (Part 2) **156**

Introduction 156
Comparisons with local authority accommodation and custody 156
Comparisons with being remanded on bail at home 159
Involvement with other professionals during the placement 160
The end of the placement 164
After the placement 170
Overview of the placements 172
Summary 173

11 Foster carers' experiences of providing care for young people on remand **174**

Introduction 174
Profile of the foster carers 174
Becoming a remand foster carer 175
Parenting styles and carer strategies 179
Girls 195
Additional needs and vulnerability 197
Management of family relationships 198
Inter-agency working 200
Support 201
Ending placements 204
Summary 207

12 Research summary, conclusions and policy implications **209**

Introduction 209

Research summary 209

References **232**

Index **253**

Foreword

In this significant and timely study, Jo Lipscombe explores the contribution of remand fostering schemes for rational and humane youth justice practice. Drawing on an extensive survey of the literature as well as her own fieldwork within a remand fostering scheme in the south of England, she concludes that the recent resurgence of such schemes may well take hold. In other words, an idea that first surfaced in this country during the reductionist 1980s might now, some two decades or so later, find a fuller and more focused expression.

Jo Lipscombe's exploration is grounded in extracts from interviews with magistrates, foster carers and the youngsters themselves. These accounts reinforce her starting point that remand is located at a crucial juncture within the criminal justice process. They also provide a graphic reminder of how complex and challenging such work is for everyone involved. For foster carers, there is the inherent tension between nurturing and regulatory roles. For the youngsters, there are profound difficulties of adaptation and loss when placement comes to an end. However, that the easier institutional option should, wherever possible, be avoided is explicitly accepted by the author and she charts a way forward for remand fostering that may avoid some of the previously encountered pitfalls. In particular, the national structure of Youth Offending Teams now provides the potential basis for support, training and development

The implications of this study reach beyond remand fostering to encompass the emerging range of settings and programmes that provide viable alternatives to penal institutions and children's homes. By definition, remand fostering is of relatively short-term duration but, as Jo Lipscombe emphasises, ways have to be found of bridging the discontinuities imposed by the criminal justice decision-making process. This scholarly exposition not only highlights the daunting nature of working with young people on remand but it also points to connections with youth justice as a whole, and with the wider context of nurturing and regulation.

Andrew Rutherford
The Law School, University of Southampton
August 2006

Preface

Children and young people who have been charged with an offence and are awaiting trial, and those who have been convicted of an offence but are awaiting sentence, will spend a period of time on remand, either being remanded on bail, to local authority accommodation, or to secure or custodial institutions. This book explores the use of foster care for young people on remand, as an alternative to custodial and residential accommodation. The research is situated within a penal reductionist framework that challenges the incarceration and confinement of children.

Offending by children is a politically contentious issue that attracts considerable public concern and controversy. The book reflects upon negative public and political attitudes towards young people and the impact of these beliefs on criminal justice policy. It documents the development of remand legislation for young people, highlighting the erosion of the rights of young defendants, at a time when responses to both adult and youth offending are moving away from a rehabilitative ideal towards populist punitivism.

The empirical research on which this book is based is an interpretation of 18 young people's narratives about their backgrounds and experiences of the criminal justice system, in particular their experience of remand foster care. These narratives are supplemented by the perspectives of eight foster carers who provide placements for young people on remand, and interviews with 13 lay youth court magistrates. The research considers the processes by which young people become involved in offending behaviour, how this behaviour can be exacerbated by involvement with the penal system, and how community interventions, such as remand foster care, can have a positive impact on a young person's conduct, self-esteem and sense of identity.

The findings of the research have implications for politicians, policy-makers and professionals working with young people in both the criminal justice system and the care system.

1 Introduction

Written in a political and public climate more sympathetic to the needs of children, the Criminal Justice Act 1991 acknowledged the need to abolish the remands of young people, aged 17 or under, to prison service custody in England and Wales. However, the Act was in itself contradictory, and has been superseded by more punitive legislation that has prolonged and indeed widened the use of custodial remands for children and young people. For example, the Criminal Justice Act 1991 made provision for court-ordered secure remands, giving magistrates the power to order a remand directly to secure accommodation, and the Criminal Justice and Public Order Act 1994 extended the applicability of court-ordered secure remands to include 12- to 14-year-olds and girls. The Criminal Justice and Police Act 2001 effectively lowered the threshold at which children and young people can be remanded to custody by allowing courts to order a secure or custodial remand or a remand for a young person where the defendant has a recent history of offending on bail or remand, or where the court is satisfied that only a secure remand is adequate to prevent the commission of further offences by the alleged offender.

The fall in the number of children being remanded to custody witnessed during the 1980s has therefore been halted and indeed reversed, with the number of children being remanded to custody having risen by more than 60 per cent, from 1,098 in 1992 to 1,772 in 2002 (NACRO, 2004). Youth Justice Board (YJB) figures (2002) indicate that the number of children remanded to secure facilities each month in England and Wales increased by over 25 per cent, from 452 in April 2001 to 567 in April 2002. Although the YJB introduced a target to reduce the use of secure remands to no more than 30 per cent of all bail remand decisions by 2004 (Audit Commission, 2004), this is contradicted by the implementation of section 130 of the Criminal Justice and Police Act 2001, which further relaxes the criteria for a secure remand, as outlined above (Goldson, 2002a; NACRO, 2002a).

Custodial remands

There is a clear need for alternatives to custodial remands for young people, particularly in light of the continued expansion of the use of incarceration, with the concomitant problems of overcrowding, unacceptable levels of suicide and self-harm, bullying and the inadequate provision of appropriate activities for prisoners (Hollis and Cross, 2003). Prison regimes are widely acknowledged as being ineffective in preventing re-offending, as being stigmatising and as causing harm to the individual (see, for example, Her Majesty's Inspectorate of Prisons [HMIP] 1997, 2000a,b,c; Crowley, 1998; Howard League, 1998, 1999a, 2001a,b,c; Goldson and Peters, 2000; Moore, 2000; Neustatter, 2002). Regimes and conditions in remand centres and remand wings of Young Offender Institutions (YOI) are often the worst within the prison system and the effects of incarceration are therefore even more detrimental for those on remand than for sentenced prisoners (Howard League, 1995a, 1997a; Goldson, 2002a; HMIP, 2002a).

Many young people on remand have experienced numerous difficulties and disadvantages in their lives (Audit Commission, 1996; Farrington, 1996; Goldson, 1998), the effects of which may be exacerbated whilst they are incarcerated. The inherent emphasis on security and control, combined with overcrowding and limited resources, means that few prisoners can engage in meaningful activity; many young remand prisoners spend over 20 hours per day locked in their cells (Howard League, 1995b, 1997a; HMIP, 2002b). Educational provision for young remand prisoners is sporadic due to limited resources and the relatively short-term nature of most remand placements (HMIP, 2000b), and the obligation to provide at least 15 hours education each week or for those aged under 17 is not always met (Penal Affairs Consortium, 2000). Furthermore, the national curriculum does not operate within prison service establishments, and the range of subjects that would be available at school may not be provided (Howard League, 1997a, 2001c). Young people also have limited opportunities to participate in physical exercise, particularly outdoor activities, which is in breach of their rights and arguably contributes to increased conflict between young people (Lord Carlile, 2006). Bullying, including verbal abuse, physical and sexual assaults, has long been recognised as a major problem within prisons and YOIs (Howard League, 1995b), perhaps in part due to the high levels of boredom and frustration resulting from restricted regimes and activities. Self-harm is pervasive in many YOIs and young remand prisoners are disproportionately involved in self-harm and suicide. The rate of suicides in prison custody is much higher than in the community (HMIP, 1999): between 1994 and 2005, at least 61 young people under the age of 21 have committed suicide whilst they were on remand in prison service custody, with another child committing suicide in a Secure Training Centre in 2004 (Inquest, 2006).

A large number of young people on remand have mental health problems that can make adjusting to prison life particularly difficult and which may be intensified by being remanded to prison (Moore and Peters, 2003). Her Majesty's Inspectorate of Prisons (1997) noted that over 50 per cent of young people on remand had a diagnosable mental disorder, and a study of the mental health and welfare needs of young male remand prisoners found that 57 per cent had problems with depression (Caddle and White, 1994). However, mental health difficulties are not always recognised when a young person is admitted to custody, and there is a grave shortage of mental health expertise and provision within criminal justice institutions (Farrant, 2001; Kearney, 2001; Kurtz *et al*, 1998), so young people's needs are often not met.

Some young people's problems whilst remanded to prison may be compounded by drug misuse, either through an existing drug habit or through taking drugs for the first time whilst in prison. There is often little help with "de-toxing" and only patchy availability of drug-related counselling for young people who do have a drug addiction when they enter prison service custody (Howard League, 1997a). Furthermore, prison service staff often have no background in child care or child welfare and their priorities are inevitably focused on containment and institutional security rather than on how to deal with the complex needs of vulnerable, damaged and troubled young people who may be also suffering mental illness or be withdrawing from drug use (Howard League, 2001b; Goldson and Peters, 2000; Paton, 2003).

Incarcerating children and young people damages family relationships and community ties, which can make re-integration into society much more difficult. Young people interviewed about their experiences of custody described incarceration as 'a dislocating experience' that was unconnected to their lives outside prison (Lyon *et al*, 2000, p. xi; see also Howard League, 1998). Maintaining links with the community is important to support the young person whilst they are on remand, and also to help them adjust to a non-offending lifestyle after they have been released, yet it can be difficult for young people to remain in contact with their family and friends whilst they are on remand in custody. Her Majesty's Inspectorate of Prisons (1997) reported that increasingly young people were being held over 150 miles from their home, which can make it very hard for family members and friends (as well as Youth Offending Team [YOT] staff) to visit regularly; in July 2004 more than a third of imprisoned children were held over 50 miles away from their home (Prison Reform Trust, 2005). Furthermore, a quarter of the young people on remand in prison service accommodation are parents themselves and are therefore separated from their own children, which is detrimental for both the young person and their child (HMIP, 2000b; Lyon *et al*, 2000).

The above examples clearly show that being incarcerated whilst on remand can be detrimental to the well-being of the young person, and that the practice is in stark contrast to the principles of both the Children Act 1989 and the United Nations Convention on the Rights of the Child (UNCRC) 1989 (see Lipscombe, 2003 for a full discussion of these breaches). Furthermore, it has long been recognised that, for the majority of young people, custodial remands are unnecessary. There are a significant number of young people remanded to custody, either prison or local authority secure accommodation, who do not need to be held in conditions of security. For instance, interviews with the managers of a number of secure units revealed that 60 of the 193 children surveyed could have been safely placed in open accommodation had the necessary alternative provision been available (Hodgkin, 1995).

Furthermore, in 1999, nearly three-quarters of the children held in prison on remand had been accused of non-violent offences (that is, offences which did not involve violence, sex, robbery or drug-trafficking). This suggests that 3,818 children were held in custody when they could have been held in open accommodation without presenting a risk of serious harm to the public (Table 1.1). Furthermore, statistics have consistently shown that less than half of the young people remanded to custody are subsequently given a custodial sentence (Howard League, 1995a, 1997a; NACRO, 1996a; Youth Justice Board, 2002; Prison Reform Trust, 2005), which suggests that the seriousness of the offence does not warrant custody.

Table 1.1
Receptions into prison on remand of young people aged 15–17, 1999

	Offence	*Number of young people*	*Percentage of remands*
	Violence against the person	570	11%
Violent offences	Sexual offences	113	2%
	Robbery	650	12%
	Drug offences	126	2%
Total violent offences		**1,459**	**27%**
	Burglary	1,240	23%
Non-violent offences	Theft and handling	1,539	29%
	Fraud and forgery	26	<1%
	Other	1,013	19%
Total non-violent offences		**3,818**	**72%**
	Not recorded	37	<1%
Total offences		**5,314**	**100%**

Figures taken from Home Office, 2000; see also Goldson and Peters, 2002.

Indeed, the National Remand Review Initiative found that the majority of refusals to grant bail were not related to the seriousness of the offence but were due to the perceived risk of the young person offending whilst on bail, or their failure to surrender to court (Moore, 1999; Goldson and Peters, 2002). Both of these issues potentially are addressed through appropriate interventions within community settings. If alternative community-based facilities were made available, the number of young people who are remanded to inappropriate and unacceptable custodial institutions could be dramatically reduced. Removing children inappropriately placed in secure accommodation also creates space within secure units for those children who truly need to be held in conditions of security but who may be prohibited from doing so due to the limited availability of provision (Goldson, 2002a).

Remands to secure and non-secure accommodation

Although there are some differences, secure and non-secure residential accommodation have similar implications for children and young people on remand and so will be discussed concurrently. Young people remanded to secure or non-secure accommodation are likely to be subjected to a number of the negative consequences inherent in prison service custody, albeit to a lesser degree. For example, bullying is prevalent within both secure and non-secure units (Sinclair and Gibbs, 1998; Renold and Barter, 2003), and young people who have been charged with sex-related offences remain particularly vulnerable to bullying and physical attacks. The problems of labelling and stigmatisation exist for young people held in local authority accommodation as they do for young people in custody, and there are similar difficulties in re-integration back into the community. Moreover, there are a number of adverse effects that are specific to secure and non-secure residential accommodation, for example, the heterogeneity of the resident population, which creates an ambiguity of purpose. Local authority residential units are typically occupied by young people who are "looked after" by the local authority under welfare proceedings as well as "section 90 and 91 offenders" and young people on remand. The role of local authority accommodation, including secure accommodation, is therefore ambiguous as it aims to adhere to the conflicting philosophies of welfare and juvenile justice (Harris and Timms, 1993; O'Neill, 2001; Goldson, 2002a).

Differential association and theories of learned behaviour (Sutherland and Cressey, 1960) also suggest that mixing non-offenders with young people on remand and convicted offenders within residential institutions can lead to problems of "contamination", with non-offenders acquiring criminal attitudes and taking part in offending behaviour (see also Hucklesby and Goodwin, 2002). Sinclair and Gibbs (1998) found that 40 per cent of the young people admitted to residential care without any previous cautions or convictions were cautioned or convicted whilst in the unit, and 75 per cent of those with a previous conviction were either cautioned or re-convicted. Although not all, many of these young people said that they had been encouraged to join in delinquent behaviour by others in the unit. Young people in open units might also relieve tension by running away, which occurs frequently (Wade *et al*, 1998) and there is a strong link between absconding and offending whilst absent from the unit. Brown (1998) found that offending on remand was higher for young people remanded to local authority residential accommodation than for young people remanded on bail. Fifty-eight per cent of the young people remanded to local authority accommodation offended whilst on remand compared with 35 per cent of those granted bail.

Whilst better than provision within most YOIs, the educational facilities for young people in both secure and non-secure residential accommodation are still inadequate compared with mainstream education (Jackson and Martin, 1998; O'Neill, 2001). Many young people in residential care are excluded or are frequently involved in truancy and, in some units, there is little structure to their day, resulting in boredom and lethargy (Berridge and Brodie, 1996). The marginalisation of girls within the prison system is echoed in secure and non-secure residential accommodation. Government policy promotes mixed-gender units, arguing that they provide a more "normal" and beneficial living experience for young people, but girls are disadvantaged particularly as they are in the minority (Gabbidon, 1994; Hodgkin, 1995; O'Neill, 2001).

Again, there is a lack of mental health expertise amongst staff employed in secure and non-secure units (Farmer and Pollock, 1998; Sinclair and Gibbs, 1998) yet self-harm is widespread within residential accommodation as it is in prisons, particularly amongst young women, some of whom may be in secure conditions precisely because they were self-harming (Howard League, 1995b).

Residential care, however, is more child-centred and less detrimental than prison service custody and is an important facility for the youth justice system, if used appropriately. It is important to acknowledge that the complete abolition of all residential care is not being advocated. There have been improvements in the way residential units are run (Triseliotis *et al*, 1995a), and there are a number of children for whom residential care is a suitable, and indeed preferable, response. Residential care should be utilised instead of prison service custody so that no young people, especially those on remand, are subjected to the negative effects of prison. To enable the transfer of young people on remand in prison custody to residential accommodation, sufficient space needs to be created within residential units to receive them, which could be achieved by developing community alternatives such as bail support and remand foster care. As already stated, it is possible that many young people currently remanded to local authority accommodation and prison service establishments could safely be granted bail or remanded to foster care if sufficient provision was made available.

Community alternatives to custodial and residential remands

Bail support schemes have achieved considerable success in maintaining children within the community whilst they are remanded (Allen and Maynard, 1999; NACRO Cymru, 2002; Youth Justice Board, 2005), but there is a group of children and young people who, for a variety of reasons, cannot return home. These children include those who have no home, those whose alleged offence is deemed too serious to allow a return home, those who live near to, or with, the alleged victim, those whose parents refuse to accept them back into the home and those whose return home is inadvisable for the protection of their welfare. The development of a range of effective alternatives is required to meet the needs and rights of these children. One such option is the provision of remand foster care placements, which is in direct accordance with the UNCRC. Article 40(4) states that:

> *A variety of dispositions, such as care, guidance and supervision orders; counselling; probation; foster care; education and vocational training programmes and other alternatives to institutional care shall be available to ensure that children are dealt with in a manner appropriate to their well-being and proportionate to both their circumstances and the offence.* (Article 40(4), UNCRC 1989)

A number of recent publications have included reference to the need for more remand foster placements to be made available by local authorities (for example, NACRO, 1999a; Moore, 1999, 2000; Home Office, 2002a, 2003) and the use of foster placements for children on remand is becoming an essential part of YOTs' remand management strategies.

However, with the exception of the evaluations of the National Remand Review Initiative (The Children's Society, 2000a, 2000b; Goldson and Peters, 2002; Moore and Peters, 2003) and a review of pre-trial accommodation for young people (Hucklesby and Goodwin, 2002), there has been a dearth of research on the specific circumstances of juvenile remands and the alternatives that may be available to courts, including remand foster care. It is therefore not yet known how appropriate or effective it is to utilise foster care placements for children and young people on remand.

The extension of the boundaries of foster care

Since the 1970s, the use of foster care has been extended to new populations of children who were previously thought to be too difficult to be placed with families. Research evidence has demonstrated that, given sufficient support, remuneration and recognition, fosters carers can be recruited and retained to look after children with more than average difficulties, enabling children who would typically have been placed in institutions to be looked after within the community (Triseliotis et al, 1995a, b; Walker et al, 2002). The implementation of the Children Act 1989 raised the threshold for the compulsory care of children, so that those who enter by this route present a greater concentration of serious problems than formerly (Farmer et al, 2004), and many of those in foster care today would in the past have been placed in residential care. The children now placed in foster care include those with physical disabilities and/or mental health difficulties, those with more complex psychological and social needs, and those involved in offending or anti-social behaviour.

However, whilst research on mainstream and specialist foster care for adolescents outwith the criminal justice system has highlighted the ability of foster care to address a wide range of adolescent needs (Shaw and Hipgrave, 1983; Berridge and Cleaver, 1987; Triseliotis, 1989; Reddy and Pfeiffer, 1997; Farmer et al, 2004), recent research on remand foster care is minimal. Although the implications are largely still relevant, the pioneering work of Nancy Hazel (1978, 1980, 1981a,b; see Chapter 4) is becoming outdated due to the rapid changes in criminal justice policy and the growing emphasis on confinement. Walker and colleagues (2002) documented the development of a Community Alternative Placement Scheme (CAPS) in Scotland that aimed to provide foster care for young people as an alternative to secure accommodation. However, whilst many of the young people included in their evaluation had criminal records, offending behaviour was not identified as a key issue for the foster placements and ultimately these placements were seen as a welfare resource rather than a criminal justice resource.

The studies that have been conducted on remand foster care have generally been reviews conducted by the remand schemes themselves, rather than independent evaluations. These reviews have identified some difficulties with remand foster placements, for example, young people finding it hard to readjust when they return home or to settle if they are moved to a long-term foster placement after sentencing (Fry, 1994). Remand foster care is more cost-effective than secure or custodial provision (Fry, 1994; Walker *et al*, 2002) but there is a need to determine whether or not it meets its objectives. For example, remand foster care needs to provide a safe environment for young people on remand, to ensure their appearance at court hearings, to prevent them from absconding and to reduce the incidence of offending on remand, thereby protecting the public. The immediate and long-term implications for young people on remand in foster care, in terms of education or employment, housing, family relationships and the sentence they receive, need to be evaluated as well as the impact on rates of offending whilst on remand, and the effect of foster care on ensuring appearance at court. The findings could then be used to improve foster care services for young people on remand, and to increase the level of confidence the courts and the public have in remand foster care.

Remand foster care – an anomalous concept?

Remand foster care is potentially an anomalous concept: foster care is traditionally seen as a welfare-based model of caring for children, yet remands are part of a controlling criminal justice system. Its position on the care-control continuum is far from clear, either in policy or in practice, as the task of fostering children and young people on remand is complex: remand foster carers have to bridge the divide between providing the care of the welfare system and the control of the criminal justice system. At the most basic level, to meet the requirements of the criminal justice system, remand placements need to provide a safe environment for an alleged offender whilst they await trial or sentencing. During this time, the alleged offender should not be involved in offending or anti-social behaviour or absconding, and should attend court at the requisite times. The particular characteristics of the remand placement are determined more to suit the demands of the criminal justice process than to meet the needs of the defendant. For instance, the end of the remand period is dictated by the court process rather than because the needs of the individual have been met. Conversely, the welfare considerations of short-term foster care place more emphasis on finding an appropriate placement for the individual, within timescales that facilitate the development of positive relationships and enable positive behavioural change. Placement endings are based on the needs and wishes of the carers and the fostered individual, rather than artificially imposed legislative deadlines.

The study on which this book is based aimed to assess the effectiveness and appropriateness of foster care as a form of provision for children and young people on remand, and to determine whether it is possible to bridge the gap between care and control. The research set out to evaluate the feasibility of remand foster care, both from a policy perspective and the perspective of the young people it affects, to ensure that it is a preferable option to institutional remands.

The research context

The research study took a developmental approach to youth justice (Rutherford, 1984, 1986; Mathiesen, 1990) and was situated within a penal reductionist discourse, as outlined by Rutherford (1984); this is discussed further in Chapter 2. The basic principles of the reductionist agenda include: reducing the physical capacity of the prison system; establishing a precise statement of legally enforceable minimum standards within prisons; and structuring sentencing discretion towards the use of the least restrictive sanctions. This book continues this argument by advocating a new emphasis within the remand system that actively promotes the use of the least restrictive remand options. Through depenalisation (the widening of the range of non-imprisonable offences) and decarceration (Mathiesen, 1990), the number of young people inappropriately remanded to prison service custody could be significantly reduced. The research aimed to investigate the importance of supporting young people on remand within the community through the provision of remand foster care. The current penal emphasis is on removing children from the community into either Young Offender Institutions or secure accommodation, when in reality the causes of, and the solution to, youthful offending lie largely within the community itself.

Research is an inherently political process and can have political consequences (Hughes, 2000; Liebling, 2001). All research is informed by personal, political and social sympathies, which renders it impossible to hold a value-free or neutral position (Becker, 1967). Indeed, much social research, particularly feminist and rights-based research, actively seeks to promote change in both policy and practice through the development of knowledge and theoretical understanding (Mackinnon, 1987; O'Neill, 2001). To contextualise the research and limit criticisms of bias it is therefore necessary to acknowledge the political and social value-position held by the researcher. The author of this book adheres to a stance which promotes society's obligation to achieve children's rights and which rejects the criminalisation and incarceration of children.

The book begins with a discussion of the theoretical and political background to current youth justice policy, before outlining the specific legislation and practice surrounding juvenile remands. The book then explores the history of remand foster care, within a discussion of community alternatives, prior to setting out the methodology and aims and objectives of the research that forms the basis of the book. The quantitative and qualitative findings from the research are presented and the conclusions for both policy and practice are drawn together in the final chapter.

2 The theoretical and political background

The reductionist agenda

As noted in Chapter 1, the research on which the book draws was situated within a penal reductionist framework that argues against the use of imprisonment and against prison expansion. The prison service in England and Wales is witnessing a prolonged growth in the use of incarceration, with the concomitant problems of overcrowding, increased levels of suicide and self-harm, bullying and the inadequate provision of appropriate activities for prisoners. Between 1990 and 2005, the total prison population increased by almost 85 per cent from 42,000 to just over 77,000, including over 11,000 young people aged under 21 (Prison Reform Trust, 2005). This increase is envisaged to continue, with statistical predictions indicating that the prison population could reach 110,000 by 2009 (Councell and Simes, 2002). These figures are the more remarkable because this period has seen a steady decline in the crime rate (Hough *et al*, 2003; Pitts, 2003).

The expansion of the prison system is both harmful to and counterproductive for the individuals caught up within it, and also threatens the basic values of a democratic society, including liberty, justice and humanity:

> *Far from protecting citizens from crime, the massive growth of incarceration undermines the essential values which distinguish free and authoritarian societies.* (Rutherford, 1984, p. v)

Significant sections of the population are increasingly physically repressed through the use of incarceration (Mathiesen, 1990) and subordinate groups are progressively more segregated and controlled through the power inherent in the criminal justice system (Foucault, 1977). Prison serves to fulfil a social or moralistic function for society, by isolating and punishing individuals who threaten the accepted structure of society, rather than rehabilitating the offender (Miller, 1973,

1991; Foucault, 1977). Prisons, together with asylums and workhouses, have been consistently used to 'confine and discipline the poor, the unemployed, the unemployable, the socially disadvantaged and the socially inept' (Carlen, 1983, p. 209; see also Foucault, 1977).

Policy makers who perpetuate the myth that prison can either rehabilitate or deter conveniently ignore the high rate of recidivism by ex-prisoners. Indeed, Foucault (1977) argues that this "failure" of the prison system has been used politically to provide a rational justification for the extension of methods of surveillance and control within society. The inefficiency of imprisonment is used as a pretext for building more, larger prisons and incarcerating more people (Mathiesen, 1983; Miller, 1991).

The most visible symptom of expansionism is the poor conditions experienced by people held in custodial institutions (Rutherford, 1984). Whilst Hudson (1993) argues that the physical conditions could be improved by the provision of more, newer and better-resourced prisons, experience has demonstrated that increased funding rarely, if ever, results in improvements (Rutherford, 1984). The Government has embarked upon an extensive, and expensive, prison building programme, yet the prison system is still overcrowded (Prison Reform Trust, 2002). Furthermore, as Rutherford (1998) commented:

The prison population crisis extends beyond a lack of resources, critical as this is, and reaches to issues of fundamental principle . . . What does it say about our society if, within a generation, we double the proportion of inhabitants held within the prison system? (Rutherford, 1998, p. 8)

Politicians and criminal justice administrators imply that prison expansion is the inevitable result of forces beyond their control and deny the fact that changes in the prison population are the consequence of policy decisions concerning the scope and direction of criminal justice (Rutherford, 1984). Conversely, the reductionist discourse acknowledges that policy choices are available and that prison expansionism can be reversed through the restriction of the use of imprisonment for all but those accused of or sentenced for the most serious offences (Miller, 1973, 1991; Rutherford, 1984;

Mathiesen, 1990; Hodgkin, 2002). The prison system has become "bogged down" with people charged with or convicted of relatively minor offences who could, and should, be dealt with via community-based alternatives.

The reductionist agenda has been proven to be effective in reducing the adult prison population in a number of countries, including Sweden and Denmark in the 1980s (Mathiesen, 1990), England in the period between 1908 and 1938, and Japan and the Netherlands between 1950 and 1975 (Rutherford, 1984, 1986). The successful reduction of juvenile incarceration was demonstrated in the 1970s by Jerome Miller, the first commissioner of the State Department of Youth Services in Massachusetts (Bakal, 1973; Coates et al, 1973; Rutherford, 1978; Miller, 1991). After becoming disillusioned with attempts to "humanise" the youth training schools in Massachusetts, Miller began a process of decarceration through the closure of the state's maximum security facility, shortening custodial sentences by increasing parole eligibility and facilitating transfers to a flexible, broad network of programmes within the community, including mentoring, "tracking" and youth-led groups (Rutherford, 1978; Miller, 1991).

Miller realised that a "deep-end" strategy was vital to prevent "net-widening", in which programmes described as alternatives to incarceration are used to supplement, rather than replace, custodial institutions, thus increasing the number of people drawn into the penal system. By addressing the needs of the young people involved in the "deepest end" of the criminal justice system first and closing the training schools in which they were held, Miller effectively eliminated the possibility of "net-widening" (Bakal, 1973; Rutherford, 1978; Miller, 1991). The closure of youth justice institutions in Massachusetts demonstrated that young people could be successfully placed within the community, with no major repercussions (Coates et al, 1973; Bakal, 1973; Miller, 1991).

However, past experience in England has shown that reductionist attempts to reduce imprisonment through developing alternative sanctions and/or by establishing principles of non-imprisonment through judicial guidelines have largely been unsuccessful (Hudson, 1993). Whilst temporary decreases in the prison population have been achieved, for example, through the process of "systems management" in the 1980s (Thorpe *et al*, 1980; Tutt and Giller, 1987),[1] these decreases have not been maintained. Therefore, reductionists advocate the dual strategic approach utilised by Miller: the negative strategy of restricting prison capacity through the closure of prisons and/or a moratorium on building new prisons, augmented by the positive provision and promotion of alternatives to custody (Rutherford, 1984; Hudson, 1993; Hodgkin, 2002). Unfortunately, the juvenile secure estate in England has recently experienced an extensive and prolonged expansion of capacity, with the development of more secure places for children sentenced and remanded to custody (Goldson, 2002b).

Prison expansion occurs both in the absence of any coherent justice policy and as a reaction to the perceived demands of various groups within society, including politicians, the media and the general public. The current youth justice system is characterised by both of these factors, which are discussed below: changes in legislation and practice are influenced by an increasingly negative public and political attitude towards young offenders with the result that there is no coherent youth justice strategy.

Public and political attitudes towards young offenders

The creation of "folk devils" and "moral panics" has been widely documented (Young, 1971; Cohen, 1972, 2002; Carlen, 1996; Davis and Bourhill, 1997; Goldson, 1999, 2000a), and this process has been apparent in the recent "crusade" against children who are involved in offending behaviour, seemingly triggered by the murder of James Bulger in 1993 (Muncie, 1999). A political campaign, reproduced and sustained by

---

[1] The systems management approach recognised that the operation of the criminal justice system comprises a series of decisions and that each decision has implications for future decisions and outcomes. By changing individual decisions, the way the system deals with individual offenders can be altered (Thorpe *et al*, 1980). However, systems management techniques can be utilised to change decisions in any direction (Haines and Drakeford, 1998) and will only decrease the number of people incarcerated if applied within a reductionist framework.

the media, was launched against so-called persistent young offenders,[2] including purported "bail bandits", who were held publicly responsible for the majority of crime committed by juveniles (House of Commons Home Affairs Committee, 1993). This campaign has been continued, intensified and broadened to include all young offenders, creating an inaccurate representation of juvenile offending (see Muncie, 1999 for an overview). Whilst the majority of juvenile crime is non-violent and directed at property rather than people – juvenile offending is mainly theft and handling stolen goods, vehicle crimes or vandalism (Rutter *et al*, 1998) – the dominant ideology is of young people as "anti-social monsters" (Grewcock, 1995) who need to be incarcerated to protect the public.

The portrayal of crime as a pervasive threat to public safety is used to vindicate an authoritarian, punitive crime control policy (Cohen, 2002), which has been implemented through the Criminal Justice Act 1993, the Criminal Justice and Public Order Act 1994, the Crime and Disorder Act 1998, and the Criminal Justice and Police Act 2001. The consensus that existed in the 1980s about the need to divert young people from custody has evaporated (Thorpe *et al*, 1980; Rutherford, 1986), with increasing numbers of children being remanded and sentenced to custody for longer periods of time. For example, during the 1990s, the average sentence length for 15–17-year-olds doubled, as magistrates responded to the prevailing climate of popular and political punitivism (Muncie, 2004). Goldson contends that the representation of children as violent and hardened criminals has served to sanction subsequent policy and practice that 'rides roughshod over the welfare needs of children and negates their claims to justice' (1997, p. 77), and that the perceived need to protect the public now takes precedence over the need to protect children (Goldson, 2002a).

---

[2] It is important to note that "persistent" and "serious" are not the same, although the terms are often confused within the media (The Children's Society, 1993). Many of the young offenders who commit the most serious of crimes will not have extensive criminal histories and, in contrast, most frequent offenders will not commit the most serious crimes (Hagell and Newburn, 1994).

Weijers (1999) argues that, because justice officials and the general public remain convinced, albeit erroneously, that juvenile crime is at an exceptionally high level,[3] responses to serious juvenile offenders are "toughened up". This "toughening up" is then expanded to encompass all responses to youth offending, so that no lenient sanctions are available. In this situation, justice professionals are often forced to choose between doing nothing, which is unacceptable to the general public, or punishing offenders harshly, which is inappropriate for the offenders. Moral panics, orchestrated and amplified by the mass media, and a high intolerance of crime influence each other in a cyclical relationship (Cohen, 1972, 2002; Tonry, 2001), resulting in the increased confinement of children.

The developmental approach

In contrast to the highly interventionist policies promoted by the government (Monaghan, 2000; Muncie and Hughes, 2002), the developmental approach to youth crime regards crime and anti-social behaviour by children and young people as a transient and integral part of the process of growing up:

Offending for many young people is a passing phase. To allow the young person to grow out of his/her offending without acquiring a serious criminal record, sentencing disposals should be kept to a minimum and involve the minimum intervention in the offender's life. (Ashford and Chard, 2000, p. 327)

This approach emphasises inclusion and absorption within the community, rather than exclusion. It is based upon evidence which

---

[3] The public perception appears to be that juvenile crime has increased and that children are becoming involved in offending at a younger age. However, it is difficult to obtain an accurate figure of the crimes attributable to young people: crime is a moving target and official statistics are estimates, not facts; definitions of criminal offences change over time and place; police recording techniques vary, as does the compilation of official statistics; the willingness of victims to report crimes is not static and is influenced by a number of factors, including the need for crime report numbers for insurance claims, access to telephones and the nature of the offence (Rutter *et al*, 1998, Burrows *et al*, 2001).

demonstrates that formal, professional involvement through the network of criminal justice, welfare and mental health services, particularly that which results in incarceration, disrupts the normal growth and development of the child and can exacerbate involvement in criminal activity through a variety of mechanisms, including labelling and differential association (Becker, 1963; Lemert, 1967; Rutherford, 1986, 1992; Stein and Carey, 1986; Malek, 1993; Giller, 1999; Smith and McVie, 2003).

For instance, Malek (1993) interviewed key workers in a range of institutions, including secure accommodation, residential schools, children's homes and psychiatric units, who believed that the great majority of young people do not benefit from the time they spend in institutions:

At best their time in institutions serves to contain them. At worst it intensifies and adds to their difficulties and denies them the experience of mainstream society to which they are expected to return. The cost to these young people and to society is huge in financial as well as emotional and human terms. (p. 91)

The developmental approach, which argues that delinquency is a typical part of adolescent behaviour that would dissipate if young people were allowed to mature without negative intervention, is supported by studies of self-reported criminal behaviour. Approximately two-thirds of all boys and a third of all girls will commit an offence before they are 25, although obviously many will not be arrested or convicted (Graham and Bowling, 1995; Flood-Page *et al*, 2000; Tables 2.1 and 2.2).

Table 2.1
Percentage of population admitting to have committed an offence during their lifetime, by age

Age	Males	Females	Total population
12–13 years	33	25	29
14–15 years	50	42	46
16–17 years	60	40	50
18–21 years	66	39	53
22–25 years	62	36	49
26–30 years	62	37	49
Total aged 12–30 years	**57**	**37**	**47**

Table 2.2

Percentage of population admitting to having committed an offence during the previous year, by age

Age	Males	Females	Total population
12–13 years	15	12	14
14–15 years	33	18	26
16–17 years	26	16	21
18–21 years	35	15	25
22–25 years	28	8	18
26–30 years	19	7	13
Total aged 12–30 years	**26**	**13**	**20**

Figures taken from Flood-Page *et al* (2000). Percentages have been rounded.

With support and encouragement, most young people mature out of crime (Friday, 1983; Rutherford, 1986, 1992). That some young people do not "grow out" of crime as they enter adulthood can be explained partly by the levels of familial and social deprivation that they have experienced during their childhoods and adolescence, and the lack of employment opportunities available to them. Adolescence is a transitional period but the length of adolescence will depend upon whether a young person has the social and economic ability to proceed to the next stage in the life cycle. Young people who, under other, less disadvantaged circumstances, would have grown out of crime, are unable to do so and are 'locked in a state of perpetual adolescence', becoming more seriously embedded in a criminal way of life (Pitts, 2001a, p. 106).

Juvenile offending, "race" and ethnicity

It is beyond the scope of this book to discuss the complexities of why young people from black and minority ethic groups, particularly African-Caribbean young men, are continually over-represented within the criminal justice system and in custodial institutions (see Phillips and Bowling, 2002 for an overview). However, it must be acknowledged that it is essential to address issues of institutional racism and discrimination to reduce the number of black and minority ethnic young people drawn into the criminal justice process.

Juvenile offending and gender

There is a customary belief that females commit fewer offences than males, and certainly they are convicted of fewer offences: only six per cent of the prison population are female (Hollis and Goodman, 2003). The relatively small number of females who are involved with the criminal justice system has meant that the characteristics and needs of female offenders have been ignored, and females as a group within the criminal justice system have been marginalised. Whilst it is the typical crimes of boys that have most impact on everyday perceptions of victimisation and anxiety about crime, there are still a considerable number of girls involved in the criminal justice system whose needs should be recognised.

In accordance with the developmental approach, the most effective resources for coping with and resolving youth crime are located in the home and school, not in custodial institutions. Adolescents in the community learn to manage their own affairs, to make responsible and informed decisions about their future, and to relate to people of different class, age or gender – opportunities that are denied to a young person in custody (Kagan, 1979; Rutherford, 1986). Young people in custodial establishments are unable to make choices about their own lives but must live by rules and regulations imposed by professionals who are trying to maintain control. This means that the young person's social development may be hampered, even if they experience only a short period in custody. Allowing young offenders to remain within the community enables them to mature and develop, avoiding the stigma and isolation of confinement (Zimring, 1978).

Community-based alternatives provide a compromise between custodial responses and radical non-intervention (Schur, 1973) by combining elements of reparation and restitution through, for example, community service, with welfare inputs such as those focusing on the young person's education or employment, whilst avoiding the negative effects of incarceration and institutionalisation. However, the current political and media climate has not been conducive to promoting public confidence in community-based sentences. There is a tendency for community alternatives to be seen as a "soft option" for the offender, even though research has shown that young offenders find reparation and mediation emotionally difficult (Roberts, 2000; Wright, 2000).

Having now outlined the political and theoretical background to the research study, the following chapter focuses specifically on the history of custodial remands and remand legislation for children and young people awaiting trial or sentence.

3 Remanding young people

Introduction

The decision to remand a suspect on bail or in custody may be encountered at any, or all, or the following stages of the criminal justice process: after arrest at the police station whilst awaiting the first appearance in court; between the first and final appearance in court if an adjournment is necessary; between conviction and sentencing if pre-sentence reports are required; and pending an appeal. The decisions made at each stage of the remand process are likely to influence decisions made at later stages of the criminal justice procedure (Thorpe *et al*, 1980), with more people remanded to custody receiving custodial sentences than those remanded on bail (Bottomley, 1970; Haines and Drakeford, 1998).

Any person charged with an offence is presumed innocent until proven otherwise, and as such should not be punished or deprived of any rights that pertain to a non-accused person (King and Morgan, 1976). However, young people on penal remand are deprived of their liberty, and also suffer the further deprivation of their rights to, for example, education, physical and mental health care, and protection from abuse, as outlined in Chapter 1.

The remand period may last from a week to six months or more, with the majority of young people being remanded for less than three months (Howard League, 1998). However, some young people will spend much longer on remand, particularly if they are being tried alongside an adult offender. The decision made by the magistrates will therefore have significant consequences for the young person, not only in terms of future decisions made within the justice process, but also in terms of the influences exerted upon the young person whilst they are on remand. The remand period can:

> . . . present a unique opportunity to help young people and their families in a direct and positive way or, conversely, it can lead to a dramatic escalation of the situation in a most damaging and unnecessary way. (Fletcher, 1992, p. 8)

Yet, the importance of the remand period for young people has often been neglected by policy-makers and academics, who have tended to focus on the implications of sentencing options instead.

The history of custodial remands

The use of custody for remand prisoners has a much longer history than the punitive use of custody. Common gaols were established in the 12th century by Henry II to provide for the safe custody of people awaiting trial. The judges who went on circuit aimed to empty the prisons by passing non-custodial sentences such as fines, banishment, ordeals, corporal punishment or execution. The granting of bail was first written into the law in the Statute of Westminster in 1275 (Winfield, 1984). By the end of the 13th century, imprisonment began to have a coercive function, particularly for debtors, but it was not until the late 18th century that imprisonment became the most serious sanction, with the exception of the death penalty (King and Morgan, 1976). Special privileges were first accorded to untried prisoners in the late 19th century, with the Prisons Act 1865 specifying that remand prisoners should be protected from contamination by the more criminally sophisticated by being separated from convicted offenders. Remand prisoners were allowed to obtain their own food, clothing and bedding, albeit at their own expense. These privileges were extended by the Prisons Act 1877 which gave remand prisoners the right to retain possession of books and papers, to have private communication with friends and legal advisers, and the right not to be compelled to work within the prison (Bottomley, 1970). However, remand centres specifically for young male offenders were not introduced until the following century, with Ashford Remand Centre being the first to open in 1961 (Bottomley, 1970).

Historically, there has always been a legal presumption in favour of bail, with the burden of proof lying with the prosecution. The prosecution should have to justify a remand to custody rather than the accused having to defend their right to bail. However, there has been a slow erosion of the rights of defendants over the 20th century that has picked up speed in recent years and grounds to justify a remand in custody have been added within recent legislation. The limitations to the right to bail are mainly contained within the Bail Act 1976, with considerable revisions in the Police and Criminal Evidence Act 1984, the Criminal Justice Acts of 1988, 1991 and 1993, the Bail (Amendment) Act 1993, the Criminal Justice and Public Order Act 1994, the Crime and Disorder Act 1998, the Youth Justice and Criminal Evidence Act 1999 and the Criminal Justice and Police Act 2001. The number of recent changes in the law with regard to bail is indicative of the complexity and contested nature of the debate surrounding the use of custody for offenders, particularly pre-trial custody (see Lipscombe 2003 for a full discussion of the development of remand legislation).

Remanding children and young people

The legal provision for remands for children and young people varies according to their age and gender.[4] Seventeen-year-old girls and boys are treated as adults within the context of remands and as such are either granted bail, with or without conditions attached, or remanded to a YOI. Fifteen- and 16-year-old boys can be bailed or remanded with or without a security requirement. If a security requirement is imposed, 15- and 16-year-old boys can technically be remanded either to local authority secure accommodation or a YOI. However, to be remanded to secure accommodation, the court must consider the boy to be "vulnerable" (discussed below) *and* be notified that a place in local authority secure accommodation is available. The provision for all young people aged between 12 and 14 and girls aged 15 or 16 is the same: they may either be granted bail or remanded to local authority accommodation (RLAA), with

---

[4] Whilst there is evidence that women are treated differently from men within the criminal justice system, in most areas of the law this is due to underlying notions of patriarchy and prejudices based upon stereotypical images of women, rather than legal edicts. However, within the remand system for juveniles, differential treatment for boys and girls is enshrined within the legislation. The provision for remands for young female offenders is based upon more patriarchal, protective notions than the provision for young male offenders, in that where a security requirement is imposed, girls aged 16 or under cannot be remanded to prison service establishments. Conversely, boys aged 15 or 16 who are remanded to custody are automatically placed in prison remand centres unless they are considered "vulnerable".

or without a court-ordered security requirement. The court has no power to remand young people aged 12–14 or girls aged 15–16 to prison service custody.

Similarly, young people aged ten and 11 cannot be remanded to custody, so a refusal to grant bail results in a remand to local authority accommodation. The court can impose conditions on the remand, but cannot impose a security requirement. However, the local authority can apply to the court for a secure accommodation order under section 25 of the Children Act 1989, once bail has been refused, for any young person aged ten to 16. The court may grant such an order if it finds that:

a) (i) he has a history of absconding and is likely to abscond from any other description of accommodation; and
(ii) if he absconds, he is likely to suffer significant harm; or
b) if he is kept in any other description of accommodation he is likely to injure himself or other persons.

A secure accommodation order empowers the local authority to place the child in secure provision, whereas a court-ordered security requirement obliges them to do so.

If a young person is remanded to local authority accommodation without a security requirement, the placement is at the discretion of the authority: the young person could be placed in a secure unit if a secure accommodation order is granted, a residential unit, with foster carers or returned home. An exception to this is if the court places a condition on the authority not to accommodate the young person with a particular named person. This is a measure mainly designed in response to concerns expressed by magistrates that the local authority would simply send children home and prevents placement at home where the court feels that the circumstances in which the child has been living may have contributed to the alleged offence (NACRO, 1993; Morgan and Henderson, 1998; Moore and Smith, 2001). If the young person is granted bail, the YOT may provide a system of bail support for them.

Vulnerability

As with much of the legislation, what constitutes vulnerability is not clearly specified. The guidance given states that boys of 15 or 16 should continue to be remanded to prison service custody, rather than local authority secure accommodation, unless:

> ... by reason of his physical or emotional immaturity or a propensity of his to harm himself, it would be undesirable for him to be remanded to a remand centre or a prison.(Crime and Disorder Act, 1998)

In some cases there may be clear-cut evidence of vulnerability arising from a history of abuse, exploitation, substance misuse, personal or psychological problems, but this will not always be so and it is extremely difficult to anticipate the likely reaction of a young person to being locked up, possibly for the first time (Moore and Smith, 2001; Goldson, 2002a).

Moreover, even 15- and 16-year-old boys deemed "vulnerable" will only be placed in secure accommodation if a placement can be found; in practice, this has often meant that a vulnerability assessment has not been made unless a secure placement was available (Moore and Peters, 2003). There have rarely been enough secure facilities available for the number of young people on remand (Moore, 1998; NACRO, 1999a; Goldson and Peters, 2002; Moore and Peters, 2003) and this situation has been intensified by the legislative amendments mentioned above. "Vulnerable" 15- and 16-year-old boys therefore are in competition for secure places with 12–14-year-old boys and 12–16-year-old girls, and the former group are likely to lose out as there is no legal alternative for the latter (Ashton and Grindrod, 1999; Goldson, 2002a).

The court's decision

The court thus has to decide whether to remand a young person on bail, to prison or secure accommodation or to the care of the local authority. As the local authority has placement discretion over children remanded to the care of the local authority, magistrates may favour a remand to secure or prison service accommodation as they can then retain control over where the young person is placed. The court's primary duty is to protect the public and so magistrates must have knowledge of and confidence in the alternatives available to them. The Howard League (1995a) found that there was a clear correlation between the provision of comprehensive community-based packages, particularly remand fostering schemes, and the willingness of the youth court to grant bail or an RLAA at an early stage. Magistrates' confidence in remand foster care placements will be influenced by their personal experience of remanding young people but also by research and evaluations of remand foster care schemes. As discussed earlier, there is insufficient independent research in this area, an issue that this book aims to address.

In many areas, the problem of high numbers of young people being remanded to custody is compounded by the scarcity of alternative provision within the community (Goldson and Peters, 2002; Hucklesby and Goodwin, 2002). The National Remand Review Initiative (NRRI) found that only 27 per cent of the local authorities involved in the Initiative were able to provide a range of remand schemes, including bail support and remand foster care (Moore, 1999) and, although there are an increasing number of remand foster care schemes across the country, many of these can only cater for very small numbers of children. The development of remand foster care schemes is discussed in more detail in Chapter 4.

The inappropriate use of custodial remands is aggravated by the lack of information available to magistrates about both the young person and the provision of alternative bail support and remand schemes within the area. The Association of Chief Officers of Probation and NACRO found that 63 per cent of juveniles remanded in custody were received from courts other than specialist youth courts (ACOP/NACRO, 1993). Magistrates in youth courts receive specialist training about the provision for juveniles whilst magistrates in adult courts may not be aware of the alternatives for young people in the area. The NRRI found that approximately 13 per cent of the young people in the Initiative had been remanded to custody without the knowledge of the relevant YOT, and in 40 per cent of the cases the courts had not been given the opportunity to consider either a community-based programme or a placement in secure accommodation (Goldson and Peters, 2002; Moore and Peters, 2003).

Summary

The history of custodial remands has been described and the current remand legislation has been documented within this chapter. The next chapter considers the potential benefits of community alternatives to secure and custodial remands, including remand foster care. The history of remand foster care is discussed, and a summary of the current availability of remand foster care schemes in England is given.

4 Community alternatives: bail support and remand foster care

Introduction

Some of the negative consequences of custodial and residential remands were outlined in Chapters 1 and 2; in addition, institutional remands are unlikely to have any long-term positive effects for young people. Removal to custodial accommodation will protect young people temporarily from the environments that elicited and maintained their delinquent behaviour, but does little to alter the original environmental factors. It is therefore probable that delinquent behaviour patterns will be resurrected once the alleged offender returns to the community (Cornish and Clarke, 1975; Lyon et al, 2000). Community-based alternatives such as bail support and remand foster care can reduce the disruptive impact of a period on a penal remand, and can offer wide-ranging assistance to young people on remand. For instance, young people remanded in the community can continue with their existing educational provision, or if no provision exists, can more easily be found alternative education. Similarly, a community remand makes it possible for those who are in employment to continue working or for the unemployed to find work by building upon existing community links. Furthermore, young people remanded on bail or to foster care remain within the community so the damage caused to family and community ties by incarceration is reduced.

Pitts (2003) summarised the findings of comprehensive meta-analyses of interventions with young offenders undertaken in the USA (Altschuler and Armstrong, 1984; Howell et al, 1995), concluding that successful rehabilitative programmes:
- are often conducted outside the justice system;
- are holistic, dealing with many aspects of young people's lives simultaneously as needed;
- are informed by an underlying developmental rationale;
- offer diverse opportunities for success and the development of positive self-image;

- build on young people's strengths rather than focusing on their deficiencies;
- are intensive, often involving weekly or even daily contact;
- adopt a socially grounded rather than a "treatment" approach and emphasise reintegration;
- involve young people in programme planning and decision-making;
- include enriched educational and vocational programmes;
- utilise forms of counselling matched to the young person's needs, including opportunities for young people to discuss childhood problems;
- provide opportunities for the development of links between young people in trouble and pro-social adults and institutions;
- give frequent, timely and accurate feedback for both positive and negative behaviour;
- demonstrate clear and consistent consequences for misconduct;
- provide a forum in which young people are enabled to recognise and understand thought processes that rationalise negative behaviour;
- offer opportunities to engage with problems and deficits which contributed to the young person's offending behaviour.

It is argued that community-based alternatives to penal remand, particularly remand foster care, are based on such principles and it is therefore predicted that they will have more rehabilitative impact than custodial remands.

Bail support

Bail support is, at its simplest, 'the provision of services designed to facilitate the granting of bail where bail would otherwise be denied' (NACRO, 1998, p. 2). Bail support schemes for young people are sometimes run by voluntary agencies under partnership agreements with Youth Offending Teams, or are provided by specialist staff within the YOT. The schemes typically include a programme of community-based activities, developed to ensure that defendants awaiting trial complete their time on bail successfully, that is by returning to court when required and by not committing offences whilst on bail. The activities may be provided by the scheme itself, or through referral to specialist organisations, and aim to improve social and life skills, develop anger management strategies, reduce drug and alcohol misuse and tackle difficulties with family relationships, education, employment or accommodation. For example, if a young person has educational problems, a bail support officer may liaise with schools, education welfare officers and organisations providing support for disaffected pupils to arrange help and services for the young person (NACRO, 1998).

As activities can be provided for a group of young people or for individuals, the programme of activities can be closely targeted to the specific needs of the young person. Individualised bail support packages mean that unnecessary criminal justice intervention is kept to a minimum and the adverse consequences of intervention are reduced.

However, as already indicated, there has been concern over the level of offending whilst on bail, which can be higher for young people than for adults. Different studies have reported varying rates of offending on bail by young people: for example, Morgan and Henderson (1998) reported a rate of 29 per cent and Brown (1998) a rate of 38 per cent. The Youth Justice Board (2002) found that 18 per cent of young people with bail support and supervision committed an offence whilst on bail.

Offending during the remand period could be reduced by giving young people increased support and encouragement whilst they are on remand. Hirschi (1969) argues that the likelihood of committing offences is largely a function of the degree to which a young person is bound to the conventional moral order. Those least likely to be delinquent are those who have most to lose by offending, whilst those with only a loose attachment to society are more likely to be delinquent, believing that they have nothing to lose. Morgan and Henderson (1998) found that having weak community links was one of the factors contributing to offending on bail. If young people can be helped to strengthen family and community ties, they might be deterred from offending. Some bailed to return home will not be encouraged or motivated by their families after a court appearance, particularly where difficult family relationships contributed to the initial offending behaviour or where other family members are involved in criminal activities. Support and encouragement therefore need to be provided by people outside the young person's family.

Moreover, as already indicated, bail is not available to all young people on remand and there is a group who cannot return home. These children include those who have no home; those whose alleged offence is deemed too serious to allow a return home; those who live near to, or with, the alleged victim; those whose parents refuse to accept them back into the home; and those whose return home is inadvisable for the protection of their welfare (see also Hucklesby and Goodwin, 2002). These young people could be placed with remand foster carers.

The history of remand foster care

Remand foster care is not a new phenomenon but began in England and Wales in the late 1970s, following initiatives in Sweden and the USA (Hazel, 1981a; Shaw and Hipgrave, 1983; Rutherford, 1986). Until the early 1970s it had been widely accepted that adolescents could not be placed in foster homes:

> On the one hand, it was believed that foster carers would not accept them [difficult adolescents] into their homes and would not be able to cope with the anticipated difficulties (although untrained residential staff were expected to do so). On the other hand, it was believed that adolescents do not want to be fostered. (Hazel, 1993a, p. 51)

However, research was beginning to accumulate that showed residential provision to be expensive and often counter-productive and that adolescents could be successfully looked after in foster care placements (Colton, 1988; Triseliotis, 1989). The initiatives in Sweden and the USA supplied evidence that foster care could provide for young offenders and that a community-based system was a workable alternative to institutionalisation (Shaw and Hipgrave, 1983; Hazel, 1993b). Models of "professional" fostering started to develop, with an emphasis on the therapeutic and caretaking aspects of foster care. Foster carers were recruited and trained specifically to work with children who had previously been considered unsuitable for foster care, such as disabled children, children from minority ethnic backgrounds and disturbed or delinquent adolescents (Stone, 1995).

Sweden and the "Kent Project"

The progressive thinking in Sweden was encapsulated in 1974 in the findings of the Swedish Royal Commission for the Placement of Children (Hazel, 1978, 1993b), which outlined four basic principles that should be used when determining children's placements in care:

- normalisation – a child's placement should be as "normal" as possible, so living in a family in the community is more appropriate than living in an institution;
- localisation – a child should be placed near to his/her own home and social network;
- individualisation – the child is offered a committed individual relationship by the carers, who listen to and advocate for the child;
- participation – all parties involved in a care placement should be included in decision-making.

Hazel (1978, 1980, 1981a) documented the development of the Kent Family Placement Project, a foster care scheme for young offenders based upon the principles advocated in Sweden. The Kent Project aimed neither to punish nor to "treat" alleged young offenders, but intended:

> ... by treating the young people as normal and capable of running their own lives, to maximise their strengths and deal with their weaknesses, whilst at the same time their environment was changed to facilitate this process. (Hazel, 1993c, p. 8)

The placements with the Kent Project were deliberately time-limited. As such, foster carers were not expected to help to "reconstruct" the young person's personality, but to help them acquire life skills and to address environmental factors that could help the young person desist from delinquent behaviour, such as education or employment and housing. The basic structure of the Project included written reciprocal agreements between the carer and young person. Foster carers had an enhanced status with payment of fees, compulsory support groups and a support worker (Hazel, 1993b).

The Kent Project was evaluated on four separate occasions, by Yelloly (1979), Hazel (1981a), Smith (1986) and Fenyo and colleagues (1989). Whilst the evaluations used different methodologies and measures of outcome, all concluded that the placements could contain delinquency and limit absconding. Although the placements did not prevent offending completely, Hazel's (1981a) evaluation concluded that less than 15 per cent of the young people placed with the scheme were convicted or cautioned during their placements.

Specialist, professional and treatment foster care[5]

There was also a rapid expansion of specialist or "treatment" foster care in the USA, following the de-institutionalisation movement in the 1970s (Wells and D'Angelo, 1994). Specialist foster care was increasingly seen as a viable alternative to residential care for young people with emotional and behavioural difficulties, including those who had been involved in offending (Chamberlain, 1994, 1998; Reddy and Pfeiffer, 1997). In most schemes, professional foster carers are provided with training and support services to design and implement interventions for the children and young people in their care, and are also responsible for helping them to access community resources, including mental health and medical professionals.

Chamberlain (1994, 1998) described a specific treatment foster care programme, developed by the Oregon Social Learning Center, which began in 1983 as an alternative to residential and group care placements for serious and chronic juvenile offenders. It provides adolescents with close supervision, fair and consistent boundaries and a supportive relationship with at least one mentoring adult, and reduces the young people's exposure to delinquent peers. In addition, the programme attempts to reinforce the young person's appropriate and positive behaviour, to encourage the development of academic skills and work habits, and to decrease conflict between family members. Chamberlain (1998) summarised the results of four studies conducted on the effectiveness of

---

[5] Historically, the terms "specialist", "treatment", "therapeutic" and "professional" foster care have often been used interchangeably (Kelly, 2002); the main distinguishing feature of a "treatment" or "therapeutic" scheme is the inclusion of specific techniques such as cognitive, behavioural or family therapies (Scott et al, 2004). However, some schemes offer a similar package of support services and interventions for individual young people, yet reject a medicalised notion of "treatment". For example, the Kent Project and the Oregon Social Learning Center treatment programme were based upon analogous models, but the Kent Project rejected the epithet of "treatment" foster care.

this approach, and concluded that treatment foster care was not only feasible but, compared with alternative residential and group care treatment models, was cost-effective and led to better outcomes for children and families. One evaluation found that young people who had experienced treatment foster care had half as many subsequent arrests and spent fewer days incarcerated during the follow-up period than those who had been in group care (Chamberlain and Reid, 1998).

Different judgements of progress and development and varied outcome measures mean that comparing assessments of individual foster care programmes, or comparing these studies with the results of evaluations of young people remanded in custody or to residential accommodation, is complex. Nonetheless, Curtis and colleagues (2001) conducted a review of the literature comparing therapeutic foster care with residential group care in the USA and concluded that the young people in each setting had similar levels of behavioural difficulty, although those in residential group care were more likely to be older and to have had prior contact with criminal justice agencies. However, with the exception of the study cited above, they found no studies that produced results in which young people in specialist foster care appeared to achieve better outcomes than those in residential group care.

Conversely, Reddy and Pfeiffer's (1997) systematic review of treatment foster care in the USA supported the view that treatment foster care can serve as an effective alternative to both residential care and custody. Chamberlain (1998) argues that treatment foster care has a number of advantages for young people, including the opportunity to tailor the treatment programme to a person's individual needs, problems and strengths. Young people are not placed with others who have similar problems and who may be a source of negative influence, as occurs in residential and custodial establishments. It is not yet clear whether specialist foster care offers particular benefits for girls, a traditionally marginalised group, but the Oregon Social Learning Center has received funding to evaluate a modified treatment foster care programme aimed at addressing the specific needs of adolescent girls.

The Scottish Community Alternative Placement Scheme (CAPS) compared the progress of 20 young people placed with CAPS specialist foster carers with that of 20 young people placed in secure accommodation

(Walker *et al*, 2002). Whilst the initial aim of CAPS was to provide placements for young people as a direct alternative to secure accommodation, the profiles of the young people actually placed suggest that not all were candidates for secure units. However, the backgrounds and behavioural difficulties of both groups were generally analogous. The evaluation concluded that, whilst the overall outcomes for the young people were similar in terms of being in education or employment and having stable move-on accommodation, the experience of living in foster care was much more positive for young people than living in a secure unit and that, for many, 'finding themselves accepted by the carers was a profoundly empowering experience' (Walker *et al*, 2002, p. 141).

There are a number of differences between treatment or specialist foster care and remand foster care, although many of the underlying principles and objectives are similar. For example, both specialist foster care and remand foster care aim to provide young people with a positive relationship with an adult, close supervision and consistent boundaries and to reduce young people's interaction with delinquent peers. Both aim to reinforce appropriate and positive behaviour, to decrease conflict between family members and to promote education and employment. However, remand foster care is, by default, time-limited whereas the length of specialist foster care placements can be determined by the needs of the child. The average length of placement with the Oregon Social Learning Center treatment foster care programme was seven months whilst the average period spent on remand is less than three months (Youth Justice Board, 2002). Walker and colleagues (2002) concluded that, whilst some derived considerable benefit from short placements, the best outcomes were achieved for young people who remained in their placements for over 18 months. The CAPS project also introduced the young person to the placement over a period of 10 to 12 days (except in emergencies) whilst remand foster care placements generally commence immediately the court hearing has been concluded.

The potential benefits of remand foster care

Remand foster care can potentially offer solutions to the problems of bail support, whilst employing the individualised, flexible approach of bail support systems (Allen and Maynard, 1999). The research outlined above suggests that foster care can provide a stable home for young people on remand, and can give a young person support and help that might not be forthcoming from their birth family. Remand foster care placements occur within the community but can, if necessary, be at a reasonable distance from friends or family members who might exert a negative influence on a young person. In this way a young person can maintain (or rebuild) and strengthen community links whilst not being drawn back into a delinquent sub-culture with their peers (Colton, 1988; Walker *et al*, 2002). Fry (1994) cites an extract from the East Sussex Remand and Intensive Lodging Scheme (RAILS) literature:

> *The young people feel it easier to keep out of trouble in an individual placement as they are not under pressure to go out in groups at night. The individual placement has the advantage of isolating them from the group they were offending with and their personal problems . . . [they] found it easier to keep out of trouble, and liked the family environment that they lived in.* (RAILS, cited by Fry, 1994, p.18)

All of the activities and programmes, outlined above, that operate within bail support schemes can be provided for young people in foster care, with additional support given by dedicated foster carers. The aim of remand foster care is to offer young people a constructive environment where they can build a relationship and work together with carers and YOT staff to address their social and personal needs and their offending behaviour (Fry, 1994). Young people are thereby given the opportunity to begin to "grow out" of crime without being unduly harmed by the labelling and stigmatising effects of institutionalisation (Rutherford, 1986; Hoare, 1992).

Foster families can be more flexible than residential units in adapting to difficult and disruptive behaviour (Colton, 1988; Walker *et al*, 2002) and, it is hoped, can provide individualised care for girls on remand who would otherwise be marginalised within residential units or prison service custody (Fry, 1994; O'Neill, 2001). Young people whose behaviour could potentially endanger the welfare of other children in residential units can be safely cared for in foster families where there are no other children (Colton, 1988; Farmer and Pollock, 1998), as can young people who would be vulnerable in secure accommodation or prison custody (Goldson, 2002a). Placing young people individually in foster placements avoids problems such as bullying and intimidation, and they are not encouraged by others to participate in delinquent behaviour. Accommodating young people together in residential units can create situations in which status is gained through deviant behaviour, whilst in normal family groups anti-social behaviour does not increase a young person's status (Hazel, 1990; Walker et al, 2002).

The low staff to inmate ratios in prison service establishments makes it virtually impossible for any members of staff to develop a beneficial relationship with individual young people (HMIP, 1997). Foster carers, however, may be more able to form positive relationships with the young people, as they tend to care for only one at a time. The foster carers can potentially become a responsible adult role model for the young person and positively influence their behaviour (Chamberlain, 1994; Walker et al, 2002). Furthermore, young people living in a family situation can learn life skills, such as budgeting, accessing benefits, basic cooking and self-care, which are often neglected in custodial and residential units (Howard League, 2001a; Walker et al, 2002).

Remand foster care is in accordance with the principles of the Children Act 1989 and the United Nations Convention on the Rights of the Child 1989, which promote the welfare of the child as paramount. However, studies of specialist and treatment foster care have identified a range of potential difficulties that may also affect remand foster care schemes. For example, the CAPS carers encountered a number of problems, including finding appropriate educational or employment provision for young people, particularly those over the school-leaving age. The CAPS placements were originally time-limited, as were the Kent Project placements, but it became clear that many young people were not ready to move on when anticipated and the placements were extended indefinitely. This clearly is not an option for young people on remand and may prove problematic: the termination of remand foster care placements is dictated by the court process, not the needs of the young person. The availability of foster carers may mean that young people are placed further away from their families than would be desirable (Walker *et al*, 2002), which can have implications for the development of community ties, particularly if the young person returns to their home area after the placement. Furthermore, appropriate move-on accommodation for the young people in the CAPS placements was rarely forthcoming; this has already been identified as a difficulty for remand foster care schemes (Fry, 1994). There are also concerns for the protection of the public, as the numbers of young people remanded to foster care who commit offences, abscond or fail to attend trial are currently unknown.

It is also widely accepted that it is more problematic to provide foster care for adolescents than for younger children and there is a high rate of disruption in adolescent placements (Berridge and Cleaver, 1987; Rowe *et al*, 1989; Triseliotis *et al*, 1995a; Farmer *et al*, 2004). As remand foster care caters specifically for adolescents, it is logical to assume that there will be a high level of placement disruption. Furthermore, a recent study of teenage fostering highlighted the importance of preparation and planning in preventing placement disruptions (Farmer *et al*, 2004) and, as noted, the CAPS study (Walker *et al*, 2002) introduced the young people to their foster placements gradually to help them prepare for moving in. However, there is often limited notice that a remand decision is going to be made and little to indicate how the decision is likely to fall, so it is difficult to make adequate preparations for a remand foster care placement.

There are also potential implications for black and minority ethnic children who may be placed with white foster carers. There are no figures available for the number of remand foster carers who are from black or minority ethnic backgrounds; Bebbington and Miles (1990) found that only five per cent of mainstream foster carers in England and Wales were from black or minority ethnic backgrounds. However, there has been increasing recognition that the needs of black and minority ethnic young people are best met within foster families of the same ethnic or cultural background (Triseliotis *et al*, 1995b).

The availability of remand foster care in England and Wales

Whilst the Kent Project, CAPS and international initiatives have demonstrated that foster care can be successful as an alternative to secure accommodation, historically specialist remand fostering schemes in England and Wales have been subsumed within mainstream foster care services (Hazel, 1981b; Fry, 1994). Local authorities, under pressure to find foster carers for adolescents who had not been involved in the criminal justice system, began to use remand foster placements for young people not on remand and specialist provision for young people on remand virtually disappeared until the early 1990s. The implementation of the Criminal Justice Act 1991 and the recognition of the need to divert young people from custody, combined with the need to develop more cost-effective services, has led to a re-emergence of remand foster care schemes over the last decade.

The recent development of remand foster care in England and Wales, however, has been slow and patchy. A survey conducted in 1994 found that 29 local authorities (24 per cent of the 120 local authorities that existed at the time) had developed some foster care provision for young people on remand, although only five per cent (six) said that they regularly placed young people remanded to local authority accommodation with foster carers (Fry, 1994). By 1998, it was estimated that there were 81 remand foster schemes nationwide (Butler, 2001), and more have become established since then. The majority of schemes are structured in a similar way, recruiting, training and supporting foster carers whose use is exclusively retained for remanded young people (NACRO, 1996b). Carers have training in more traditional areas of foster care, such as child and adolescent development, and in aspects of youth justice and the role that carers will play within the penal system (NACRO, 1996b).

There are recognised difficulties in establishing remand foster care schemes, particularly in rural or sparsely populated areas. For example, Thomas (1998) identified problems in recruiting and retaining remand foster carers in certain areas in Wales, as remand foster care is required only infrequently and the carers cannot afford to continue without regular placements. Foster care is thus unavailable as an option for young people on remand, because there are no carers, and young people are placed in

41

residential units when a community option might have been more appropriate.

The management of remand foster care

It is difficult to know where best to locate remand fostering schemes as they draw on and have to conform to both welfare and criminal justice principles. For instance, in England and Wales,[6] social services departments have experience of providing foster care but do not have criminal justice expertise, and there is a risk that remand foster care will be subsumed by mainstream fostering as occurred in the 1980s. Youth Offending Teams have the necessary criminal justice expertise but not the experience of recruiting and training foster carers or supporting foster care placements. A survey of pre-trial accommodation for young people found that remand fostering schemes run by social services were less favourably rated by YOTs than those run by the YOTs themselves or by voluntary agencies in terms of meeting the young people's needs, although no explanation for this difference was given (Hucklesby and Goodwin, 2002). Wherever remand fostering is situated, it is important to have strong links between social services and YOTs to make sure that the welfare needs of young people on remand are not subordinated to criminal justice demands.

Summary

This chapter has outlined some of the shortfalls of bail support and supervision in providing for all children. The history and current status of remand foster care has been documented, alongside issues around the management of remand foster care schemes. The next chapter describes the objectives and methodology of the study on which this book is based, which aimed to explore the views of young people who have experienced remand foster care and to provide independent research evidence that might assist judicial, political and policy decision-making.

---

[6] The situation in Scotland differs as social services provide for children within the criminal justice system as well as those within the care system.

5 Research aims and methodology

Introduction

This chapter discusses the theoretical framework in which the research was situated. The aims and objectives of the empirical study are outlined and the methodology utilised to achieve these goals is discussed. Specific attention is paid to the ethical and practical implications of research with children, particularly those who are involved in the criminal justice process.

Knowledge base and theoretical perspective

The theoretical perspective underpinning the research on which this book is based draws upon feminist research principles and applies these principles to research with children. Whilst feminist theories are inherently adult-focused,[7] they can be developed and mediated through a children's rights perspective to provide insights into children's experiences (Alanen, 1994; O'Neill, 2001). Children's experiences and realities have been largely ignored as have, until relatively recently, women's experiences (see, for example, Oakley, 1981, 1994; Alanen, 1994) and the children's rights movement is confronting similar challenges to those of the feminist movement. The expression of women's views has often been muted, particularly in any situation where women's interests and perspectives are at variance with those of men (Anderson and Jack, 1991), and the articulation of children's experiences is similarly subdued in situations where their views are at variance with those of adults. As women were historically seen as the property of their husbands, children have been perceived as the property of their parents who are assumed to speak on their behalf. With the exception of children who are or who become

---

[7] Indeed, certain feminist authors problematise notions of children and childhood through their ideological opposition to conceptualisations of "motherhood" and child-rearing; see, for example, Firestone (1972).

"looked after", whose views have been given more credence by both practitioners and researchers,[8] and despite the right to be consulted and listened to established within the UNCRC and the Children Act 1989, many children are still considered to be either vulnerable, incompetent or unreliable witnesses of their own lives (Qvortrup, 1994).

There has been a cultural and political reluctance to take children's ideas seriously (Morrows and Richards, 1996), particularly those who are involved in offending behaviour who have been silenced in political and policy discourses. The label of "offender" further reduces a child's power to be heard or listened to: children who are also offenders are doubly subordinate through their status as offenders and as children (Becker, 1967). Children caught up in the justice process are suppressed through being prosecuted and punished, and are then not able to voice their opinions of the system that subjugates them. They are rarely viewed as children, but are seen as "other", and are denied the rights appertaining to "innocent" children (Davis and Bourhill, 1997; Fionda, 2001), reflecting a conceptual rift between deserving and undeserving children (Goldson, 2002c).

There is a need to protect children from exploitation by researchers but there is an inherent risk of exaggerating this need which may become a convenient mechanism to protect the superordinate adult world against the intrusion of subordinate children (Becker, 1967; Qvortrup, 1994). The criticisms of research with children – that they may make things up to please the interviewer; exaggerate or under-report certain behaviours; that their accounts are socially constructed; that they do not have enough knowledge to comment on their experiences – could all equally be applied to research with adults (Mayall, 1994) and cannot justify excluding children from the research process. To understand the effect social and public policies have on children, one must ask them directly:

---

[8] Since the implementation of the Children Act 1975, child care practitioners have had a legal duty to take into account of the views of children and, following this, child care research has developed a considerable tradition of including children's viewpoints (see, for example, Rowe et al, 1989; Triseliotis et al, 1995a).

To understand why someone behaves as he does you must understand how it looked to him, what he thought he had to contend with, what alternatives he saw open to him; you can understand the effects of opportunity structures, delinquent subcultures, social norms, and other commonly invoked explanations of behavior only by seeing them from the actor's point of view. (Becker, 2002, p. 80)

In terms of policy formulation, it is only logical that the users of a service are consulted about the service that they receive (Boyden and Ennew, 1997; Renold and Barter, 2003) and it is only just that children involved in the criminal justice system are consulted about their experiences of this system (Hill, 1997; Howard League, 1998). Research in which children have taken part has shown that they are more verbally skilled, emotionally considerate and socially qualified than might be anticipated (Fine and Sandström, 1988). This research therefore aimed to allow children and young people who are involved in a particular stage of the youth justice system to express their opinions, to share their experiences, and to explain the deficiencies of that system as they perceive them. Whilst children may be regarded as lacking in wisdom because they have not had sufficient experience of life (Roche, 1999), children involved in offending generally have had considerably more experience of the youth justice system than most adults. These young people are the "experts" in their field; it is impossible for an adult to comprehend what it means to be a child on remand without asking them directly.

Research aims and objectives

The purpose of this study was to investigate the viability of foster care for children and young people on remand, as an alternative to secure or non-secure residential accommodation, through an examination of the circumstances and experiences of young people on remand. As explained above, a key objective was to explore the young people's own constructions of their lives and experiences of the criminal justice system.

There were six main aims within the research:

* to create a profile of the young people referred to a specific remand foster care project to enable a comparison of the demographic

characteristics and offending histories of young people accommodated by the project and those not accommodated;

- to explore the young people's experiences of being on remand in a foster care placement and how this period of involvement in the criminal justice system fitted into the "story" of their lives;
- to consider these young people's views about the impact on them of the remand foster placement, including the interventions and supports provided to them during this time;
- to investigate the differences between "successful" remand foster placements and "unsuccessful" remand placements (that is, those that lasted until the young person was sentenced and those that did not last this long), and to consider factors that may contribute to the success of a placement;
- to investigate the perspectives of the remand foster carers on the needs of the young people on remand, the value of the placements and their views on the role and function of remand foster care;
- to discuss the remand decision-making process with local youth court magistrates and to discover their opinions of remand provision for young people in their area, including remand foster care.

Methodology

The project

The research was conducted with a specific remand foster care scheme in the south of England. The project is part of a national child care charitable organisation, with ring-fenced funding from social services, and provides remand foster care placements for four local authorities across the county in which it is based. This particular scheme was selected mainly due to the willingness of staff to be involved in the research but also because it is one of the most established remand fostering schemes in the country. The scheme is additionally one of the largest in that, at the time the research commenced, it employed eight foster carers – some more recently developed schemes have only one or two. Each foster carer within the scheme studied provides a placement for only one young person at a time, with the placement ending a week after the final court hearing. This is in contrast to other remand fostering schemes that allow the placement of more than one young person on remand with the foster carers or where carers are also able to provide placements for "mainstream" fostered children, and those which allow the placements to continue indefinitely. In addition to the eight foster carers, the project employed three remand fostering officers who were responsible for providing 24-hour support and assistance to the foster carers. Support for the placed young person was provided by the YOTs and social services. The foster carers were paid a relatively generous weekly allowance when a child was placed with them but did not receive a retaining fee if a child was not placed.

The project provides foster care placements for young people aged ten to 17 who have been remanded to local authority accommodation or bailed to reside as directed by the courts. At the time of the research, the initial referral to the scheme would generally be made by a YOT officer who was with the young person either in the police station or at his/her first court hearing. If a young person was remanded in custody, referrals to the scheme could be made prior to subsequent remand hearings. The remand fostering officer would identify a potential carer with whom the young person could be placed and this information would be presented to the court. If the court agreed that the young person should be remanded to local authority accommodation and thus placed with remand foster carers or bailed to reside as directed with the carers, a more detailed referral form would be completed with the young person. The young person and foster carer would also sign a placement agreement outlining the expectations of the carer and young person during the course of the placement. Once the placement had begun, a series of meetings would occur including the 72-hour statutory review for looked after children, home visits and weekly or bi-weekly placement reviews. Accounts of all contact and meetings were written by the remand fostering officers; this information was held within case file records which provided the basis for the quantitative data collection.

Case-file analysis

As comparatively little is known about remand foster care placements, it was important to gain contextual information about a relatively large number of placements and the characteristics of the young people in those placements. One objective was therefore to develop a profile of the young people referred to the scheme, collating quantifiable details about the duration of the placements, the frequency of absconding from or offending whilst in the placement, and more subjective data such as the quality of the relationship between the carers and young person. Analysis of this material enabled the identification of factors that influenced the success of the placements. This information provided a situational framework in which to locate the interviews with the young people and carers.

The study thus began with an examination of all the case records held by the project of the young people referred to it within the preceding 15 months.[9] Some of the young people were referred to the scheme more than once during the study period, which resulted in a total of 127 case records relating to 101 young people. Forty-six of these young people were placed with the project but 55 were not. Details of their backgrounds, demographic characteristics and offending histories were documented, together with specific information relating to the remand foster care placement for the 46 young people who were accommodated by the scheme during the study period.

Interviews with young people

Accessing participants

Of the 46 young people accepted by the project, one absconded on his way from court to the placement and so was not followed up for interview. However, attempts were made to trace the remaining 45 young people who had been placed with the scheme during the study period, through the YOTs with whom they had been registered.

There were a number of difficulties in tracing the young people, for example, the YOTs did not have current addresses for three of them and three were known to be homeless but were not in contact with any statutory organisations that could facilitate contact (Table 5.1).

---

[9] The initial time period chosen was 12 months, but this timeframe yielded only 92 cases, so the study period was extended for an additional three months to increase the overall sample.

Table 5.1
Reasons for young people not participating in the study

Reason for non-participation	Number	Percentage of non-participation (n = 27)	Percentage of total sample (n = 45)
Did not respond to contact made by letter	12	44	26
Did not respond to contact made by YOT	3	11	7
YOTs unable to provide current address	3	11	7
Known to be homeless	3	11	7
Did not attend appointments	3	11	7
Parental consent withheld	2	8	4
Direct refusal to take part	1	4	2
Total	**27**	**100**	**60**

Of those contacted by post, there can be no assumption that they received the letter as many have transient lifestyles and may have moved from the address provided. Furthermore, many socially excluded young people do not have "formal" daily routines as they may be attending neither school nor work and might be unused to responding to institutionalised approaches such as letters. Unfortunately there were no alternative approaches that were thought likely to be more effective. For example, many of the young people were no longer involved with the YOT so contact could not be facilitated by YOT staff and there were no youth clubs or groups common to the young people through which they could be contacted.

Consent

In addition to these difficulties, 31 of the potential participants were aged under 16 and consent had to be sought from their parents before they could be approached. Two parents withheld their consent; neither was asked to explain why but both voluntarily gave similar reasons for their refusal. One explained that her son was currently undergoing a mental health assessment and the other stated that her daughter was involved in a convoluted legal dispute. Both of these parents felt that participating in a research interview would be disruptive for the child at that particular time.

Ultimately, 21 young people agreed to take part in the research but three of them missed their appointments. "Failure" to keep appointments may of course be an indirect way of refusing to participate (Mahon *et al*, 1996) and discretion is required in deciding whether or not to try to arrange another interview. On two occasions a second appointment was arranged but again the young person did not attend. On the advice of the YOT officer the third young person who did not arrive at the pre-arranged meeting place was not contacted a second time.

Interview format

Narrative interviews (discussed below) were therefore conducted with 18 of the young people who had been placed in remand foster carer, six to 12 months after their placement had concluded. It was decided to conduct retrospective interviews, rather than talking to the young people during the remand period itself, for a number of reasons. Firstly, the remand period is only one part of the criminal justice process and cannot be seen in isolation from the rest of the system. What happens when the remand ends and in the immediate aftermath may be of importance to the young person, for example, in terms of accepting the sentence passed and adjusting to either custody or a move to alternative accommodation. Interviewing young people during the remand period would therefore decontextualise the significance of this time. Situating the remand period as a specific time within the totality of the young person's life allowed a more objective understanding of the "meaning" of the remand period for them, in the context of their previous and subsequent experiences. There is obviously the potential for *post hoc* rationalisation of behaviour, actions and events by the young people but this is seen as advantageous rather than detrimental to the research as the young people were able to reflect upon and evaluate their experiences of remand foster care within the context of their lives.

Secondly, the remand period tends to be relatively short and is an intense period of time for the young person who often has numerous and frequent appointments to attend. Some young people may not have the time, emotional strength or desire to become involved in academic research during what is often a period of considerable anxiety. Furthermore, any delays in contacting the young person, obtaining parental consent and arranging a convenient time to meet could mean that it is not possible to arrange an interview during the remand period. This problem would be enhanced for any placements that broke down, especially within the first few days of the placement, and so it would be difficult to recruit participants who had had particularly negative experiences of remand foster care. Interviewing the young people some time after the court case had been concluded allowed them to reflect upon their time on remand with potentially fewer external pressures and demands on their time by criminal justice agencies. It also enabled the possibility of interviewing young people whose placements broke down in the early stages of the remand period, thereby achieving a more balanced account of young people's experiences of remand foster care.

The third reason for conducting retrospective interviews was to allow the young people to be as honest and open about their experiences as possible. If a young person has any fear that what they say to the researcher during the interview may jeopardise the remand placement or influence the outcome of the trial, they could understandably be reluctant to share their views honestly (see also Fisher *et al*, 1986). By conducting the interviews after the conclusion of the trial, the young people could be confident that what they said could not affect their remand placement, their trial or sentence.

As mentioned above, tracing the young people to request their participation in retrospective interviews proved to be problematic. However, this difficulty was not considered sufficient to outweigh the benefits of contacting the young people after their court case had been concluded rather than during the remand period.

Narrative interviews

The interviews took the form of narratives of the young people's lives, asking them to tell the researcher their "story". Narratives are accounts of past events, held together either through a chronological or thematic sequence, in which the teller takes the listener to a previous time and recapitulates what happened to them (Riessman, 1993). Narratives are situated contextually and the respondent's social and political values will enter into the "metastory" about what happened (Riessman, 1993).

An interview guide was developed and specific questions were used as prompts if the young person was finding it difficult to start or continue their narrative and to probe issues further (Riessman, 1993; O'Neill, 2001). This process of narrating a story of previous events with targeted questions overcomes some of the potential causes of bias. For instance, allowing the young people to talk freely about what is important to them in the context of their lives prevents both negative bias (that is, the researcher excluding or undervaluing important issues) and positive bias (the researcher including or over-valuing unimportant or non-existent issues) (Fisher et al, 1986). Standard interview techniques can suppress the respondents' stories by limiting their responses to "relevant" answers to narrowly defined questions (Mishler, 1986). The use of narrative techniques moves beyond this process of stimulus and response and invites the respondents to describe and explain their stories in their own words. This requires skill on the part of the researcher in knowing when not to interrupt and when to stay silent to allow the respondent the opportunity to speak (Anderson and Jack, 1991).

Narrative interviewing is a particularly appropriate methodological tool to use with children as not all have the same ability to verbalise their experiences in response to specific questions, but the ability to construct narratives develops early and rapidly in children (Gee, 1985). Narrative interviewing provides the opportunity for children to talk about what is important and meaningful to them, sometimes with more eloquence than when answering specific questions: 'When space is made for them, children's voices express themselves clearly' (Mauthner, 1997, p. 21).

The interviews explored the young person's family and educational background, peer relationships, experience of the criminal justice system and, if appropriate, of social services and other agencies. The young people explained how they first became involved in offending behaviour, how their criminal career developed and their past and current attitude towards offending behaviour. They talked about their experience of the remand process and how they felt their time in a remand foster care placement had affected them, in terms of its impact on their behaviour, educational or employment status, family and peer relationships and also on the sentence they received. Although this was not a comparative study,[10] the young people described their previous experiences of the care system and of remand provision and how these compared with their experiences of remand foster care.

Validity[11] and the reliability of narrative research

The narrative approach allows respondents to have control over the material they include, which can result in incomplete coverage of the research questions and inconsistent data. However, as the aim of the research was to identify and explore rather than quantify themes and issues, this was not problematic. The quality of the information shared by the young people enabled the identification of patterns, relationships and issues common to their experiences of remand foster care and the wider criminal justice process.

Oral history and narrative methodologies clearly rely on the ability of the respondent to recall events and experiences. Memory is selective and many people will only remember what they considered to be of consequence or significant to them, but this in itself is notable: '*what* someone remembers can be a good indicator of what has been most important to that person over time' (Gittins, 1979, p. 92, original emphasis). The events that the young people recollected would not represent all of the experiences they had whilst involved in the criminal justice process, but the events that they do recall might be crucial in terms of their own understanding and interpretation of their lives.

Conducting the interviews

The interviews were conducted in a variety of settings. Nine of the 45 young people who had been placed with remand foster carers were in custodial institutions when they consented to participate in the research (see Lipscombe, 2003 for a full discussion of the ethical, logistical and

---

[10]The complexities of criminal legislature and the disparity in young people's offending histories makes comparisons difficult unless a very large sample can be obtained. However, many of the young people had previous experience of care and/or custody, which makes broad comparisons possible.

[11]The representativeness of the sample of young people interviewed and the implications of this for the validity of the research findings are discussed in Chapter 6.

practical implications of research with young people in custody). The remainder of the interviews were conducted in public settings, for example, fast-food restaurants, coffee shops and youth clubs. The researcher discussed with each young person where they would like to meet initially and then, once they had met, where they would like the interview to take place.[12] Although it was thought that these public settings would not be conducive to maintaining confidentiality, the young people seemed comfortable with the openness of the settings. There were a number of ways in which the young people contested and challenged the power of the researcher, for example, by turning up late for the appointment, calling the researcher at the last minute to change the meeting point, or having their friends waiting outside (see also Burman *et al*, 2001). Some of these mechanisms can provide a potential "escape clause" for respondents so that if, having met the researcher, they decide that they do not want to participate or continue the interview, they have an "excuse" to end it.

Rapport was facilitated by explaining to the young people that from the research perspective they were the "experts" and that the researcher knew virtually nothing about themselves or their lives and was learning about how the remand process worked and what it meant to be on remand. This approach was utilised successfully by Scully (1990) in her work with convicted rapists, and appeared to be beneficial here. The young people were reassured that they could withdraw from the research at any time without experiencing any adverse consequences and that they would not have to talk about any areas of their lives or specific events that they did not wish to.

Clearly the implicit power of the researcher, as an adult and as a researcher, over the young person cannot be ignored. Whilst the young person had control over what they included in their narrative during the interview, the researcher arranged, began and concluded the meeting and the young person's control was limited once the interview was completed (Gluck and Patai, 1991). As explained later, the interviews were transcribed so that the young people had a copy of the conversation and they

---

[12] See Davies (2000) for a discussion of the process of selecting an appropriate setting for interviews with offenders in the community.

were able to edit this script if they so wished, but they had no control over the analysis of the material.

The researcher's position, identity, gender and ethnicity will always influence the content and presentation of the respondent's narrative. Creating a narrative also creates an identity for the participant: 'In telling about an experience, I am also creating a self – how I want to be known by them' (Riessman, 1993, p.11). The young people in the study might have wanted to promote their identity as a young offender or as someone no longer involved with the criminal justice system and might have selected specific experiences to include in or exclude from their narratives. However, this subjectivity is an important factor in itself as it represents what the individual young people considered to be significant to their identity.

Confidentiality, disclosure and guilty knowledge

As with any research with children, it was possible that the young people in the study might disclose sensitive information about themselves during the interviews that they had not previously revealed to another adult. It was explained to the young people at the start of the interview, both verbally and through a written agreement, that they could only be offered partial confidentiality in this respect. Should they disclose anything that led the researcher to believe that they or any other young person were at risk of harm, this would be discussed with them to decide upon an appropriate course of action.

In addition to disclosure of risk or harm, the young people might share information about offences that they have committed but for which they have not been convicted. Whether researchers have a legal, ethical or moral obligation to report such "guilty knowledge" has been the focus of considerable debate (see Feenan, 2002). Due to the researcher's ideological stance against the criminalisation of children, a conscious decision was made not to report any past offending behaviour to the authorities. This position was conveyed to the young people so that they felt empowered to discuss their experiences without the threat of any adverse consequences.

Transcribing the interviews

The interviews conducted with children at liberty were, with the young person's consent, tape-recorded and later transcribed. The scripts were sent to the young people so that they could edit, add to or remove anything that they had said and had a record of the conversation for their own interest. The researcher was prevented by prison staff from tape-recording the interviews conducted within YOIs and so hand-written notes were taken during the interview, supplemented by a summary of the interview written immediately afterwards. These notes were written up fully and sent to the young people,[13] again asking for any amendments. The young people were informed at this stage that they could withdraw all or part of the information they had shared at any time. However, none made further contact with the researcher.

Interviews with foster carers

Semi-structured qualitative interviews were conducted with seven of the eight foster carers[14] employed by the project during the study period, plus one foster carer who had recently resigned from the project. This interview was particularly interesting as it enabled a more detailed discussion of the negative aspects of remand fostering and provided an insight into key factors that could influence a carer's decision to cease fostering. All of the interviews were conducted in the carers' homes. One interview involved both carers within a couple; the others were either with single carers or the main carer within a couple. Demographic details about the foster carers are presented in Chapter 11.

These taped interviews explored the carers' experiences of looking after young people on remand and their opinions about the goals, aims, and objectives of remand foster care. The emotional and behavioural difficulties presented by the young people were discussed, together with

---

[13] The researcher and young people discussed the possible consequences of having their mail opened by prison staff, but none felt that this would be problematic and all wanted to have copies of the interview notes sent to them.

[14] The eighth foster carer initially agreed to participate in an interview but later withdrew from the research due to constraints on her time.

the strategies the foster carers used to manage difficult behaviour. The carers' involvement in facilitating contact with the young person's family and friends and in arranging education, employment and other activities was considered. The foster carers were asked to talk about the training and support, including financial help, offered by the project and how satisfied they were with this. Early discussions with staff from one of the participating YOTs and with staff at the project suggested that gender might be a significant factor in the success of placements, as girls appear harder to manage within the placements. This echoes findings by O'Neill (2001) who found that staff in local authority secure units had a more negative attitude towards working with girls than with boys. A similar negative attitude to girls has been found to prevail among male residential workers in children's homes (Farmer and Pollock, 1998). The interviews therefore explored possible reasons for this, such as the similarities and differences between caring for girls and boys, and the carers' explanations of any gender differences in the management of young people.

Interviews with magistrates

Letters were sent via the Justices' Chief Executive of the Magistrates' Court Committee to the 220 lay youth court magistrates working within the geographical area encompassed by the study. The letters invited the magistrates to participate in a discussion about the remand process for young people. The magistrates were informed that the aim of the research was to explore children's and young people's experiences of being on remand and that their comments would give context to the study. They were not told that the main focus of the study was on remand foster care for reasons of methodological rigour. The objectives of the interview were to assess the general level of awareness of remand foster care within the youth court magistracy, to gauge magistrates' attitudes towards remand foster care as an alternative to custodial remands and to situate remand foster care within the range of provision available for young people on remand. Alerting potential respondents to the main thrust of the research could deter magistrates who knew very little about remand foster care from responding to the research request or promote active research of remand foster care provision prior to the interview. Similarly, it could encourage magistrates who have a particularly strong view of remand foster care, be it negative or positive, to respond to the invitation to participate. These factors have the potential to create a biased sample that would thereby affect the validity and reliability of the research. It can be argued that this approach is not entirely ethical as the magistrates were not fully informed about the research before they gave their consent, but in this instance it was considered necessary so that the results were not invalidated (see Kent, 2000). The magistrates were informed shortly after the interviews had been conducted that the research was going to focus specifically on remand foster care and that their views on this were welcomed.

Nineteen magistrates responded to the initial contact letter, of whom 13 were interviewed (a total response rate of 6 per cent). Three felt they did not have enough experience of the youth justice system to be able to contribute to the interview, having only very recently become youth court magistrates, and three were too busy to participate at that time. There are clearly implications for the representativeness of such a small sample. It might be that the magistrates who did respond to the contact letter were more concerned about the inadequacies of the remand system for young people or conversely had a more punitive attitude than those who did not respond, but there was no way of assessing this. Again, it is important to recognise that the interviews and corresponding analysis are not being advanced as established conclusions but as illustrative of some of the issues relevant to the remanding of young people.

The magistrates who did participate in the research were interviewed either in their own homes, offices or in the magistrates' court buildings. Their views of remand provision in the region were sought, including their knowledge and opinion of remand foster care as an alternative to secure accommodation. The factors that influence their decisions about remand outcomes were discussed to expound the findings from the case file analysis.

All of the interviews were tape-recorded and transcribed, with the transcripts sent to the participants to allow them to edit their comments.

Payment

The young people and foster carers who participated in the study were given a token payment of £10 for their time and assistance with the research. Whilst there are ethical debates about the appropriateness of doing so, it was believed that paying the participants would demonstrate that the researcher valued their experiences, views and opinions.

In accordance with their code of conduct, magistrates should not profit from their position as magistrates. The magistrates were therefore asked to nominate a charity to which a donation would be made on their behalf.

Discussions with other professionals

Discussions with YOT staff and the remand fostering officers employed by the project were held at the beginning of the research, and subsequently throughout the study. These discussions informed and guided the interviews with other participants and the analysis, and gave an insight into policy and practice issues. However, the research did not aim to consider in detail the role of the remand fostering officers nor how this differed in nature or impact from that of local authority social workers or YOT staff.

Analysis

The quantitative data obtained from the case-file analysis were analysed statistically, using SPSS, against a number of outcome measures. For example, the demographic characteristics and offending histories of those who were accommodated by the scheme were compared with those who were not, to identify any factors that differentiated the two groups. Similarly, demographic information was correlated with the likelihood of the remand foster placement disrupting before the young person was sentenced. The statistical analysis was not meant to be a positivistic reduction of the young people's experiences but was intended to identify themes, patterns and traits that may be influential in the outcome of the placement. The results of these analyses are presented in Chapter 6.

The qualitative data obtained from the interviews with young people were examined using a form of thematic analysis, identifying themes and categories that emerged during the interviews and the relationships and patterns between them (Ely *et al*, 1991), using the computer package NUD*IST as an aide to the analysis. The findings from these interviews are discussed in Chapters 8, 9 and 10.

The data from the interviews with magistrates and foster carers were subject to a more structured analysis, reflecting the more structured nature of the interviews. A framework of core concepts was created, including aspects specific to each group of respondents but also including generic concepts that were relevant to all of the participants. These findings are presented in Chapters 7 and 11, respectively.

Parameters of the research study

There are limits to the generalisability of the empirical research and caution is therefore necessary in the interpretation of the findings and the conclusions drawn. For example, it has to be acknowledged throughout the subsequent chapters that there were a relatively small number of participants, and that both girls and minority ethnic young people were under-represented in the empirical study, although they present particular issues that have numerous implications for policy and practice. As mentioned above, the involvement of remand fostering officers in the research was deliberately limited, and the birth children of the foster carers were not included in the research, although their views of and involvement with particular placements can be critical to the outcomes of the placement (Farmer *et al*, 2004). Furthermore, only one remand foster care scheme was studied and there may be differences between this and other schemes due to the management structure and staffing of the schemes, and their geographical locations. It is necessary to reiterate that the research aimed to identify issues, themes and patterns surrounding the use of remand foster care and was conducted with a primarily qualitative, rather than quantitative, intent.

Summary

This chapter has outlined the knowledge base and theoretical framework in which the research was situated, the aims and objectives of the study and the methodological approaches used. The next chapters consider the findings from the research, which are drawn together and discussed, with reference to policy and practice implications, in Chapter 12.

6 Characteristics of the young people on remand

Introduction

The case-file records of all 101 young people referred to the scheme over a 15-month period were scrutinised. Nineteen of the young people had more than one referral to the scheme during the study period (Table 6.1) and for these instances details of the most recent referral or placement were recorded. Information about the young people's backgrounds, demographic characteristics and offending histories was documented. The young people referred to the scheme were aged between 10.5 and almost 18 years (see Figure 6.1, p. 68); 46 of the 101 young people were placed with remand foster carers with their placements lasting between two and 144 days (Figure 6.2).

Table 6.1
Number of referrals to the scheme during the study period

Number of referrals (including index referral)	Number of young people
One	82
Two	14
Three	3
Four	2
Total number of young people	101
Total number of referrals	**127**

The 101 young people referred to the scheme

Information was collected on a number of current difficulties and past adversities that the young people might have experienced, including sexual, physical and emotional abuse; difficult family relationships;

previous experience of the care system; and mental health difficulties[15] in order to determine whether there were identifiable characteristics that influenced whether a young person was actually placed with the scheme. Young people were only considered to have experienced a particular difficulty or adversity if it was clearly mentioned in the files. This is likely to have resulted in an underestimation of the levels of adversity and difficulty experienced, as instances of suspected but unproven adversity were not included. However, it is clear that, as research on young offenders has previously shown (West and Farrington, 1973; Farrington, 1996; Rutter *et al*, 1998; Moore and Peters, 2003), the young people had frequently encountered considerable adversity during their childhood and that the majority had experienced difficult relationships with their parents or step-parents. Being looked after in the care system is associated with adolescent offending (Stewart *et al*, 2002);[16] 52 per cent of the young people referred to the scheme had been looked after at some stage in their lives. As previous research has shown (Hester *et al*, 2000; Higgins and McCabe, 2001), many of the young people had suffered multiple patterns of disadvantage.

Of the 101 young people referred to the scheme, ten were girls and nine were of minority ethnic origin. The proportion of minority ethnic young people referred was higher than in the population of the specific

---

[15] The difficulties and adversities the young people experienced need to be interpreted and understood in light of the wider societal conditions and structural inequalities (such as poverty, access to education and employment, the provision of state benefits, housing conditions, standards of health care provision, discrimination and so forth) which they may have endured and which are known to be associated with offending behaviour (see, for example, Graham and Bowling, 1995; Foster, 2000; Social Exclusion Unit, 2002). However, information regarding the environmental, cultural and economic backgrounds of the young people was not consistently documented within their case-file records and therefore the analysis here is focused on individual experiences and characteristics.

[16] There is a complex relationship between being looked after in the care system and adolescent offending: Stewart and colleagues (2002) found that children who had "out-of-home" placements were more likely to offend than children who had experienced similar adversities but who had not had an "out-of-home" placement, but this is likely to be related to the severity of the factors that precipitated a child's placement in care as well as a child's experiences whilst they were looked after (see also Sinclair and Gibbs, 1998).

county (Office for National Statistics, 2003).[17] In a further six cases, the ethnicity of the young person was not recorded. All but 14 of the young people had previously been sentenced by a youth court; the previous sentences varied in tariff from conditional discharges to custodial sentences. Sixty-six of the young people were classified as persistent offenders, having been convicted on at least three separate occasions, although some had committed many more offences, 12 having over 20 previous recorded convictions.

The current charges facing the young people are listed in Table 6.2 (see also Goldson and Peters, 2002). Thirteen young people were charged with a single offence and the majority (78) were charged with between two and six offences, with nine young people being charged with between seven and 20 offences.

The differences between those children who were and were not remanded to foster care will now be considered, before looking in more detail at the characteristics of those placed with the scheme and of the placements themselves.

Who was and who was not placed with the scheme?

As explained above, of the 101 young people referred to the scheme, 55 were not placed with remand foster carers. The reasons why varied, although in 11 cases the reason was not recorded. In ten cases (22 per cent of the 44 cases where information about the decision was available) the magistrates granted bail and the young person returned home or to other relatives (Table 6.3). In another ten cases (22 per cent) the magistrates imposed a secure remand and the young person was thus placed in either a secure unit or a YOI. In 13 cases (30 per cent) the scheme was either unable or unwilling to offer a placement for the young person. This is discussed in detail later.

---

[17] This might be due to a higher proportion of black and minority ethnic young people becoming involved with the criminal justice system due to inherent racism (The Children's Society, 2000a, 2000b), or might be an attempt by criminal justice agencies to provide minority ethnic children with a greater chance of being remanded to foster care. Further research would be necessary to clarify this.

Table 6.2

The current charges facing the young people

Offence	Referred and placed	Referred but not placed	Total number
Theft/attempted theft	26	17	43
Burglary (dwelling)	18	17	35
Common assault/violent disorder	12	21	33
'Taking (a vehicle) Without the Owner's Consent (TWOC)/aggravated TWOC/ allowing self to be carried	20	13	33
Criminal damage	14	13	27
Public order offences	7	18	25
Other vehicle offences (including driving without insurance, driving whilst disqualified, etc.)	10	14	24
Breach of bail	9	10	19
Actual Bodily Harm /Grievous Bodily Harm	7	11	18
Burglary (non-dwelling)	6	9	15
Breach of community penalties	6	9	15
Robbery/attempted robbery	3	10	13
Shoplifting	9	3	12
Assaulting a police officer	9	1	10
Arson/arson with intent*	10	0	10
Rape/indecent assault	3	7	10
Attempted murder*	7	1	8
Handling stolen goods	2	5	7
Conspiracy to burgle	2	4	6
Obstructing police (including resisting arrest, perverting course of justice, escape from lawful custody)	1	4	5
Possession of offensive weapon	0	4	4
Possession of class B drugs	1	3	4
Deception	1	1	2
Other	1	1	2
Total number of offences	**184**	**196**	**380**

* One young person had been charged with seven counts of attempted murder and seven counts of arson with intent

Table 6.3
Why young people were not placed with remand foster carers

Reason	Number of young people	Per cent of young people
Scheme unable or unwilling to offer a placement	13	30
Granted bail	10	22
Remanded to secure accommodation/YOI	10	22
Young person rejected remand foster placement	5	11
Young person did not meet criteria	2	5
No bail application made	2	5
Young person changed plea	2	5

$n = 44$

Five young people (11%) themselves rejected the opportunity to have a remand foster care placement and were remanded to either non-secure or secure residential accommodation. Whilst remand foster care is seen by many professionals and academics as preferable to residential or secure facilities (see Chapter 4), some young people might be apprehensive about being placed with a family, particularly when their previous experiences of family life have been negative or if they are to be placed with carers of a different cultural or ethnic background. The attitudes of young people towards remand foster care is discussed further in Chapters 9 and 10.

In two instances (5%) the young person did not meet the criteria necessary to allow a remand to foster care, for example, because although their alleged offence was committed within the area served by the project, their usual residence was outside its remit. In another two cases (5%) the young people changed their plea to guilty and were thus sentenced, rather than remanded, at their court appearance so a decision about their remand was superfluous. In two cases (5%), however, no bail application was made, which suggests that the defence solicitor might not have realised that alternative provision was available and the young people were remanded to a YOI. This was an issue raised by the National Remand Review Initiative (Moore, 1999; Goldson and Peters, 2002), which noted that, in over a third of the cases studied, the court had not been given the opportunity to consider alternative arrangements. It is clearly essential to provide the court with adequate information about remand foster care so that bail applications are not seen as futile or as foregone conclusions.

Factors influencing the decision to place a young person with the scheme

A simple statistical analysis was undertaken to determine whether there were particular factors that appeared to influence the remand decision made by the magistrates. This analysis excluded the two young people mentioned above, who were sentenced at the court hearing and so for whom a remand decision was not made, and the two who did not meet the criteria for a remand to foster care, and is therefore based on 97 cases.

The quality and quantity of information about the defendant that is presented to the magistrates will vary enormously, depending upon the advocacy of the solicitors and/or YOT officer. Certain information, such as the nature and seriousness of the offence, and the defendant's previous response to bail (where applicable), will be presented in all contested bail decisions, either by the prosecution or the defence. Other information may be provided by the defence solicitor to address objections to bail raised by the prosecution, for example, to demonstrate evidence of strong community links if the prosecution argues that the young person is likely to abscond. The prosecution may also present details about the young person's home background if they feel that bail should be refused for the protection or welfare of the young person, for instance, if there is a history of domestic violence or other family problems. The information presented to the magistrates was therefore unlikely to be consistent across different cases,[18] but a few trends in decision-making were apparent whilst the influence of other factors, expected to influence decisions, was noticeably absent.

---

[18]It was beyond the remit of this study to document precise details of the information provided to the court about each young person; however, it seems fair to assume that the information available to the scheme at the time of the referral was also available to the YOT officer and/or defence solicitor and therefore would have been presented to the magistrates.

Age and gender

There were no statistically significant differences between the ages of the 46 young people placed with the scheme and the 55 referred but not placed with the scheme (Figure 6.1), nor did gender appear to affect the decision whether or not to place a young person with remand foster carers.

Figure 6.1

The age of the young people referred to the scheme

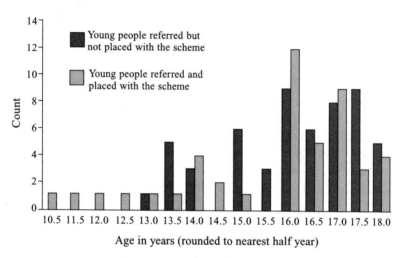

Age in years (rounded to nearest half year)

However, the girls referred to the scheme were significantly younger than the boys: the mean age of the girls was fractionally over 15 years ($x =$ 180.3 months, $sd = 16.12$) compared with a mean age of 16 years and two weeks for the boys ($x = 192.5$ months, $sd = 18.85$ months) ($t = 2.24$, $df = 11$, $p < 0.05$). This reflects previous research (see, for example, Flood-Page *et al*, 2000) that the peak age of offending is lower for girls than it is for boys. Furthermore, girls were significantly more likely than boys to have experienced physical abuse (Fisher's exact test, $p = 0.023$) and emotional abuse (Fisher's exact test, $p = 0.008$), and to have either self-harmed or attempted suicide in the past (Fisher's exact test, $p = 0.011$). Although not statistically significant, girls were more likely to have previously been looked after in the care system than boys. They were also significantly more likely to have experienced higher numbers of previous adversities overall ($\chi^2 = 13.35$, $df = 2$, $p < 0.01$).

Exceptions to the right to bail

The Bail Act 1976 outlines the exceptions to the right to bail and the reasons for which bail may be refused (Chapter 3). The latter include the nature and seriousness of the offence, the accused's previous record when granted bail (for example, absconding or committing offences whilst on bail) and the character, antecedents and community ties of the defendant. Somewhat surprisingly, there was no clear relationship between the nature of the offence allegedly committed and the likelihood of the young person being granted bail. There was a slight tendency for young people who had been charged with a violent offence to be refused bail but this was not statistically significant. Young people who had previously breached bail were no more likely to be refused bail on this occasion than those who had not done so. Neither the number of previous convictions nor the highest tariff sentence that the young person had previously received were significantly related to the likelihood of the young person being granted bail. It thus seems that the magistrates' decisions were being influenced more by factors about the young person's character and background than by factors about their offending behaviour.

Education or employment

Young people who were not involved in any form of education, training or employment were significantly more likely to be remanded into secure accommodation or custody than those who had some sort of educational or employment provision. Thirty per cent (17) of those who were not in education or employment were remanded to secure accommodation or custody compared with only seven per cent (3) of those who were in education or employment ($\chi^2 = 10.038$, $df = 4$, $p < 0.05$). This suggests that the lack of appropriate education, training and employment for young people of this age has a detrimental effect on the remand decision, perhaps because these young people are seen as being less responsible or having fewer positive links with their community, and are considered to be at more risk of absconding or failing to surrender to custody at the requisite time.

Previous residence

Where the young people had been living during the few months prior to their arrest was recorded, as was their residence immediately preceding the remand hearing. For some young people this was the same; for example, they had been living with their family prior to their court appearance and were still living there at the time the remand decision was made. For others this had varied; for instance, they may have been homeless prior to their arrest and were initially remanded in custody before being referred to the scheme. Interestingly, there appeared to be no relationship between the young person's residence prior to their arrest and the outcome of the remand decision, which is contrary to previous research findings in the adult court (Bottomley, 1970; King, 1971). However, 47 per cent of those who were initially remanded in custody were then remanded to foster care, which suggests that these young people did not need to be held in custody for this period and alternative accommodation should have been provided.

Adversities

Young people who had experienced a high number of background adversities were more likely to be remanded to local authority accommodation and placed in foster care than those with less difficult backgrounds. Eighty per cent (8) of those who had experienced between six and eight types of adversity were placed with remand foster carers compared with 53 per cent (31) of those who had experienced between three and five types of adversity, and only 25 per cent (7) of those who had experienced two or fewer types of adversity (χ^2 = 11.024, df = 4, p <0.05). These are issues that might be raised by the prosecution solicitor to prevent the granting of bail for the young person's protection or welfare.

These findings suggest that remand foster care is seen as a "welfare option" for children who have had particularly disadvantaged backgrounds. The magistrates were asked about this in interviews and there was some suggestion that the background of the individual child could influence the remand decision regardless of the nature of the alleged offence or their previous offending history (Chapter 7). It is possible that these young people were already known to social services, which might have influenced the court's decision.

Self-harm

Given the prolonged attention to the high levels of self-harm and suicide by young people in custody (Chapter 1), it was of some concern to note that magistrates did not appear to take into consideration a young person's history of self-harm or suicide attempts when deciding on the most appropriate form of remand. Again, the magistrates' knowledge of a young person's propensity to self-harm is dependent upon the information provided by the defence or YOT, but these findings suggest that the risk of self-harm is not being seriously considered within the court. Indeed, only four of the magistrates, when interviewed, mentioned the vulnerability criteria.

Justice by geography

Conversely, recent figures show that there are geographical and regional differences in remand and sentencing rates (Youth Justice Board, 2002) and it was expected that these differences would be reflected across the areas served by the four YOTs. However, there were no significant relationships between the court that the young person attended and the remand outcome.

The 13 young people not offered a placement by the scheme

As mentioned above, a remand foster placement was not always forthcoming, with 13 young people being refused a placement by the scheme. On one occasion all of the remand foster care placements were occupied and the scheme was unable to offer a placement for the young person, who was then subject to a custodial remand. In the remaining 12 cases the scheme was unwilling to offer a placement for the specific young person. The case-file records generally stated that a placement could not be offered due to the potential risk to the foster carers or their families. For example, on four occasions the young person had been charged with a sexual offence but the only foster placements available were in families with young children who were deemed to be at risk. However, statistical analysis suggested that the decision to offer a placement was not significantly related to whether or not the young person was charged with a sexual offence; indeed, a number of young people who had been charged with sexual offences were placed with foster carers.

Similarly, a number of young people who were thought to present a physical risk to the foster family were refused placements by the project, but this appeared to be based on their previous history of violent offences, rather than whether or not they were currently charged with a violent offence. Twenty-four per cent (7) of those who had previously committed a violent offence were not offered a placement by the scheme compared with only nine per cent (5) of those who had not committed a violent offence in the past, although this is not a statistically significant difference.

The only significant indicator of whether or not a young person was likely to be refused a placement by the scheme was whether they had experienced mental health problems. Twenty-four per cent (7) of those who were recorded as having mental health difficulties were not offered a foster care placement compared with only seven per cent (5) of those who did not have mental health problems (Fisher's exact test, $p =$ 0.028). Mental health services provision is a problematic area for many organisations and institutions working with young offenders, with 40 per cent of YOTs reporting considerable dissatisfaction with access to Child and Adolescent Mental Health Services (Youth Justice Board, 2001a). It is therefore unsurprising that the remand foster care project is reluctant to accept young people who are unlikely to receive the mental health support they need. Unfortunately these young people are unlikely to have their needs met by alternative forms of remand provision either. This suggests that, even in areas where remand fostering schemes exist, there is still a particular need for additional mental health resources and support for young people on remand. The views of the foster carers and young people about mental health provision is discussed in later chapters.

Of the three cases where the scheme refused to offer a placement and the remand outcome was known, one young person remained with the respite foster carers with whom he had previously been living, another was remanded to a secure unit and the third was remanded to a YOI. The latter instance was a cause for considerable concern as the young person had a history of self-harm and had made recent suicide attempts. A placement in secure accommodation had been requested but none were available. The subsequent remand placement for nine of the young people who were not offered a foster care placement by the scheme was not recorded, so it is not clear whether a refusal to offer a remand foster placement was detrimental for the young person.

The 46 young people accommodated by the scheme

Forty-six young people were placed with the project during the 15-month study period: 40 boys and six girls. The ages of the young people ranged between ten-and-a-half and almost 18 years (see Figure 6.1). Forty of the young people were classified as white (36 boys and four girls), four (two boys and two girls) were of minority ethnic origin and one boy was of dual heritage. The ethnicity of one boy was not recorded. As noted above, many of the young people on remand had experienced a wide range of difficulties and past adversities (Table 6.4).

Table 6.4
Current difficulties and past adversities experienced by the young people

Type of adversity	Number	Per cent
Poor family relationships	42	91
Drug/alcohol misuse	36	78
Experience of care system	26	57
Self-harm/suicide attempts	19	41
Mental health difficulties	16	35
Learning difficulties	16	35
Physical abuse	9	20
Emotional abuse	7	15
Neglect	4	9
Sexual abuse	3	7

n = 46

Fourteen of the 46 young people were living with a parent at the time of the referral to the scheme, including only three who were living with both birth parents. The majority of young people were in care, custody or were homeless. Thirteen were on remand in Young Offender Institutions, with a further two in secure units (Table 6.5).

Table 6.5
Young person's residence at time of referral

Residence	Number	Per cent
Young Offender Institution (YOI)	13	28
Homeless	11	24
Lone parent	4	9
Residential care	3	7
Birth parent and step-parent	7	15
Secure unit	2	4
Both birth parents	3	7
Friends	1	2
Foster care	1	2
Adoptive parents	1	2
Other	0	0
Not known	0	0
Total	**46**	**100**

Education and employment

Poor educational or employment attainment has consistently been associated with offending behaviour (Graham and Bowling, 1995; Haines and Drakeford, 1998; Rutter *et al*, 1998; NACRO, 1999c). For example, truancy and school exclusions have been related to anti-social behaviour (Audit Commission, 1996). Whilst young people may be excluded specifically because of their offending behaviour, at another level, there has been a substantial increase in the number of permanent school exclusions, partly as a result of the publication of league tables and the introduction of other market type mechanisms. This has placed schools under pressure to reduce the number of "difficult" and disadvantaged children (Jackson and Martin, 1998; NACRO, 1999c); children who are disengaged from school may be more disaffected generally and feel that they have nothing to lose by offending (The Children's Society, 1993). Furthermore, other factors are likely to influence both educational attainment and offending behaviour, such as social exclusion, discrimination, poverty, poor housing, large family size and inadequate parental supervision (NACRO, 1999c). The majority (24) of the 46 young people placed in remand foster care were in neither education nor employment (Table 6.6), only ten being in mainstream school or college.

Table 6.6
Young person's education or employment status at time of referral

Type of education or employment	Number	Per cent
Mainstream school/college	10	22
Pupil referral unit	6	13
Special day school	2	4
Home tuition	0	0
Full-time employment	1	2
Training scheme	2	4
Combination of education and employment	0	0
Neither	24	53
Not recorded	1	2
Total	**46**	**100**

The placements

The median length of placements was 28 days (mean length 37 days), with the shortest being two and the longest 144 days (Figure 6.2). One placement effectively never began as the young person absconded on the way to the carers' home from his court appearance.[19] This immediately raises questions about whose responsibility it is to co-ordinate effective transport arrangements for young people leaving court – whether this responsibility lies with the YOT, social services, the remand foster care scheme or the individual foster carer.

Whilst one of the aims of the placements is to maintain the young person until they are sentenced, 50 per cent (23) of the placements ended before the young person was sentenced, mainly due to the young person's difficult behaviour within the placement (39 per cent, 9), absconding (30 per cent, 7) or offending (22 per cent, 5). One placement ended when the young person made an allegation of sexual assault against the foster

---

[19] n will therefore vary between 45 and 46 depending on which factors are being analysed.

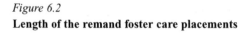

Figure 6.2

Length of the remand foster care placements

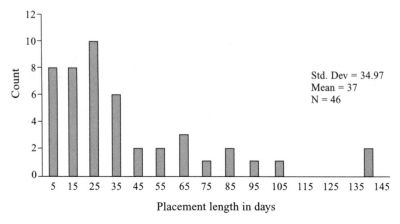

Std. Dev = 34.97
Mean = 37
N = 46

Placement length in days

carers (the allegation was subsequently withdrawn) and another when the young person found himself alternative accommodation and elected, with the court's consent, to move out of the foster placement. Factors that were related to the likelihood of the placement ending before the young person was sentenced are discussed later in this chapter. Although placements that broke down tended to be slightly shorter than those that did not (mean lengths were 31 days and 42 days respectively), this difference was not statistically significant. Indeed, one placement lasted for 112 days and another for 84 days before disrupting.

Conditions

Conditions were attached to the remand for 27 of the 46 young people (61 per cent), with 12 being subject to curfews, four being subject to conditions of non-association and 11 being subject to both. Non-association was typically with other young people with whom they had allegedly committed the offence but also included relatives, in one instance the young person's mother. Having conditions attached to the remand is a double-edged sword in that the foster carers generally appreciated the additional control they were afforded by the conditions (see Chapter 11) but over half (15, 56 per cent) of the young people breached the conditions of their remand. Whilst failure to comply with a condition of remand is not an offence in itself, it does mean that a young person can be returned to court. Any breach of conditions can then constitute an exception to the general right to bail and the young person can be remanded in custody. In effect, therefore, attaching conditions to a remand can result in the young person being remanded to custody, whereas if no conditions had been attached to the remand they would have remained on remand in the foster placement.

The "success" of the placements

In relation to the Bail Act 1976 and the objections to bail, the main criteria by which the success of remand foster care placements should be judged are the levels of offending whilst on remand, absconding and interfering with the course of justice. There were no recorded instances of interfering with the course of justice as such, although some young people when interviewed admitted to breaching conditions of non-association which, in some circumstances, could amount to interfering with the course of justice, for example, if they associated with witnesses.

Absconding

As noted above, seven (15 per cent) of the 46 young people absconded from the placement. One young person absconded on his way from the remand hearing, another within 48 hours of arriving at the placement. Two young people appeared initially to settle well into the placement but absconded after five days, one of whom returned home to her mother. One placement lasted for 15 days before the young person absconded, although he had been displaying disruptive and difficult behaviour throughout the placement. He did not return to the placement, was reported missing to the police who located him in an amusement arcade in a drunken and abusive state and the placement was subsequently ended. The other two who absconded did so after 28 and 46 days, both with relatives (one his mother, the other his half-brother). Both of these placements had been considered to be progressing well but it appears that the "pull" of their families was too strong to resist.

Young people who had previously been in care were significantly more likely to abscond (Fisher's exact test, $p = 0.012$); indeed all seven of those who absconded had been looked after at some stage. These young people may have become used to absconding as a way of dealing with difficulties (see, for example, Farmer and Parker, 1991).

Offending in placement

It is notable that only 11 (24 per cent) of the 46 young people were known by the police to have offended whilst they were in the remand foster placement and, of these, only one was considered to have committed an offence more serious than the original charge. This is a considerable achievement in light of the young people's previous offending histories and backgrounds. This level of offending is considerably lower than has been found for young people remanded to local authority accommodation (58 per cent) and young people granted bail (35 per cent) (Brown, 1998; Chapter 4).

Six of the young people were known to have committed offences on only one occasion during the placement. These offences included shoplifting (two young people), TWOC (taking [a vehicle] without the owner's consent), theft, burglary and "going equipped for theft". The remaining five young people committed offences on more than one occasion, with two committing thefts, and one committing a burglary and also numerous driving offences. The details of one young person's offending were not recorded but it was noted that he was arrested three times during the placement. The fifth young person was involved in a series of physical attacks against women.

Young people who were subject to a curfew were significantly more likely to commit an offence during the placement than those who were not, with 39 per cent (9) of the young people who had a curfew committing an offence compared with 11 per cent (2) of those who did not (Fisher's exact test, $p = 0.038$). This suggests that magistrates were fairly accurate in their concerns about offending whilst on remand when deciding whether to impose a curfew, but that curfews are relatively ineffective in preventing the commitment of offences.

Young people who were known to have difficulties with their peers, for example, being easily led, were significantly more likely to offend than those who did not have such difficulties (Fisher's exact test, $p = 0.019$). This implies that an emphasis on helping young people to negotiate and manage their peer relationships might be beneficial in reducing incidences of offending whilst they are in foster care. Similarly, young people who were either currently involved in substance misuse or had a history of drug or alcohol misuse were more likely to commit an offence during the placement (Fisher's exact test, $p = 0.045$). Whilst some did have drugs or alcohol counselling during the placement, others did not. Arguably, increased counselling provision might help young people manage their substance use and could have a knock-on effect on the likelihood of them committing offences whilst on remand.

Young people whose educational or employment situation was considered by the fostering officers to have been enhanced during the placement were significantly less likely to offend (Fisher's exact test, $p = 0.012$), as were young people whose family relationships were believed to have improved (Fisher's exact test, $p = 0.005$). These figures emphasise the importance of viewing the young person holistically and dealing with issues of peer and family relationships, education and employment, substance misuse and social inclusion, rather than merely focusing on their offending behaviour.

The wider benefits of remand foster care

The remand foster placements had the potential to begin to address these wider issues of social integration or exclusion. Ratings were made by the researcher, based upon written information from the case-file records, of how beneficial the foster placements were for the young people in terms of promoting good behaviour during the placement, improving family relationships and developing opportunities for education, training or employment. The records were, as a whole, very detailed and appeared to be reliable and coherent accounts of the placements.

Behaviour in placement

Nineteen (42 per cent) of the 46 young people were rated as displaying good behaviour during the placement, 13 (29 per cent) as showing acceptable behaviour and 13 (29 per cent) as showing poor behaviour. Young people were rated as displaying poor behaviour if details of repeated negative behaviour were recorded in the files. For example, one young person was described as manipulative, an habitual liar (including faking injuries to himself to create an excuse for coming home late), and having problems with gambling. Another young person was described as uncommunicative, being verbally abusive to the carers and project staff, and having no commitment to the placement.

Examples of young people rated as showing acceptable behaviour include a young person who lied to the carers about smoking and who showed poor personal hygiene, but for whom there were no other reported behavioural difficulties. Another young person was described as not causing any problems as such but as being difficult to motivate and reluctant to join in activities. One young boy developed a good relationship with his carers but was involved in a number of minor but irritating behaviours, such as drawing pictures with the carer's lipstick and needlessly wasting toiletries.

Young people for whom there were no recorded behavioural difficulties and for whom positive behaviour was documented were rated as displaying good behaviour. Examples of this included having settled in well, obeying the house-rules, being polite and well-behaved, being considerate and courteous, and developing good relationships with the carers' family.

Relationship with carers

The relationship between the young person and the carers was also rated. Six young people (14 per cent) were rated as having a very negative or negative relationship with the carers, 11 (25 per cent) had a neutral or mixed relationship and 27 (61 per cent) had a positive or very positive relationship with them.[20] Unsurprisingly, young people who showed good behaviour in the placement were more likely to develop a positive relationship with their carers, but some carers were still able to develop positive relationships with a number of those who displayed poor behaviour (Table 6.7). This suggests that some carers are able to see beyond (or behind) the child's actions and not judge them solely on their behaviour.

---

[20] As noted above, one young person did not arrive at the placement and there was not sufficient information on another young person's relationship with the carers for the researcher to make a judgement.

Table 6.7
Young person's behaviour in the placement and their relationship with the carers

Behaviour in placement	*Relationship with carers*					
	Negative		*Neutral*		*Positive*	
	No.	*%*	*No.*	*%*	*No.*	*%*
Poor	5	39	5	39	3	23
Average	0	0	5	42	7	58
Good	1*	5	1	5	17	90

n = 44

* The carers who had a negative relationship with the young person, even though her behaviour was good, were the carers against whom an allegation was made.

Education and employment

As already acknowledged within this book and in much other research, there are strong associations between low educational status and inadequate educational and employment provision and offending behaviour. It is therefore recognised by the scheme that education and employment are important factors to be addressed. As shown in Table 6.6, at the start of the placement 24 of the 46 young people (53 per cent) had no educational or employment provision.

The timescale for establishing or rebuilding educational and employment links is very short, with the mean length of the placements being only five weeks. However, 18 (39 per cent) of the young people made positive changes such as attending school more regularly, registering with employment agencies, joining training schemes or finding part-time or temporary jobs. Twenty-five (54 per cent) maintained their existing educational or employment status, which could be either in education or employment (9) or neither (16). Although these young people's situation was not improved, it was not detrimentally affected. Home tuition was arranged for two (4 per cent) young people but delays in providing this meant that the remand period had ended before the tuition was in place.

Unfortunately, however, three (7 per cent) young people's education was negatively affected by their placement. One had been attending a

81

mainstream school but it was too far from the placement for him to continue attending. The other two were sporadically attending Pupil Referral Units prior to the placement but did not attend at all during the placement.

As detailed above, young people who had seen a positive improvement in their educational or employment status during the placement were significantly less likely to offend whilst they were on remand. It is important, therefore, that continued emphasis is placed on encouraging and assisting the young people to find employment or education. The young people's views on their education and employment and the foster carers' experiences of helping the young people access education and employment opportunities are discussed in later chapters.

Family relationships

If the foster placement was beneficial for the young person in terms of maintaining or improving family relationships, they were also significantly less likely to commit an offence during the placement. Sixteen (35 per cent) of the young people were able to re-negotiate their relationships with key family members, often actively assisted by the foster carers. Most of the foster carers saw family relationships as pivotal to changing the young person's behaviour and were therefore keen to become involved in repairing these relationships (Chapter 11).

Factors affecting breakdown

A simple statistical analysis was also conducted to determine whether it was possible to identify factors that were associated with placement breakdown. As previously detailed, 23 of the placements ended earlier than ideally planned. One did not even begin because the young person absconded on his way from court; another ended on the day sentence was passed due to deterioration in the young person's behaviour during the few days preceding the trial.

Neither the age nor the gender of the young person seemed to influence the likelihood of the placement disrupting.[21] Indeed, exactly half of the

---

[21] The number of minority ethnic young people placed with the scheme was too small to determine whether ethnicity is related to the likelihood of placement breakdown.

placements of girls and half of the placements of boys disrupted before sentencing. None of the adversities that the young people had experienced were significantly related to the likelihood of the placement disrupting, with the exception of whether or not they had previously been looked after in the care system. Seventeen (65 per cent) of the young people who had previously been in care experienced placement disruptions compared with six (30 per cent) of those who had not been looked after (Fisher's exact test, p = 0.018). This association is largely due to the seven young people with care histories who absconded from their placements. It may be that these young people have more fragile relationships with their family and less family support or, as already noted, that they have become used to absconding as a way of dealing with difficulties.

Melvin and Didcott (1976) found that being charged with theft and having multiple charges were both related to the likelihood of bail being breached.[22] There were similar findings in this study in that young people charged with theft were more likely to experience the breakdown of their placement. Seventy-three per cent (11) of those charged with theft experienced a disruption compared with 39 per cent (12) of those not charged with theft (Fisher's exact test, p = 0.029). Similarly, young people who were charged with more than five offences were more likely to experience a placement disruption than those charged with fewer than five (Fisher's exact test, p = 0.029). However, there was also a correlation between theft and the number of charges faced: young people accused of theft were more likely to be charged with five or more offences than those not accused of theft (Fisher's exact test, p = 0.003). A larger research sample would be necessary to determine which factor is the most influential in affecting placement breakdown.

Both offending whilst on remand and absconding from the placement were significantly related to the likelihood of the placement disrupting (Fisher's exact test, p = 0.018 and p = 0.005, respectively), although breaching court-ordered conditions was not. The factors that were associa-

---

[22] However, Melvin and Didcott (1976) acknowledge that these "high-risk" factors are still poor distinguishers of risk, and to select people for bail or custody on this basis would not be efficient due to the large number of false negatives and false positives that would be identified.

ted with offending whilst on remand and absconding were documented above.

The interview participants

As explained in Chapter 5, 18 of the 46 young people who had been placed in remand foster care participated in an interview. These young people were aged between 13 and 18 at the time of the interview. Two were female, two were black and one was of dual heritage. The charges they faced at the time of their remand included TWOC and aggravated TWOC, theft, burglary, robbery, common assault, ABH, arson and indecent assault. There were no statistical differences in the demographic characteristics, backgrounds or offending histories between those who agreed to participate in the research and those who did not, although, as discussed earlier, young people who were in prison service custody at the time of the initial contact were significantly more likely to participate in the interviews than those who were at liberty.

There were also a number of placement-related differences between those who declined to participate and those who did take part in the research. The young people who took part were significantly less likely to have breached the conditions of their remand (if conditions had been applied) than those who did not participate (Fisher's exact test, $p = 0.045$). Conversely, although not statistically significant, the young people interviewed were more likely to have experienced a placement disruption than those who were not interviewed. Participants were less likely to have experienced an improvement in their educational or employment status during the placement ($\chi^2 = 6.507$, $df = 2$, $p < 0.05$) and were less likely to have had a beneficial change in their family relationships (Fisher's exact test, $p = 0.038$). It is possible, therefore, that the experiences of remand foster care for the young people interviewed might have been more negative than for those who did not participate.

Summary

This chapter has provided a profile of the young people referred to the remand foster care project over a period of 15 months, and highlighted the few differences between those placed and those not placed with the scheme. Details of the placements have been recorded, including factors that appear to be associated with placement success. The following chapter investigates the magistrates' views of remand foster care and the remand decision-making process, before the experiences of the young people who were placed in remand foster care and the carers who looked after them are described.

7 Interviews with magistrates

Introduction

Lay magistrates are a central element in the administration of the youth justice system (Vernon, 2000); interviews therefore were conducted with 13 lay youth court magistrates[23] to discuss remand decisions and the availability of remand provision in the area. The interviews were not designed to be a rigorous examination of the decision-making process but aimed to obtain a broader picture of the magistrates' knowledge of bail and remand options, their opinions about which were the most influential factors in the decision-making process and their attitudes towards the remand alternatives available. Whilst the case-file analysis (Chapter 5) did not reveal any disparity between the different courts, there was a large amount of inconsistency in the comments made by the magistrates.[24] Courts have

---

[23] District judges (previously known as stipendiary magistrates) were not invited to participate in the research due to the limited number of district judges in the country and the relatively small number of remand hearings over which they preside. Ninety six per cent of all criminal cases are heard within magistrates' courts, and approximately 91 per cent of these cases are adjudicated by lay magistrates (Morgan and Russell, 2000; Morgan, 2002). Less than one per cent of the magistracy are district judges (Dhami and Ayton, 2001). However, it should be noted that previous research (albeit conducted in adult courts, rather than the youth court) is ambiguous about the consistency of decisions made by lay magistrates and district judges. Some research suggests that there is little difference in the decisions district judges and lay magistrates make in adult courts (Doherty and East, 1985; Dhami and Ayton, 2001), but others argue that district judges are more likely to impose a remand to custody than are lay magistrates (Hucklesby, 1997; Morgan, 2002). It is currently a matter of chance whether a case is heard by lay magistrates or a district judge: although some courts have a full-time district judge, most do not and it is the luck of the draw if the defendant appears in a court in which a district judge does sit (Morgan, 2002). Magistrates' courts, as a whole, impose more custodial remands and sentences than does the Crown Court (Sanders, 2002).

[24] It must be noted that the comments made are not a criticism of any of the individuals that took part in the research, but are a reflection of problematic issues within the youth justice process itself. Many magistrates will sit only infrequently on a youth bench and thus, understandably, might have limited experience or knowledge of youth court procedures.

considerable scope for the exercise of discretion and individual judgements, which result in discrepancies between courts (Hucklesby, 1996;
Sanders and Young, 2002). The implications of this for young people on
remand are obvious – one court might consider a remand to custody to be
appropriate whilst another might impose bail with stringent conditions.

The magistrates

Four of the magistrates who participated in the research were male and
nine female; all were of white British origin. Nine of the magistrates
chaired the youth bench, but four did not. Other details about the participants and their length of service as a magistrate are presented in
Table 7.1.

Table 7.1
Characteristics of the participating magistrates

	Minimum	Maximum	Mean
Age of magistrate	44	69	56
Years' experience on adult bench	4	30	12.8
Years' experience on youth bench	2	15	7.5
Number of days sitting in youth court per month	1	5	2

This sample is not representative of the magistracy as a whole, which is
gender balanced and ethnically representative of the population at national
level (Morgan, 2002). Fewer of the participating magistrates (4) were
retired than would be expected although, as predicted, they were over-
whelmingly drawn from professional or managerial occupations (Morgan,
2002).

Importance of the remand decision

It was recognised by magistrates in the study and those writing elsewhere
(Wates, 2003) that remand decisions are amongst the most problematic
decisions made and that the consequences of the pronouncement are far-
reaching:

> . . . *they are some of the most difficult decisions we make . . . because*

you have only heard the prosecution's case at its highest and you've had a very limited input from the defence and so you are usually left with two fairly different stories of a particular circumstance and it's then having to make a judgement about which way you go, knowing how important bail is . . . initially it's remanding for a week, if you are going to remand them into custody it's a week, but for a young person that is a heck of a long time.

I find it the most difficult because you have got too little information to base it on and you do get the strongest opposing views . . . in other circumstances, because you've got much more evidence, you've probably had longer to come to a judgement and I think, you know, if it's a case then you are going to have to decide guilt or innocence and bail . . . it's deciding, trying to avoid thinking, 'This person is guilty'. It's actually saying, 'Are they [going to abscond/commit offences] . . . ?'. That's what the question is.

However, the magistrates explained that they had only sporadic training in the youth court, few opportunities to discuss the remand process and no feedback on the decisions they had made. In addition, the magistrates interviewed appeared to make inconsistent use of the written guidance issued by the Judicial Studies Board (2001), had incomplete knowledge of the remand provision in their area, and had varying attitudes towards the different remand options available.

Training, guidance and feedback

All magistrates who wish to become youth court magistrates must complete three years' service in an adult court and then undertake distinct induction training prior to becoming a youth court magistrate (Magistrates' Association, 2003). Further training, however, is *ad hoc* and not compulsory. Whilst the youth court magistrates undergo an appraisal to assess their competency and identify any training needs, these appraisals only occur every three years (Magistrates' Association, 2003). There have been rapid changes within the criminal justice system recently, with numerous new pieces of criminal justice legislation being passed, many of which have implications for the remand process. However, it was apparent that few of the magistrates recalled having received formal training or being provided with opportunities to discuss these legislative amendments. Three magistrates said that they had never received training specifically on remand or bail decisions, five had received training but not within the previous two years, and only five had received training within the preceding two years.

Doubts about the capacity of the current training provisions to create a youth justice magistracy that is fully conversant with the legislation and policy objectives have previously been raised (Vernon, 2000) and it was clear that confusion existed amongst the magistrates. Indeed one magistrate was unaware that the youth court dealt with remand decisions at all:

No, I've not had any training on remands, not specifically. We don't deal with them, you see. We just hand down sentences.

In some instances, training was provided through presentations by agencies, such as probation or the local bail support organisation, at the quarterly youth bench meetings. Again, attendance at these meetings was not obligatory; lay magistrates are volunteers and many have competing demands on their time that may prevent them from attending training sessions or meetings. Nonetheless, such meetings would provide an opportunity at which the magistrates could be informed about the remand foster care project, for example, through a presentation by the remand fostering officers. None of the magistrates recalled attending such a presentation, and those who were aware of the scheme had obtained their knowledge of it largely through direct contact with the foster carers in court.

Magistrates' decision-making is guided by the *Youth Court Bench Book*, published by the Judicial Studies Board (2001 – updated regularly). However, the amount of use the magistrates made of the *Bench Book* varied and some were unaware of what it included. For example, whilst the *Bench Book* includes a section on 'Adjournment: Bail and remand to local authority accommodation and prison', one magistrate did not realise this and another thought that the guidance only covered bail decisions but not what should happen if bail were refused. One was unclear as to whether written guidance existed and said, 'If we have written guidance, I don't usually refer to it.'

Of those who did utilise the *Bench Book*, some were critical of its content. For example, one magistrate explained that, whilst the Book gave general guidance, it was not sufficiently detailed to be of use in more complex decisions: 'the things that are difficult are never, ever in the Book'. It was also acknowledged that the *Bench Book* did only give guidance and the rules were 'not set in stone, they are guidelines . . . we can deviate up or down'. It was apparent that the guidance was subject to different interpretations by the magistrates and the resulting judgements varied between benches.

Clearly, the legal adviser can advise and correct magistrates on points of law, but s/he cannot direct the magistrates' decisions:

> *We are told the law, we are not told how to apply it . . . You are told the law by the legal adviser but they are not allowed to say what you are going to do, obviously. They can just advise us on the law.*

Six of the magistrates complained about the absence of any feedback about decisions that they had made and felt that feedback would help them feel more confident about making pronouncements. Two magistrates said that a 'general comment' might be made if the courts' Chief Executive or the YOTs became concerned that a particular trend was developing or that a specific bench was making more use of custodial remands than other benches, but that no detailed feedback was provided. Without feedback, magistrates cannot know if they made an appropriate decision and this may restrict their ability to learn whether they are using the right information in the right way (Dhami and Ayton, 2001) or which forms of remand provision are more apposite in particular circumstances.

Remand provision

The decision magistrates can make is clearly limited by the range and availability of community resources at their disposal (Beaulieu and Cesaroni, 1999), but is also constrained by a lack of knowledge of those resources. The level of understanding the magistrates had of each type of bail and remand provision varied, but there were a number of common themes which were identifiable. As noted above, one magistrate was unaware that remand decisions were made in the youth court; another was unclear about the average length of a remand period and her estimation was markedly less than the actual time a child could spend on remand: 'I really have no idea. I would say as short as possible, no longer than a week.'

Conditional bail and bail support

Bail was considered to be the most frequent outcome for children appearing in the youth court. Estimates of how often conditions were attached to bail ranged from 10 per cent to 60 or 70 per cent of cases, possibly reflecting variations in practice between different youth court benches. One magistrate said that they would:

> . . . normally be looking for conditions because . . . of the nature of the characters we see . . . and the nature of the cases, so it's either assault or it's shoplifting or it's harassment, so you are tending to say you have to do something about stopping them repeating it.

However, the majority of the magistrates were cautious about imposing conditions on a young person's bail:

> Because a lot of the time you'd be setting them up to fail and you don't want to do that . . . You've got to strike a balance between protecting them and society but also not setting them up to fail.

The most common conditions imposed were conditions of residence (which could be with remand foster carers), curfews and "exclusion zones", or geographical restrictions. Parents (or foster carers) might request conditions that could give them additional control over the child but magistrates were divided over whether to impose such conditions. For example, one magistrate said that, if a child's parents explained that they could not keep him/her in at night, they would impose a curfew to aid the parents, regardless of whether this was appropriate to the offence allegedly committed. However, another magistrate argued that this was improper because conditions have to be proportionate to the offence.

Granting a young person conditional bail was recognised as having advantages for the young person that a remand to local authority accommodation or custody did not:

> If you're trying to persuade a young person to take responsibility for

themselves then imposing bail with conditions on them, even though the condition may only be of residence, then you're encouraging them to take responsibility for themselves . . . whereas if you remand them into the care of the local authority you're not.

The majority of the magistrates were aware of and had a good understanding of the bail support provision in the local area. The bail support scheme was generally believed to be a very effective resource that could help young people adhere to their bail conditions and to "de-chaos" their lives. However, the frequency with which the magistrates had encountered the bail support scheme varied: some magistrates said that the bail support team was often represented in court and therefore regularly utilised but others believed that bail support provision was much more limited and rarely available.

Dealing with a young person who has breached the conditions of their bail was an area of considerable confusion for a few of the magistrates. Failing to surrender to bail (that is not returning to court at the appointed time) is a criminal offence for which a warrant can be issued, although this is not applicable to children remanded to local authority accommodation. Breaching any other bail condition is not an offence in itself, although the young person can be arrested and held in police cells until the next available court hearing. The magistrates can then make a remand decision afresh.

Some of the magistrates did not know that breaching conditions could warrant a change in the remand status, and others erroneously believed that breach was a separate, criminal offence for which the young person would be sentenced. It was the general consensus that very few children did breach their conditions and that, on the occasions where this did occur, the remand status was unlikely to be altered but that the child would be given a "second chance".

Remand to local authority accommodation

Remands to local authority accommodation (RLAA) were the most contentious form of remand provision because the magistrates were unable to stipulate where the young person should reside. The decision was seen as a 'frustrating . . . paper exercise' because the local authority then had the power to place the young person with foster carers, in a children's home or back at home. The latter two options were seen as largely inappropriate in many situations. For example, magistrates may be reluctant for a child to return home:

Sometimes you really don't want the youngster to go back to the environment that the child is living in because that obviously has a reflection on why the offences are taking place.

It seems pointless to me to have to go through the hurdle of remanding someone to the care of the local authority who, in turn, remand him back to where he came from. You might just as well give him unconditional bail, which is what we often do.

Children's homes were deemed unsuitable for children on remand for a variety of reasons, including the limited control staff in children's homes had over the young people, the impact on other children in the homes (particularly children placed for welfare reasons), the "deviant subcultures" that existed in some homes, which encouraged further offending, and the problem of children being brought before the courts having committed a misdemeanour in the children's home:

Children's homes can be considered a volatile cocktail waiting to explode . . . They [the children] seem to wind each other up to re-offend.

Sometimes they get brought to court for such stupid things . . . slamming a door, kicking a door. What teenager doesn't slam or kick a door? . . . There is no way that they [the staff] can discipline these children. They can't send them to their rooms . . . certainly they can't smack them . . . they can't even stop their pocket money, so their only option is to call the police and send them to the youth court.

The alternative option would be for the local authority to place the child with remand foster carers, which is clearly central to this research. All of the magistrates understood that children on remand might be placed with foster carers, but six were unsure how this happened or who the carers were, generally assuming that they were mainstream foster carers managed by the local authority. Three magistrates were aware that a specialist remand foster care scheme existed but were unclear about who managed it or who was eligible to be placed there. For example, one magistrate said that 'the [remand foster care placement] is only after conviction and pre-sentence', not realising that children could be placed there prior to their trial. The remaining four magistrates were more conversant with the scheme and how it could be accessed, namely either through remanding the child to local authority accommodation with the implicit understanding that they would be placed with the remand project, or by remanding them on bail with a condition to reside with the foster carers.

However, only one was able to recall details of the process through which a remand foster placement would be accessed, which suggests that it is an uncommon occurrence:

> *I think, from my recollection . . . I am assuming that the YOT officers will identify a child that could be placed . . . the representative [from the remand foster care project] will come into court and introduce the lady or gentleman with whom the child would be placed and ask that we allow it.*

The Home Office suggests that remand foster care is not often utilised as magistrates do not have confidence that it is an available option (Home Office, 2003) and these comments indicate that the magistrates are infrequently made aware of its potential use.

However, in general, remand foster care was perceived to be a very positive and successful alternative to being remanded home or to a children's home. The foster carers were seen as 'devoted', 'enthusiastic', 'tolerant' and 'quite remarkable' people who were able to develop a 'rapport . . . with the young people, after a very short time'. They were perceived to provide a 'one-to-one' relationship with the young person that they would be unlikely to have in a children's home, offering support and guidance, and keeping the young people occupied:

> *They [the foster carers] probably do what proper parents do . . . Take them out and about, work with them, play with them, talk to them, treat them as part of the family. They are not left too much on their own . . . They seem to actually look at what interests the child.*

> *The truth is that the remand foster placements are so good. The people are so well trained that they can get inside these kids' heads and they will come in completely different children.*

A few of the magistrates were aware that foster carers could provide placements for children charged with sexual or violent offences, but most thought that this was not possible (see also Hucklesby and Goodwin, 2002). This clearly has implications for whether a bench would agree to an RLAA or enforce a secure remand for a young person charged with such offences.

A range of difficulties with remand foster care was identified by the magistrates. Although not a factor that should influence their decisions, one morally problematic issue for them was that the young people had to leave the foster carers almost immediately after they were sentenced: 'that can be devastating for them and they just go back to offending'.

She'd built up a trust, she'd built up a relationship . . . and it was all taken away from her. It's unfair. And doesn't that make you think that this child is going to think that whatever she does in life it's going to be taken away?

I think it's a wonderful system, but it would be really lovely if it could continue for some of the youngsters once they are convicted and sentenced. They are still very much at risk and they may only have had a six- or eight-week break in that sort of environment with someone who really straightens them out, makes them aware of what's important, and then for that to be stopped is quite sad.

Of more direct relevance to the decision-making process, magistrates were aware that some placements would break down, particularly if the young person was unco-operative:

Sometimes you can have a foster carer who's very keen to have the child with them, who's very enthusiastic but the young person doesn't want to co-operate. I've seen that.

They seem to work quite well and they seem to be successful but there are always going to be the ones that break down.

Furthermore, although the majority of magistrates believed that the young people were unlikely to offend or breach their conditions whilst they were in foster care, one magistrate was more sceptical of the ability of remand foster care to prevent offending:

I'd like to say that it was effective . . . The foster carers that come into court all seem very caring and very nice people but we see these children back time and time and time again . . . I can think of one in particular who's probably in court on a fortnightly basis and he's in foster care . . . I'm sure this lady is giving him the best care that she can but it's not solving the problem because he has contact with his family and he offends when he goes to see his family . . . I think the children probably get more care, if they've been placed with a foster carer. I think they probably get the stability that they need but it doesn't always stop them offending.

The magistrates were also aware of a lack of foster carers, meaning that placements might not be available or that the young person would be placed a considerable distance from home, which could affect their ability to comply with conditions or fulfil other responsibilities, such as completing previously imposed community sentences.

Some magistrates discussed the frustration caused by their inability to impose a remand directly to foster care. Whilst in practice a young person could be bailed to reside with the foster carers and thereby be assured of a remand foster placement, one magistrate explained that if the criteria for an RLAA were met, an RLAA had to be imposed, regardless of how unsatisfactory the ultimate placement may be. The magistrates desired a return to the now-redundant procedure of being able to stipulate where a young person remanded to local authority accommodation would be placed, but recognised the local authority's need for flexibility in placements due to their limited resources.

One magistrate indicated that the lack of an appropriate remand foster care placement could lead to a young person being remanded into secure accommodation or custody:

A child or young person that was very problematic, home circumstances were difficult and given that there was no suitable alternative, yes, the young person might go into custody if they didn't come up with a foster placement.

Secure accommodation

The main concern the magistrates had about secure accommodation was its limited availability, particularly within the county, saying that the nearest secure unit was 'invariably full'. They recognised the problems for children who were placed out of the county, both in maintaining family contact and in having to travel considerable distances to attend further court hearings. However, they all felt that their 'hands are tied', that they were unable to intervene in any way and were resigned to accepting the difficulties:

> *If we say that we want someone to go into secure accommodation, that is for others to find, and I know that that sounds a bit cold and hard but that is totally beyond our world . . . It is incredible because of the distances involved . . . but we have to just trust other people's judgement. I mean we can't get involved.*

> *I have never known secure accommodation to be available . . . after 15, 20 years on the youth bench . . . You are supposed to wait while they make a telephone call and then it always comes back saying 'There is no bed available'. I don't really know [what happens then]; they'd either go outside the area or they find themselves in Holloway or Feltham or Reading or somewhere. So this has never been satisfactory.*

It must be acknowledged that magistrates cannot be expected to become involved in what was described by one as 'the worst aspect of the youth justice process'. However, the problems of overcrowding and expansionism will continue whilst magistrates maintain the belief that a secure or custodial place can and will always be found for the young person. This issue is discussed further in later chapters.

Two of the magistrates were unaware of the legislative changes that meant that they could direct a secure remand and still believed that the local authority had to request a secure accommodation order. Another magistrate said that, until very recently, she was not aware of this but that the legal adviser had requested an adjournment whilst s/he clarified the situation.

Custody

Whilst six magistrates did not express strong opinions in favour of or against imposing custodial remands, four said that they were extremely reluctant to impose a custodial remand on a young person, due to the 'catastrophic' effect it could have and the appalling conditions they had witnessed when visiting various YOIs. One said that he wished such places were not available as a remand option so that magistrates could not be responsible for sending children there. However, three of the magistrates favoured custodial remands, believing them to be necessary to protect the public or to remove young people from the difficulties they faced. It was acknowledged that the latter would not be a consideration for adults:

> *I don't have a problem in sending a youngster into custody. It's not what you're there for with adults, but certainly with youngsters . . . if their criminal behaviour is such that they are really out of control, then maybe a couple of months of relative peace and quiet . . . I mean I know it's not quiet in prison but the pressures, the tensions, the temptations that they have . . .*

Of the three magistrates who had no qualms about imposing a custodial remand, two had positive but perhaps unrealistic views of the facilities and regimes for remand prisoners in YOIs. For example, one magistrate explained that:

> *They have a lot more privileges, you know; they can make phone calls, they can wear their own clothes and I think the food is better. The lock-up is less stringent than if they'd been actually tried.*

Whilst the first two points are generally accurate, the last is not, as was discussed in Chapter 1.

Whether or not the magistrates believe the defendant to be guilty should not influence the remand decision, but one magistrate said:

> *I'm not suggesting that it would be the best place for a child to live but then they've committed a crime and they have to pay for it.*

This attitude is inappropriate and misguided: at this stage in the justice proceedings, the defendant is legally innocent and should not be punished in any way. Another magistrate understood this but still suggested that a presumption of guilt could be influential in the remand decision:

There's just a chance that you might be found not guilty, you could be innocent and . . . you've got to be fairly certain that there's a good chance that somebody has done something before you would remand them to somewhere like that.

The different attitudes towards and understanding of the consequences of their decisions means that young people are likely to be subject to inconsistent remand decisions, with some magistrates being more willing than others to impose bail, an RLAA or custodial remand.

Remand decisions – criteria

The magistrates generally considered the seriousness of the alleged offence to be the first criterion they would consider when making a remand decision, although this was not apparent from the case-file analysis (Chapter 5) which suggested that the seriousness of the offence was not related to the nature of the remand imposed. This is perhaps because the magistrates had a different understanding of what constitutes seriousness. For example, one magistrate said that most young people are remanded on unconditional bail because the majority of crimes are nuisance crimes, such as 'car crime, driving offences, theft, burglary, drugs', yet burglary was considered by the majority to be a serious offence, warranting a custodial or secure remand, and is classified as a 'high seriousness crime' in the *Youth Court Bench Book* (2001). Car crimes (such as TWOC) were seen by other magistrates as warranting conditional bail and aggravated or persistent TWOC as justifying a secure remand:

If you have a child that is everlastingly stealing cars, for the safety of the public, you can't have somebody who can't drive endlessly nicking cars and driving them, can you?

Attempted rape or rape, attempted murder, kidnap, arson and robbery were all seen as serious offences for which custody was the only route possible.

> *If you are actually charged with arson it's very serious, then effectively*
> *[custody] is the only option that's available.*

However, the case-file analysis showed that young people charged with arson, rape and attempted murder had all successfully been placed with remand foster carers and that alternatives to custody are available.

The young person's history of complying with prior periods of remand was considered influential; if they had previously breached bail, the magistrates felt that it was unlikely that bail would be granted again. The perception of the young person's propensity to offend whilst on bail was more frequently cited as a reason to deny bail. However, the case-file analysis (Chapter 5) indicated that neither of these criteria was statistically related to the likelihood of granting bail.

Most, but not all, of the magistrates were aware that the remand options available to them were dependent on the age of the defendant, although they were not always clear about what the relevant age limits were. There was a general opinion that the court would be more reluctant to impose a custodial remand on a younger child:

> *You should see a marked going-down the younger they are, because no*
> *one wants to lock kids up.*

> *You've got to look at it much more carefully in the case of younger*
> *defendants.*

Whilst this is clearly beneficial for younger children, it is disadvantageous for the older ones as they may not receive such a considered decision, yet may be equally harmed by a custodial remand.

There was a worryingly low recognition of the vulnerability criteria; indeed vulnerability was only mentioned by four magistrates, one of whom said:

> *All the magistrates can do is note that the child is vulnerable or at risk*
> *of suicide and hope that the information travels with him.*

That the magistrates could direct the remand of a vulnerable young person into secure accommodation rather than custody was not realised by this magistrate, although the other three were more conversant with the implications. The defence solicitor, legal adviser or YOT officer can offer advice to magistrates, but they may not be aware of a child's propensity to self-harm or attempt suicide, and a YOT officer might not always be present in court, particularly if the court is sitting on a Saturday. (Saturday courts are discussed in more detail later).

The gender of the defendant was not thought to influence the magistrates' decision but most made specific comments about girls who were involved in violent offences or had 'heavy drinking problems' because this type of behaviour was not traditionally associated with girls:

It is quite frightening how much violence by girls there is, you know, group violence when a group of girls take a dislike to another group. Because one doesn't associate violence with females generally, it is more a male thing.

Violent offending by girls was also seen to be increasing, with the perception that 'the macho culture is amongst girls now', although this is not borne out by official statistics (see, for example, East and Campbell, 2000; Home Office, 2002b).

None of the magistrates considered that the ethnicity of the defendant had any impact on the remand decision, although it is likely that they were either not consciously aware of the influence it may have, or were concerned about appearing to be racially prejudiced. The over-representation of minority ethnic young people in custodial establishments has already been acknowledged, but a more subtle methodology would be required to determine the role the magistracy play in this discrimination.

As mentioned in Chapter 5, children who had experienced particularly disadvantaged backgrounds were more likely to be RLAA and to be placed with foster carers. Some magistrates appeared willing to remove children from their families, regardless of the nature of the alleged offence or other criteria, if it was thought to be advantageous for the child's or family's welfare:

If a child is the eldest in the family, then he or she is not setting a good example to the rest of the family. You need to know the background of mum, dad, whether it's a single parent, and I think that if they are committing offences at that level, or even if they are the youngest, then maybe to take them out for a short time that would be beneficial to them . . . [and] it would obviously have an impact on the family.

That can be a factor, again probably more in support of the parents, you know. If . . . this is the eldest child and mum's got three other children and really this one is causing more problems than it's worth, you might then think, 'What's in the greatest benefit to the family?' If we took the lad out for a little bit, and it's usually more lads than girls, in those sort of circumstances, might that have some effect on it?

The attitude of the young person could be influential in the decision-making process (see also Hough *et al*, 2003). For example, one magistrate was dismissive of children who appeared unperturbed by their situation: *If they're not bothered then why waste more effort on them? I mean, if somebody says, 'I don't give a monkey's, mate. I'm a persistent young offender, I'm on so many different charges' and you think 'Well, if you've jumped bail before, what's the point?'. There's no point going round the same circle. If they don't want it, then fine.*

Another magistrate felt that she would be more willing to grant bail to a young person who had initially been remanded to custody if they appeared to have 'realised the folly of his ways'. This is an issue that is likely to become increasingly influential due to the recent changes in the youth court culture, which include more direct interaction between the Chair of the magistrates and the defendant (Home Office, 2001).

It was clear that the magistrates had variable knowledge of the remand options available to them, a different understanding of the criteria used in making the remand decision and conflicting attitudes towards remanding a child to local authority accommodation or custody. As acknowledged by some of the magistrates, this means that 'any courtroom can easily come to a different conclusion' but that was seen as 'part of the game, you know'. Whilst it is assumed that this remark was made flippantly, the implications for young defendants are manifest.

Remand decisions – process

The problems of different knowledge of remand provision and the variable understanding and interpretation of the remand legislation are compounded by the perception of the magistrates' role. Whilst one magistrate had a proactive strategy of asking the YOT for any advice or help that they could offer, for example, in terms of alternative accommodation, others appeared to take a very passive role within the court process, waiting to receive information from the solicitors rather than actively seeking it:

> *We don't sort of think 'Right, what shall we do?'. It's really listening and selecting from what's offered . . . so you're given a fairly clear steer.*

Previous research has suggested that magistrates are more likely to believe the police or Crown Prosecution Service (CPS) than the defence: the former are seen as neutral whilst the latter is seen as partial (Hucklesby, 1997; Hucklesby and Marshall, 2000; Sanders, 2002). This can lead to "rubber-stamping" whereby the magistrates simply concur with the earlier decision made by the police to grant bail or to remand in custody prior to the initial court hearing:

> *If they are remanded in custody by the police, they are just coming up [to court] to just move the process on . . . if they are already remanded, then it's quite a jump back . . . we have to have exceptional reasons for giving bail.*

The CPS viewpoint has been found to be very influential in remand decisions, with magistrates agreeing with the CPS request in over 95 per cent of cases (Godson and Mitchell, 1991; Hucklesby, 1997). A number of magistrates explained that they were 'entitled to take the prosecution evidence at its highest . . . so you believe the prosecution case'. The prosecutor was believed to provide 'an indication of the direction you're going in' and the defence solicitor, with the YOT's support, would have to provide a very strong argument to convince the magistrates to take another course of action. The ability of the defence solicitor to challenge such decisions is therefore crucial:

I think normally when it is going to be secure you almost know from something fairly early on. Basically the prosecutor outlines the case and you think, 'Ooh, I'm going to need an awful lot of persuasion.'

This does not suggest that the young person's right to bail is being promoted or that the magistrates are acting in a neutral position, and reinforces the importance of the defence solicitor's and YOT's roles in advocating a less restrictive remand for the young person.

However, the defence solicitor's willingness to challenge the prosecution may be affected by the "court culture" (Hucklesby, 1997). A court culture is essentially a set of informal norms or rules within a court; participants within the court process adapt their working practices to fit their expectations of what the court is likely to do in light of these "rules". Predictable routines therefore develop, reducing risk and uncertainty and providing for the efficient disposal of cases (Paterson and Whittaker, 1994; Hucklesby, 1997). For example, defence solicitors are unlikely to advise defendants to make a bail application if they believe that it would be unsuccessful, because it would damage the credibility of the defence solicitor in the eyes of the court. Defence solicitors may "second guess" the magistrates' decisions to maintain their compliance and conformity to the court culture (Hucklesby, 1997). This clearly may be detrimental for the defendant if a more appropriate disposal is available, but the CPS has opposed it and the magistrates are perceived to be unwilling to condone it. One of the magistrates talked of her disbelief when a defence solicitor did challenge the perceived routine within the court by asking for a conditional remand for a young person accused of attempted murder:

I remember his solicitor standing up and [he] said, 'Give bail and every condition under the sun' and we just thought, you know, for that sort of thing you are not going to be in a position to give anybody bail. It doesn't matter, regardless of the pleas, it's far too serious an offence. You are almost wasting court time asking for it.

Yet there is no legal reason why a defendant charged with attempted murder (or indeed, any grave crime) should not be granted bail, unless they had previously been convicted of homicide or rape (Ashford and

Chard 2000).[25] Furthermore, as already noted, the remand foster scheme had successfully provided placements for children accused of grave crimes, and the court could impose an RLAA or bail with a condition to reside at the foster placement.

Moreover, it is vital for a child that a bail application is made, however unlikely it is to be agreed. Hucklesby (1997) found, in the adult court, that if the CPS requested a remand in custody and the defendant did not apply for bail, the defendant was almost always remanded in custody. Conversely, if the CPS requested a remand in custody but the defendant did make a bail application, 29 per cent were granted bail, albeit with conditions. It is feasible that making a bail application despite a request for custody being made could have even more of an impact in the youth court due to a wider range of alternatives being available to the youth bench, such as remand foster care.

The role of the defence solicitor is therefore critical and s/he should liaise with the local YOT to discover what alternative provision is available and attempt to persuade the magistrates to impose a less restrictive remand option.[26] However, evidence suggests that defence solicitors all too frequently fail to communicate with the YOTs, even though a YOT officer may be able to provide resources in the form of accommodation or a bail support package (Ashford and Chard, 2000). In some instances, part-icularly in "Saturday courts", no YOT officer will be present in court, which can compound the situation for young defendants.

Saturday courts
Children and young people who are arrested and held in police custody after the close of court on a Friday evening will attend court the following morning. In many areas of the country there is no emergency youth justice cover on a Saturday and so the young person's remand hearing will be

---

[25] Children and young people can be remanded to custody for their own protection; however, as this book has argued, prison service custody is neither a safe nor a protective environment for young people.

[26] Due to resource limitations, this research was not able to investigate defence solicitors' knowledge or opinions of remand foster care, but this is clearly an area that warrants further attention.

held in the adult court; the final evaluation of the National Remand Review Initiative (Goldson and Peters, 2002) found that approximately five per cent of young people remanded to custody were remanded from Saturday morning courts. This has a number of implications: for example, it is less likely that a YOT officer will be in the court and so alternative provision may not be recommended to the defence solicitor or magistrate. Saturday courts may also be adjudicated by a lone magistrate, which was recognised as problematic by one of the magistrates in the study:

In the adult court many decisions are made by one magistrate on a Saturday morning court and that could be a youth, of course. So it's quite a big decision to make and probably the one that shouldn't be done by one magistrate, but I've never heard any attempt to change that.

Conversely, another magistrate felt that this was not an issue of concern because the decision was 'only' a remand hearing:

They could also be dealt with by non-youth panel magistrates because the Saturday rota is all magistrates, and it may not necessarily be a youth court magistrate. That's not a problem because usually a remand court on a Saturday is very quickly dealing with them on remand, they are not dealing with the sentencing.

However, as already outlined, the remand decision has clear implications for the young person. It is known that adult courts remand young defendants in custody much more frequently than youth courts (Ashford and Chard, 2000), which indicates that the practice of holding children's remand hearings in an adult court should not continue.

Other influential factors

Clearly, youth court magistrates do not operate in a vacuum but function within a volatile political and public climate regarding young people who commit offences (Beaulieu and Cesaroni, 1999; Vernon, 2000; Hough *et al*, 2003). The magistrates talked about the conflicting guidance received from government departments and the reports of overcrowding in prisons:

The magistracy is getting so many mixed messages at the moment . . . On the one hand, we're sending too many people to prison, the next day the Lord Chief Justice is telling us 'Anyone who pinches a phone off someone in the street deserves two years in custody', you know. [We] disregard it. Just do the job.

In the adult and the youth court we have had solicitors who start their representation by talking about the situation in prisons and remand centres, and advice from above. And it's designed to influence your decision. And while I don't think it does influence our decision it's obviously another pressure that's there.

These comments reflect previous periods within England and Wales when the judiciary has been reluctant to amend its practice in accordance with guidance establishing principles of non-imprisonment (Hudson, 1993). As mentioned above, the magistrates believed that a custodial or secure place for a young defendant would always be found, and they were impervious to the reports that there were no places available. As Miller (1991) recognised, to reverse punitive prison expansion and achieve decarceration, the number of custodial placements available needs to be strictly limited, or the judiciary will continue to create a demand for custody that, in turn, will be fulfilled by the construction of more prisons.

Impact on sentencing

The magistrates acknowledged that the type of remand the young person had received could affect the sentence that was ultimately imposed, although this could occur in a number of ways. A few suggested that a young person might be given a more lenient sentence if they had already spent time in custody on remand:

You might think, 'Well, what good would it do, serving another two, four, six, eight months, whatever? He's done six weeks already. If that hasn't done any good what's the point of this?' . . . so that might keep a few people away from time in custody.

However, the more prevalent view was that a custodial remand would increase the likelihood of a custodial sentence:

If you are remanded in custody as a young person, if you then come up and are found guilty or plead guilty to something which is punishable by imprisonment you're more likely to end up there because it would probably be a fairly serious matter. Secondly, it would make it look as though you'd been there before, and thirdly, for some reason bail was withheld.

The Criminal Justice Act 1991 allows the court to consider any personal mitigation advanced on behalf of the child, which could include signs of reform or settling down, complying with bail or remand conditions, and responding positively to community intervention. Young people who are RLAA or granted bail are able to prove that they would respond positively to a community sentence, but young people remanded to custody are denied this opportunity:

If we're thinking of [a sentence in] custody . . . we would have to give reasons. Very often, if we come down on the side of not sending them into detention, one of the reasons could be their response to help. Now if they are remanded in custody it would be very difficult to say that, which is one of the reasons why bail support schemes are so good, because it gives them the chance to respond and that gives us an indication of how they would get on on a supervision order. So in a way what happens to them on remand can affect the sentence. I suppose that to those that have shall be given, in a way, because they're on a roll. If they don't respond then, you know . . . If they're in custody they can't.

Conversely, the impact of a custodial remand could be used in mitigation for a young person:

If they are coming back to court and saying, 'I realise that custody is absolutely dreadful, please don't send me to prison for this offence', you might be persuaded, if you felt it's genuine, to give them a non-custodial sentence.

However, this might be the result of a negative rather than a positive experience, for example, the young person might be scared of returning to prison due to being bullied or victimised (Ashford and Chard, 2000) as opposed to any rehabilitative effect of incarceration.

The comments made by the foster carers and reports written by the YOTs and remand foster scheme (usually in conjunction with the foster carers) could be influential in the sentencing decision because they demonstrated the young people's ability to reform themselves:

> *. . . because if you can see that there has been a marked change in that person from first seeing them to sentence . . . and there was a good report from the foster home . . . then yes, it can affect what we do with them . . . A slightly lesser sentence, yes . . . because you can find that that period spent in a foster home actually takes them away from their own environment and they can certainly change, because youngsters do change.*

> *There's no point putting them in if they've seen the light and they're actually beginning to behave a bit better. . . If they've done really well and if the foster parents come into court and say, 'Well, so-and-so had been absolutely wonderful', you wouldn't put them inside then.*

In essence, good advocacy on the behalf of a child, even one who has been charged with a serious crime, could result in the imposition of bail with a condition of residence with foster carers, or an RLAA. As a result of the beneficial intervention by foster carers, the child, if convicted, might then have a community sentence imposed. Conversely, a child who is remanded to custody does not have the same intervention nor the opportunity to demonstrate their ability to abide by bail conditions and not re-offend, and might be sentenced to custody.

Summary

It is clear that the magistrates' decision will have a significant impact on the young person, both in the immediate term and the longer term due to the relationship between remand status and sentencing. However, the interviews demonstrated that the magistrates had varied knowledge of the remand provision in their area and that the legislation and guidance could be interpreted very differently, leading to discrepancies between decisions made in different courts. Of particular note within this research was the lack of knowledge magistrates had about the remand foster care scheme operating within their area, and the frustration caused by the inability to direct a remand to foster care, should that be appropriate. For remand fostering to expand, magistrates must be convinced that it is an effective alternative to existing options (Butler, 2001); to be convinced they must first know of its existence and then be provided with feedback on its efficacy in specific situations.

8 Young people's backgrounds and childhood experiences

Introduction

The importance of interviewing children about the systems and processes that control them has already been emphasised. The views of the 18 children and young people interviewed about their experiences of remand fostering are therefore central to this research and are documented in this and the following chapters.

The complex associations between family background, childhood adversity, educational achievement, peer relationships, drug use and criminal behaviour have often been debated within a context of poverty, structural inequality and discrimination (see, for example, Farrington, 1996; Cullingford and Morrison, 1997; Rutter *et al*, 1998; Stewart *et al*, 2002). Chapter 6 recounted basic information held on the young people's case-file records about such aspects of their lives. This chapter begins by exploring the young people's own interpretation of their childhood experiences, and their understanding of the impact of these factors on their offending behaviour.[27] Their involvement in the criminal justice system prior to their remand in foster care is then discussed. Subsequent chapters focus specifically on the young people's experiences of remand foster care.

Childhood experiences

The narrative approach to interviewing (Chapter 5) meant that the young people were able to control what they included in their stories and it is likely that some of those who had suffered adverse experiences chose not to relay these experiences (O'Neill, 2001). However, there was a range of

---

[27] There is not scope in this book to discuss how social policies compound and exacerbate the difficulties young people face, although this is clearly of crucial importance. Rather, the analysis is specific to the areas that the young people themselves acknowledged as being influential in their lives.

common themes that arose from the young people's narratives, such as negative family relationships, disengagement from education and problematic substance use. Eighteen young people were interviewed.

Family background and family relationships

A number of family characteristics (which in turn are related to wider structural vulnerabilities such as poverty and inequality) are correlated with offending behaviour in children, including single-parent and reconstituted families, family discord, abuse and neglect (Rutter and Giller, 1983; Farrington, 1996; Cullingford and Morrison, 1997; Rutter *et al*, 1998; Stewart *et al*, 2002). In stark contrast to Hagell and Newburn's (1994) findings, which stated that the majority of persistent young offenders had positive relationships with their parents, only two (11 per cent) of the 18 young people interviewed in this study said that they had an "OK" relationship with their parents. All of the others described negative relationships, including emotional ambivalence and rejection, physical violence, or parental alcoholism and mental health problems.

Excluding being remanded to local authority accommodation, 11 (61 per cent) of the 18 young people had been looked after in the care system at some stage in their childhood, with six describing multiple moves in and out of or within the care system. Steven,[28] aged 14, had experienced the breakdown of his adoptive placement and 'about 16 different foster placements and . . . children's homes' within the previous four years. One young man had been brought up by his grandparents; two others had repeatedly moved between their mothers and fathers; and three had been homeless or "living rough" at least once during their childhood.

Some young people blamed themselves for having been taken into the care system, believing that it was a result of their "naughty" behaviour:

When I was eight I was in care for weekends, in a children's home. I went there every weekend . . . because I was naughty. And then I was in and out of care until 14.

---

[28] Pseudonyms have been given to all participants to maintain confidentiality.

I was in care from, like, 13 onwards but in and out . . .'cos I was naughty and started doing drugs and that.

Others thought that being taken into care was a trigger for their behavioural problems. One 14-year-old girl, Chantalle, described her feelings of anger and jealousy when she remained in care whilst her sisters returned home to live with their mother:

I went off the rails a bit. That's when I started offending . . . I don't forgive her for leaving me in there and getting my sisters out . . . I know for a fact what started me off is when my mum give me away.

Like a number of the other young people, Chantalle's relationship with her mother was characterised by ambivalence and a pattern of "yo-yoing" between home, care and living with friends:

I can't even count the number of times my mum's kicked me out, took me back, kicked me out.

It was clear that these young people felt hurt and let down by their parents. Craig believed that his mother resented him because her family disowned her when he was born. Lawrence felt abandoned as a young child when he was taken into care:

She got rid of me when I was three, which is fair enough 'cos she couldn't cope, but she never, until I was seven, she didn't even make contact. It was only a foster home, it wasn't adoption.

This rejection was repeated when Lawrence was 13 and his mother again stopped seeing him without explanation:

She broke off contact for no apparent reason and I couldn't cope with it. It made me feel heartbroken, to tell you the truth.

Mikey talked about his relationship with his father and the effect he felt it had had on his behaviour:

If you don't mind the language, he's an arsehole . . . he's just, he used to beat my mum up and he, it's because of that I think I'm the way I am. He's never been there for me and I've always had to prove myself . . . every time something went wrong it would be, 'Oh, pack your bags and

*go, pack your bags and leave now' and you don't need that from your
father, do you know what I mean? You want him to be there to support
you and it's just, I dunno, it's just not right.*

Similarly, Cullingford and Morrison (1997) concluded that young people
involved in offending behaviour believed that their parents were not
actively interested in them and that their parents demonstrated a passive
or neglectful attitude towards them (see also Farrington and West, 1990).

Domestic violence and physical abuse

A history of physical abuse is frequently reported by people involved in
offending behaviour (Boswell, 1995; Stewart *et al*, 2002). Ten of the 18
young people described experiencing violence within their family, either
witnessing violence between their parents or step-parents, or as victims
of violence themselves. Chantalle described the violence inflicted upon
her mother by her father before they separated and the subsequent physical
abuse she and her sisters experienced:

*That's all he knew though, to hit out all the time. I'm not sticking up for
him though 'cos he was horrible, really horrible to my mum. Horrible
to me and my sisters as well. When he took us down, like, for a break,
for a little while, a couple of days, he used to, you know, we got belts
and bars and stuff like that, all over. I don't like it. I knows he's evil and
nothing can change that.*

Rutter and colleagues (1998) argue that the family and social context
within which physical abuse occurs is more likely to be a contributory
factor to offending behaviour than the abuse *per se*. However, the young
people in this study did draw associations between their experience of
domestic violence or physical abuse and their involvement in offending
behaviour. Sometimes the violence experienced led the young people to
be violent towards the adults who were harming them. Craig talked of his
mother's long-term boyfriend as 'a piece of shit on the floor' because:

*. . . he used to beat me up when I was a little kid, all through my life,
like he's been around my whole life, beating me and beating me until I
was big enough to beat him back.*

Stewart had numerous physical fights with his mother, exacerbated by both his and his mother's alcohol use:

I've not got a too good relationship with her. If she gets drunk and starts spitting at me it makes me lose my temper. Once I came downstairs in the morning and she had a mark under her eye. She said I'd hit her but I couldn't remember doing it. I wouldn't do anything like that unless I was drunk.

He acknowledged that he should have had more respect for his mother but that he could not because she would pull his hair and spit in his face.

Parental alcoholism

A number of young people talked about their parents' problems with drugs and alcohol. Parents who have such problems may be preoccupied and unaware of the impact their substance misuse has on their children (Cullingford and Morrison, 1997). Thirteen-year-old Tom talked about the problems caused by his mother's alcoholism:

I started meeting these other people, realised that other people's mums weren't so bad . . . [I] started getting an attitude problem and I started to recognise what mum was actually doing . . . That she was drinking and that's where the money was going, and that's why we couldn't have nice things . . . Then I started playing around and going out, sort of like for days on end, not coming back . . . I couldn't be bothered to listen to her shouting.

Tom had a more positive relationship with his father although he seemed disappointed that his father was prepared to finance his wife's drinking: 'Dad's fine. He just works and spends all the money on beer for my mum.' Staying out on the streets was a way for Tom to escape the detrimental atmosphere and arguments at home, but led to him becoming involved in offending behaviour:

I was about nine then and I started meeting other people that had been in the same boat as me really, had a mum with a drink problem or drug problem . . . and I just saw what they got and how they got it, by stealing, which it was like, how great it was getting stuff for nothing.

Some of the young people thought that their own problems with alcohol or drugs (discussed later) were related to their parents' substance misuse. For example, Chantalle thought that her mother's drug use influenced her experimentation with drugs and Steven thought that his mother's alcoholism had triggered his own drinking.

Family criminality

The Cambridge Study in Delinquency (West and Farrington, 1973, 1977; Farrington and West, 1990) identified family criminality as one of the factors associated with offending behaviour in children. Clearly, criminality cannot be attributed to genetic factors alone; it is more plausible that criminality is "inherited" through the acceptance of deviant behaviour and attitudes by family members (Cullingford and Morrison, 1997), exacerbated by practices such as the targeting of members of families "known" to the police (Reiner, 1994; Sanders and Young, 2002). Eight (44 per cent) of the 18 young people interviewed had parents and/or siblings who had also been involved in criminal behaviour. Trevor believed that offending was a family trait:

It's because I'm a Smith, the whole family is cursed to always get in trouble . . . I was taught it was alright to thieve, just don't get caught. My mum used to say she didn't like me doing it, but that it was alright as long as I didn't get caught.

Luke also believed that offending behaviour was something that he had "inherited" from his father:

Me and my little brother's the only ones with the same dad, so we takes after each other 'cos my dad's a criminal as well; he's been banged up and that.

Education

As discussed in Chapter 6, an association between low educational achievement and criminal behaviour has often been identified (Graham and Bowling, 1995; Audit Commission, 1996; Haines and Drakeford, 1998; Rutter *et al*, 1998; NACRO, 1999c), and offending behaviour and drug misuse have been found to be high amongst excluded children (Audit Commission, 1996; Powis *et al*, 1998). Eleven (61 per cent) of the young people had been excluded from at least one school and ten (56 per cent) had been enrolled at numerous different schools and/or Pupil Referral Units. Five talked about having had no formal education since they were in Year 10, when they were aged 14, two had "left" school when they were aged 12, and one girl said that she had never been to senior school at all.

A number of themes emerged from the young people's explanations for their disengagement from education. For some the work was too difficult, which resulted in them misbehaving in class or truanting:

School was just too much. I mean it was easy to start off with but then it sort of got harder in the last couple of years. I sort of ended up skiving and causing trouble.

A lack of individual attention in classes was also problematic, with Pupil Referral Units seen as preferable by some young people because there were fewer students competing for the teachers' time:

I used to go to a unit, that's the only thing I can do 'cos it's only a couple of people in the class and it's people you know, but when it's a classroom of 30, you're like, 'Which one are you looking at?' It's too noisy, you tap the person in front of you and the next person and then the whole room is going. Like, if I'm writing something, someone would come over and push the pen and jog it or something and I'd go mad.

Other young people talked about difficulties with their peers at school, including bullying and intimidation. Stewart was bullied but felt let down by the teachers who were unable to stop it:

I did go to school but I had a few problems there . . . I'd hit people back because they were bullying me but then I was the one who got into trouble. They said you should tell someone if you are being bullied, but that doesn't work, you just get bullied more.

Some young people did not appreciate the purpose of school, feeling that it did not benefit them in any way, particularly as, in contrast, their offending behaviour could be instantly profitable:

I had better things to do. Why go and sit in a classroom when I can make money?

117

Educational provision for these young people could also be curtailed because of their involvement in the criminal justice system. Craig was taken off the school register because he was in custody for over six weeks. On his release no mainstream school would accept him and he was enrolled in a Pupil Referral Unit, to which he went twice in three years. Many of the young people talked about taking drugs or committing offences whilst they were truanting or excluded from school. There are obvious associations between truancy and school exclusion and becoming involved in offending behaviour – children are unlikely to be constructively occupied whilst they are not at school and are more likely to meet other excluded young people who might be involved in offending behaviour.

Peer relationships

Previous research (for example, Graham and Bowling, 1995) has demonstrated that associating with other young people who are involved in offending is related to the onset of criminal behaviour. In addition to the difficulties they faced with peers at school, some of the young people in the study had problems making and maintaining friendships outside school. Often the friends whom they did make were involved in offending behaviour, or were considerably older. Tom explained that he:

> . . . didn't really have any friends because I was naughty and the rest of them were good. I had a couple; they were in trouble as well.

The friends whom he did have were generally much older than Tom – when he was ten his "friends" were 17-year-olds, already involved in stealing from shops.

Many of these young people were isolated from their families and excluded from peer networks at school and would attach themselves to other excluded groups of young people (see also Cullingford and Morrison, 1997). Mikey started offending when he became "friends" with a much older group of boys:

> Everyone in [town] was doing it and I felt 'Yeah . . . I'm with the boys, I'm one of them' . . . They used to say, 'Yeah, come on lads, let's go and have a smoke' or 'let's go do this, let's go do that, let's go robbing,' do you know what I mean? Most nine-year-olds don't get that, they get

told to piss off but me, I was one of the boys, you know, 'Come out with
us, come robbing with us '.

Such friendships could create a sense of belonging and of status for these
young people.

Paul started offending when he was ten, shoplifting chocolate and
sweets with his friends. When he was a few years older, however, he was
taught that he could earn money through selling what he stole:

We met some older geezers who showed us that we could get more
money, and then we saw you can get money in your hand, so we were
shoplifting CDs and that.

The majority of the young people admitted that their offending generally
occurred when they were with their friends but three said that, although
they initially started offending with friends, they preferred to commit
offences alone as it was more profitable and they would look less
suspicious on their own.

Most of the young people who offended with their friends said that
they were not encouraged to start offending by their friends, but that it
was something they decided to do together. However, when they talked in
detail about the first offence that they committed, it became apparent that
they had been introduced to crime by more experienced young people.
Simon described how he first became involved in car thefts:

I started when I was 12 or 13 – the first time I was a passenger in a
stolen car. Some mates had nicked it and persuaded me to get in. I knew
it was stolen but they told me to get in. There was a police chase and
we got caught – the one driving crashed the car. Then I was taught how
to nick cars and just carried on, doing it for the buzz.

Similarly, Stewart's first arrest was as a result of riding a bicycle that had
been stolen by his friends.

Natalie explained that a school friend with whom she was truanting
taught her how to shoplift:

She'd been doing it, yeah, but I hadn't done it before, but she sort of
told me what to do and how to do it, and I got caught 'cos it was my
first time and then I got cautioned for that . . . we were skiving off

school . . . and Clare was there, 'Do you want to go shoplifting?'. I knew what it was, and I said 'Yeah, alright' . . . It was when we went in Safeways and sort of nicked Pringles and a drink of milkshake . . . this woman come up and said 'Can you come this way?' . . . she took us in the office and we got locked in and we got caught, 'cos they called the police. That's when we realised we'd been done for what we'd done.

Some of the young people talked about how hard it was to avoid getting into trouble when they were with their friends:

You see your friends doing it so you go along with them, you feel you might be missing out otherwise. Or you say you'll go along with them but not take anything, but then you do and you get caught.

It's one thing you learn round here, no one does anything on their own. If one of them gets caught, they make . . . try and make sure that you all get caught.

Luke realised that his friends had an adverse influence on his behaviour but felt that adults did not understand how difficult it could be to break old friendships and make new relationships with young people who were not involved in crime:

Everybody says, 'Move away, change your friends', but you can't. It ain't as easy as that.

Whilst adults have relative freedom to move house, change jobs or meet new people, it is much harder for children and young people to dislocate themselves from their neighbourhood and to establish new friendships, particularly when they may have the stigma of a criminal record.

Drugs and alcohol use

The use of drugs and alcohol is related to criminal behaviour in a number of ways: users may steal in order to fund their habit or steal alcohol or drugs from shops and pharmacies; substance use might constitute an element of a deviant lifestyle in which offending is also a part; and drugs and alcohol may cause disinhibition and lower young people's resistance to becoming involved in offending behaviour (Rutter *et al*, 1998). Drug use is also much higher amongst excluded young people living in deprived neighbourhoods, which are also affected by other social problems such as crime, health inequalities and pervasive unemployment (Foster, 2000).

Only one of the young people said that they had never used drugs or did not drink excessively. Seventeen (94 per cent) admitted to smoking cannabis fairly regularly, 14 (78 per cent) talked about taking other illegal drugs, including ecstasy, speed, cocaine, crack cocaine, magic mushrooms, and in one instance, heroin. Two young people also talked about taking prescription drugs such as valium and temazepam, initially prescribed to treat anxiety, depression and sleep problems, to counter the effects of the stimulant drugs they were taking. The young people's drug use often had started at a very young age: Trevor and Luke both said they had started smoking cannabis when they were aged eight or nine; Tom when he was 11; Ashley, Corey and Steven all before they were 13. The use of drugs tended to escalate quite rapidly, with the young people talking about having taken many different types of drug by the time they were 14 or 15.

The reasons the young people gave for taking drugs were encompassed by two main themes: firstly, to escape from problems at home and secondly, to impress peers. Lawrence, Steven and Craig all took drugs as a means of escape, although it was not always effective and, for Craig at least, led to addiction:

A lot of the times it was, like, I used to get a hard time and that, and feel depressed and real low . . . the only way I could think of getting out of it was either putting myself to sleep on pot or getting so high on crack you can't even remember what the problem was.

Just to get rid of all my problems, but when did they ever go away? Well, they went away sometimes but they always bloody come back.

It was just an escape for me. That's how it started out and then it turned from an escape into a need.

Mikey and Chantalle both took drugs to be part of a "crowd" and to impress older peers. Chantalle explained:

Well, first of all to, like, get in a crowd, like you know, it'll be a bit of like puff or you know, like dope or whatever. After that, you know, you get on to like the more classed like drugs, like, you know, speed or pills or something like that.

The influence of older siblings was also apparent:

It was because of my brother. He's like three or four years older than me, so he was 12 or 13, and I caught him smoking puff so he let me have some so I didn't tell, 'cos if I'd had some too, I couldn't say anything.

Alcohol was a significant problem for a number of the young people, with 11 saying that they drank large amounts of alcohol regularly. Again, drinking alcohol had begun at an early age, as a means of escape or to impress friends or siblings, and for some had become a serious problem. Natalie talked about her daily use of alcohol:

I used to drink a lot when I was about 14. I used to drink a bottle of vodka and a litre bottle of wine [each day]. I used to go home and I wouldn't be able to put myself to bed.

She then went on to describe being raped when she was drunk, walking home from a nightclub on her own. Craig had also put himself at risk through excessive drinking, becoming so drunk that he frequently could not remember how he had got home.

As well as placing the young people at risk, there was a clear relationship between the use of alcohol or drugs and committing offences. Lawrence talked about stealing to fund his drug use and also stealing alcohol when he was drunk to enable him to continue drinking. Stewart's drinking escalated after he was sexually abused by a friend's uncle and was a contributory factor in a number of the assaults that he committed:

I'd taken cannabis before and had alcohol before then but it started getting worse. I was leaving my mates behind, stealing money off my mum ... meeting up with other people who were all drinking ... Drinking was making me steal more alcohol and making me violent. I started bullying people as well, if they looked at me funny or called me something wrong. Like one time I was walking down this alley and kicked in the fence and this guy came out his house ... and grabbed my mate and me, so I battered him. I really freaked out; I thought he would hit me or call the police, so I hit him . . . I regret it now. . . I've hit too many people for no reason, just when I'm drunk, and I feel guilty, people I don't even know.

Offending behaviour and experience of the justice system

As well as the influence of family, friends and substance use on their offending behaviour, the young people gave a number of additional reasons for becoming involved in criminal behaviour and for continuing to offend. These included offending to obtain money and material goods, to relieve boredom and for the "buzz", and to promote their image or identity as a criminal (Presdee, 2000; Hayward, 2002).

Money was a motivating factor for a number of the young people, both in instigating and prolonging their offending. Chantalle and Steven both talked about not having money or material belongings due to their status as looked after children. Chantalle said:

I started thieving 'cos I never really . . . the people I was living with used to keep all the money themselves. I never used to get no new clothes or nothing, social services never called round, never checked up to see if the money was being spent properly . . . Lack of money, um, and after that, after that . . . well, you get used to it, it's a habit. You wake up everyday and like you had that, like 100 quid the day before, you want 100 quid again that day. Or you'd have 100 quid but you'd do it for the fun of it because it was a hobby.

Trevor's offences were mainly acquisitive, but were committed for the "buzz" it gave him as well as for the money he obtained:

I know it was stupid but it was for the buzz . . . I did it more for the buzz but also the buzz of having money and the stuff you can get with the money . . . In one house I found about 700 quid in a handbag – my heart was going, it was such a buzz . . . I wish I had saved all the money I got then I could buy a computer. I think I would have about 25 grand. That's what I mean, it is more than what some people earn in a year, but that's why you get addicted to it.

Simon also referred to his offending, which principally involved stealing cars and motorbikes, as 'an addiction, like an addiction'. For many, offending behaviour appeared to be a source of excitement and pleasure in neighbourhoods where more traditional activities and leisure pursuits were unavailable to them (Hayward, 2002). Young people, particularly those who are neither in education nor employment yet who are excluded from receipt of state benefits, may be "forced" to find illicit forms of entertainment (Presdee, 2000).

Ashley's sense of identity and personal fulfilment seemed to be strongly tied in with his offending behaviour. At the time of the interview he was in custody but talked about missing the excitement of being involved in car chases with the police and even missing sitting in the police station. He said that he initially became involved in offending to create a deviant identity for himself:

> When I first started it was to get a record. I was 12. I was just doing crime to get arrested. I thought it was cool to have a criminal record.

This reflects Katz's (1988) assertion that many young people involved in offending behaviour take pride in their reputations as "badmen", in a culture where crime is being increasingly represented through popular media (including films, television, "gangsta rap", video games and so forth) as romantic, fashionable, cool and exciting (Hayward, 2002).

Rationalisation or remorse
Some young people rationalised their behaviour with scant regard to the effect it had on the victims or on themselves:

> If I've got to walk home or if I'm going out with someone and I'm walking to theirs, I'll take a car. . . I won't get the bus. If I had to do that every night it would cost a tenner, so I steal a car.

Ashley stole a car to enable him to fulfil the requirements of a previous sentence:

> I had to get to the attendance centre 'cos I had an order for burglaries, cars and that, and I nicked a car so I could get there.

Others showed signs of remorse for their offending behaviour, expressing both sympathy for the victims and regret for the impact their criminal behaviour had had on their family, friends and employment opportunities. Chantalle (seven months pregnant at the time of the interview) talked about wanting a clean record so that professionals such as social workers and police officers would not prejudge her ability as a mother:

> *In the end I wish, I wish I could have a clean, clean record. I wish I had never even done my first offence at all. Gets you in so much . . . I mean people just look at you and they look at your previous convictions and assault, theft, they wouldn't trust you as far as they could throw you . . . I ain't like it no more but they're still making me look like I am like it. And they're talking about if I didn't do this, they'd take the baby off me, and if I didn't do that, they'd take the baby off me. Like police officers sitting there saying, 'Well, what makes you think you'd be a fit mother?'*

Ineffective contact with police and statutory agencies

Although all of the young people had participated in offending behaviour for a considerable time, none had been deterred by their involvement with statutory agencies.[29] Tom started offending when he was below the age of criminal responsibility but at the age of ten was taken to the police station and cautioned. He believed that the police were trying to scare him so that he did not offend again, which was effective but only for a short time:

> *. . . but then I just thought, 'Oh well, that wasn't too bad.' Then I thought, 'Oh, I won't get caught this time', and then the next time I went to the police station, 'Next time I do it I won't get caught', and so on.*

---

[29]There has been widespread evaluation of "what works" in preventing recidivism by young offenders (see, for example, Utting and Vennard, 2000). Lipsey (1995) conducted a meta-analysis of approximately 400 evaluations of interventions and concluded that those which reduced offending included programmes designed to improve personal and social skills or focused on changing behaviour, or multiple service programmes combining a number of different approaches. Conversely, vocational counselling and deterrent programmes, such as shock incarceration, could result in an increase in recidivism.

Paul's comments echoed this theme:

You get back into it without being caught for a couple of months and think you can get away with it, and then you get caught once but think you only got caught once so you do it again, and then you get caught again.

The sentences the young people received could be equally ineffective in curtailing their offending. Stewart had been given a range of community sentences but felt that they had not taught him anything nor affected his behaviour:

. . . conditional discharge, I got a supervision order, reparation order. But it don't do anything, it's no punishment. It doesn't seem to help; it's like half an hour of your time with them speaking to you, saying that it's bad, but as you already know what you're doing is bad, then it ain't helping you.

Conversely, Simon repeatedly talked about the ineffectiveness of prison and his belief that a community sentence that included a car offenders' group would be more constructive in reducing his offending:

I've been institutionalised. I've been inside more than outside. I'm not bothered about prison – I was at first but you just have to get used to it. The car offenders' group would help . . . Prison doesn't do anything, just makes the crime rate go down, it doesn't do anything to help me stop offending. They just think, 'If he re-offends again we will send him down again'. They're not worried about helping, so it will just go on and on and on.

Ashley also thought that prison was unsuccessful in preventing re-offending because one becomes accustomed to it:

As soon as you come out you think, 'That wasn't too bad', and the more you do it the more OK it is.

Darren, however, believed that a 'short, hard stint in Feltham' had stopped him committing any further crimes of violence.

Patterns of offending

Darren was unusual within this sample as all of his offences were related to violence: assaults and Grievous Bodily Harm (GBH). The majority of the young people had been involved in a number of different types of offence, including shoplifting, thefts, TWOC and aggravated TWOC, burglary, robbery and armed robbery, and assaults, although there was often some element of "specialism". In two instances the young people had previously been involved only in relatively minor crime such as shoplifting but were on remand for allegedly committing a much more serious offence. In one case this was indecent assault, in another arson.

Previous experience of detention in local authority care or custody

Only two of the young people had never been remanded or sentenced to local authority care or custody. For three young people, the most serious court order they had received was a remand to local authority accommodation, for two a remand or sentence to secure accommodation, and for 11 a remand or sentence to prison service custody.

Four of the young people talked about their experiences on remand in children's homes and all emphasised the lack of control that the staff had over the residents. One young person articulated this:

I was free to do what I liked. They don't give you no guidance, they don't say 'Don't' – well, they do say 'Don't do this, don't do that' but you just ignore them and go out the door.

Craig's comments about his experience of secure accommodation echoed this theme. He said:

I was only there for a couple of days but it seemed easy enough, secure units . . . it's just a laugh, secure. Everyone just fucks about, you do what you like really . . . more puff and that gets in, you know what I mean? You're not meant to smoke in there but there's always 20 decks of fags getting passed about on the sly.

Natalie talked about the violence and the self-harming behaviour that she witnessed whilst she was on remand in a secure unit:

There was girls there that were cutting their wrists with CDs and there

127

was violence and they used to chuck the tables and chairs around. And the first day I went there I cried.

She also described the bullying that occurred whilst she was there and how she had to defend herself against it:
I didn't want to go for my dinner 'cos I didn't know anyone and they were being horrible. They were sort of, 'Oh what's she looking at?'... They tried to act hard but then it sort of turned around because I sort of put them in their boots as I didn't. I wasn't being a bully or anything, I just didn't want two girls bullying me.

Craig talked about the culture of fighting and bullying that he had encountered within prisons and the need to establish a status as someone who cannot be bullied:
You got to go in there and you got to make yourself. You got to show yourself straight away to be someone who they're not going to be able to bully. You got to go in there, do something to show them 'Don't bully him'. Just go in there, walk on association, you know what I mean? In a way you're bullying other people.

Mikey also talked about the perceived importance of fighting within YOIs as a means of establishing a reputation and thereby avoiding victimisation. Clearly, as much other research has demonstrated, bullying is widespread within custodial institutions and young people feel they have to be physically and verbally aggressive from the outset to prevent themselves becoming the victim (King and Morgan, 1980; Howard League, 1995b, 1998; Goldson, 2002a).

The appalling physical conditions within YOIs and the lack of appropriate activities have also been highlighted by previous research (Howard League, 1995b; HMIP, 2000a) and the young people's descriptions of the YOIs in which they had been detained supported this research. Paul described one YOI as being:
... a dirty prison. It stinks, the cells are dirty, the floors are all coming up and there's woodlice underneath. You have to try to keep it clean yourself.

Other young people talked about YOIs as being 'disgusting' or 'shit-holes'. The lack of activities compounded the poor conditions in the cells. The young people explained that they were often locked in their cells all day, with no or very limited access to education or training. Most of the young people had televisions in their cells, which they appreciated, but the amount of time they spent locked up was unacceptable. For example, Stewart talked about his most recent period of detention in a YOI and said that:

> . . . in the first five days I was there I got six hours out of my cell. On one day I only got one hour out.

The young people also talked about the ease with which they could access drugs within the YOIs:

> They were just everywhere, people bringing them up. People were chucking them over the fence and when you were playing football you could go grab them.

As discussed above, only one young person thought that their experience of custody had curtailed their offending behaviour. Comments by other young people described the "revolving door" process and the effects of "contamination" by other offenders:

> I'd just carry on doing exactly what I was doing 'cos it wouldn't have give me no incentive to sort myself out, because basically when you go to jail it's just a vicious circle. You do a crime, you go to jail, you come out, you ain't got no money, you go back out robbing again. End up going back to jail. Straight like that, it's just one big vicious circle. Like round and round and round and round.

> You go to prison, right, you learn more about crime . . . it's like crime capital. You just like speak to people and they like tell you how to do this, how to do that, how to do this.

Clearly, the young people's experience of detention in local authority care or custody had been detrimental to their welfare and had often exacerbated their own anti-social behaviour.

Summary

This chapter has discussed the young people's views of the influences of their friends and family, educational experiences, and their use of drugs and alcohol, on the onset and continuation of their offending behaviour. The ineffectiveness of previous contact with the criminal justice system was apparent within the young people's narratives: overall, they felt that both community and custodial sentences had limited impact on their offending behaviour. The next chapters explore the young people's experiences of remand foster care and highlight that, whilst it is not a universal panacea, remand foster care is a more child-centred, positive mechanism for dealing with alleged young offenders that can have a considerably greater effect on reducing their offending behaviour and increasing feelings of social inclusion.

9 Young people's experiences of remand foster care (Part 1)

Introduction

The young people's experiences of remand foster care are discussed in this and the subsequent chapter. This chapter focuses on the young people's (lack of) involvement in the remand decision, the development of their relationship with the foster carers and the positive and negative aspects of remand foster care. It discusses the effect the remand placement had on the young people's friendships and family relationships, and the impact it had on their behaviour, including offending. The following chapter compares the young people's experiences of remand foster care and other forms of care and/or custody, discuss their involvement with professionals other than the foster carers, and explore how the placements ended and the outcomes post-placement.

Five of the 18 young people had been placed on remand with foster carers on more than one occasion and, unusually for the scheme, another had been remanded to live with the foster carer, returned home and then been placed back with the carer as a specialist (non-remand) foster care placement. The interview material therefore covered 23 remand placements, of which 10 (43 per cent) lasted until the week after the completion of the court hearings[30] and 13 (57 per cent) broke down before then.

A common underlying theme throughout the young people's narratives related to their sense of identity and self-esteem. Although not clinically measured, many appeared to have low self-esteem and their experiences in remand foster care could have both negative and positive effects on their self-esteem, confidence and sense of identity.

---

[30]To reiterate, the project allows the young person to stay with the foster carer for up to a week after the conclusion of the court hearing to facilitate a move to alternative accommodation.

Experiences of remand foster care

Involvement in the remand decision

Both the UNCRC and the Children Act 1989 state that children and young people should be involved in all decisions affecting their welfare. Furthermore, previous research has indicated that involving young people in planning and preparing for a foster placement reduces the likelihood of placement disruption (Farmer *et al*, 2004). The remand foster care project studied stipulates in its referral form that young people will only be offered a placement if the 'young person is, after having full knowledge of the placement and its implications on her/his lifestyle, willing to participate and abide by the placement agreement'. However, many of the young people said that they were not consulted about the possibility of being remanded to foster care, or that if they were, the discussion was merely a token gesture and did not offer a real opportunity for participation in the decision. For example, Tom was initially remanded to a children's home at which he was informed that he would be moving:

> *They put me in a children's home. And then one day they just said, 'Right, pack your stuff, you're going.' They packed it for me actually. They just said, 'Someone's come' . . . they just said, 'Go upstairs, get your stuff, you're going.'*

He was not told where he was going nor with whom he would be living until he was actually being driven to the foster carers' home by his YOT officer.

Natalie was consulted about going to remand foster care but felt that her views would not be taken into consideration by the YOT staff or magistrates:

> *It's not a choice that I could make. They don't say to you, 'Do you want to go to foster care?', they make that decision for you . . . I mean they did say, 'How would you feel about going to foster care?' and I said, 'I don't mind' but if you said you did mind you still wouldn't get a choice of going anywhere else.*

A number of young people talked about being given a choice but said that the alternative available to them, custody, was not an option they wanted to consider:

You have a choice but you're going, you ain't going to choose to stay inside are you?

[the YOT officer said] 'You've got this choice, you got to go back to Feltham and spend three to five months on remand or come out via this place.' I thought, 'Wow, what a choice.'

For Darren, the decision about whether or not he could be bailed to reside with the foster carers took place over two days whilst he remained in prison service custody. He was fairly well informed about the project and the potential placement but the initial application for a remand on bail was appealed against:

When I went to court . . . while I was in the cell, Jacqui, my foster carer, come in and saw me and we got on well and she said, 'Yeah, we're going to go for it' and then the court went for it. Well, first of all they went for it. They said 'Yeah,' then the prosecution appealed against it which meant I had to go back in the cell and go back up to Feltham that night, then the appeal was heard the next morning . . . That one night? It's the longest night I've ever had. You're just sitting there thinking, 'Look what I could do.' You've either got all or nothing, ain't you?

Alfie was also in custody when the application for his remand status to be changed was heard in court. However, he did not know the application was being made, nor where he would be going if it was successful:

We just got chucked out of Feltham and told 'Off you go.' I didn't know where to go, I had to wait for the bus and then went to the train station . . . I thought I was getting bail and going home! We were just told to pack our kit. I asked if I was going home and they said, 'No, foster care.' I didn't want to go, I wanted to go home. I didn't know where I was going, I didn't want to go to people I didn't know.

Many of the young people were extremely nervous or uncomfortable about going to the remand foster placement, particularly if they had previous negative experiences of family life or the care system, but again believed that it was preferable to custody:

You don't want to be part of a family, you just don't want to be in prison . . . I was in the court cells and someone came down and said, 'This geezer is here, if you think he is OK you can go with him'. I thought it was a bit weird but it was better than prison so I said 'Alright'.

They said I could either go to foster care or they would keep me in the cell. I weren't happy about it at first . . . I was anxious, I didn't feel I would fit in with someone else's family . . . [but] there was no choice.

Even young people who were looking forward to going to the placement said that they were nervous about moving into a different house with people whom they did not know.

Some of the anxieties appeared to be related to the young people's sense of identity and what they thought the carers would think of them. Stewart was concerned that his carers would prejudge him on the basis of his offending behaviour and "offender" identity:

I was a bit nervous . . . I was worried that they'd think I was a thief and that I'd be going round their house looking at their stuff, that they wouldn't trust me.

Meeting the foster carers beforehand, as Darren did, was beneficial in helping the young people deal with the move to remand foster care. Simon said that his foster carer had come to the court to talk to him before his hearing. He said that:

She was alright, bubbly. I got on with her straight away. She talked formal like, not holding anything back. She was really straight up . . . It was Jane's or prison – I said I would go to Jane's and try it out as, soon as I saw her, I liked her.

Similarly, Paul was able to meet the carers prior to moving to the placement but, due to the current lack of forethought within the court system, this is frequently not possible. The remand decision is often made rapidly, with little time for the carers to meet the young person. However, it is rare that a young person would be brought to court on the same day that they were arrested[31] and they would usually be granted bail by the police or held in police cells, PACE beds[32] or institutional accommodation overnight. If the young person is granted police bail there is clearly time for placement planning and for them to meet potential foster carers. For young people held overnight, the courts could organise their schedule so that all remand cases were heard in the afternoon, so that young people could meet the potential foster carers in the morning before their case is heard. Admittedly, this would allow only a brief meeting with the carers but it might be enough to allay some young people's concerns and fears.

Settling into the placements

The young people's feelings of nervousness and anxiety tended to culminate when they arrived at the placement. Lawrence said:

I was just nervous, and your head's spinning. You don't know what to say, you don't, you don't know even if you should ask to sit down or what. You don't know whether you should take your trainers off or not . . . like my second day there . . . I just laid in bed. I didn't know if I should go down and get my own breakfast or wait to be called or even make a cup of tea . . . I'd already met Kim and I'd spoken to her and I did think, yeah nice lady, and I had no problems with her but I didn't know how it was going to work. And I think she cottoned on and then she explained; she said, 'Just help yourself, oh, within reason.'

From the young people's accounts, it was clear that most of the foster carers were very aware of how anxious the young people might be and the concerns and difficulties that they might face when they first arrived at a placement. The carers appeared to have an ability to acknowledge and understand how the young person might be feeling and the capability to address this quickly and effectively. Simple actions, such as providing a meal that the young person would like or offering them a bath, were

---

[31] If a warrant has been issued for a young person's arrest, s/he may be brought to court on the day of their arrest; however this is infrequent and YOTs could have specific arrangements for dealing with these instances.

[32] Overnight accommodation with carers or in lodgings, provided for children who need to be detained by the police under the Police and Criminal Evidence Act 1984 (PACE) but who cannot be held in police custody.

important to make them feel welcomed and more comfortable. Darren's foster carer had discovered what food he liked when she first met him in the court cells, which helped to establish their relationship when he arrived at the placement:

> *I didn't really know what to do with myself so I just stood there. I was hungry and . . . I was dirty, I smelt, I just wanted to go and get in the bath but I didn't want to ask, until she turned round and said, 'Oh, you must want a bath. Take your clothes off, I'll wash them for you.' [Then]* '*I went downstairs, she'd cooked me something to eat and I said, 'How did you know I liked that?' and she said, 'Because you remember on the first meeting?'. She'd asked me what I like to eat . . . she said, 'I remember from when you told me'. So I ate that and then we went for a walk and she showed me where everything was.*

Children remanded to a YOI have a very different experience on their arrival: they undergo a Reception Interview leading to the completion of a "T1:V" form[33] and the development of a risk management plan (Goldson, 2002a). This interview necessarily raises complex and sensitive personal issues, for example, discussing any history of self-harm, family breakdown, mental and physical health problems, victimisation and bullying, but is conducted within an hour of the young person's arrival at the prison. It is also likely to be the fifth of six similar interviews that a young person remanded to custody will face within a day. As Goldson argues, this 'process can . . . be regarded as abusive and damaging' (2002a, p. 82), particularly if the young person is nervous, scared or feeling suicidal. Clearly the welcome afforded by the foster carers is, on this evidence, considerably more caring, child-centred and appropriate than is the reception procedure in YOIs.

Young people arriving at prison are subject to a very institutionalised routine that precludes responding to an individual's specific needs or anxieties (Goldson, 2002a). In contrast, remand foster carers can react

---

[33] The "T-Forms" are a series of assessment documents completed when a young person is sentenced or remanded to secure facilities; the T1:V form is a specific vulnerability assessment used by admission staff during the reception interview in a custodial institution (Youth Justice Board, 2001b).

flexibly to the particular concerns of an individual young person. Being able to have a bath after a difficult and stressful court appearance, having the opportunity to telephone family members, or having a meal without fear of bullying or victimisation by other prisoners, are options available to young people in remand foster care but not those on remand in custody.

Relationship with carers

The relationships young people had with carers developed in different ways, often related to the young person's perception of the carers' attitude towards them. The young people appreciated immensely the caring, nurturing and respectful attitudes demonstrated by some foster carers, which was often contrary to their expectations and previous experiences. The manner in which the foster carers treated them could have a considerable impact upon the young person's self-esteem, confidence and sense of worth. For example, Paul felt that he was treated with respect and dignity by the first foster carers he was placed with:

In the mornings Kate would knock the door and I'd get up, have a shower or whatever, and Kate would ask if she could go in and clean the room. Even though it is their room she would ask as if it was my room. I did have to clean the room but sometimes she would do it as a favour, like if it needed hoovering. They would always knock. I liked having some privacy. They treated me like I was actually living there.

Mikey thought that his carer considered him to be worth spending time with and valued the way she treated him as an individual rather than just another prisoner:

She's really considerate; she'd listen to your problems and that. If you wanted to talk to her about anything she'd talk to you . . . And she'd get newspapers every day and we'd sit there doing crosswords together and that, and it wasn't, it's not really me, but it was. It was good. It was just like, this person has got time for me . . . She didn't treat me like a criminal, she treated me like a person. And that's what I needed at the time, I didn't need to be treated like a criminal, like standing outside your cell, prison name and number, 'FW5016 Smith, sir' and all that . . . She weren't like that, she treated you as an individual, as a person. If you was alright with her, she was alright with you. That's the way she see it.

Similarly, Lawrence enjoyed the feeling of being trusted by his carers when they asked him to buy goods for them and entrusted him with quite considerable amounts of money. He believed that the carers liked him and actually wanted to spend time with him:

They didn't treat me like I'm different, they just treated me like someone they'd speak to, you know what I mean? And not, not just someone to speak to, someone they liked more than anything, and that was good. They used to trust me and that as well. They would go out and leave me in the house and they wouldn't worry about anything going missing.

These comments reflect the ability of remand foster care to meet the obligations towards remanded children stipulated in Article 40 of the UNCRC, specifically promoting the child's sense of dignity and worth, and promoting the child's constructive reintegration into society.

Conversely, however, Mark did not feel trusted or believed by his foster carer, particularly when her children were involved:

There were three kids and one of them went into the garden when I was smoking and broke all my fags. I told Clare but she didn't believe me. I had the money to buy some more so it wasn't that but it was the principle – Clare didn't believe me because I am a criminal, but she did believe her kids.

Trevor also had a more negative relationship with his foster carers, whom he thought did not like him because he was 'so screwed up 'cos of drugs'.

Three of the five young people who had been placed with remand foster carers on two occasions said that they had experienced one positive and one negative placement whilst two said that both placements had been positive. These differences were largely related to the way in which the young people felt they were treated by the foster carers. For example, in his second placement, Paul felt that he was continuously compared to a previously fostered child whom the carers said was better behaved than Paul, which made him feel disliked by the carers. Paul

said that the male foster carer would threaten him in an attempt to make
him behave:

*The man was always moaning about something, like coming in late . . .
I hated the second one [placement]. Not the woman but the man; he used
blackmail. He said he would call the police and get me back – not get
you back as in back to the placement but get you back in other ways.*

Tom also experienced two very different foster placements. Although his
first placement broke down on the day of sentencing, he had developed a
very strong relationship with the carers whom he saw as 'like a second set
of parents', which was comforting to him. He felt that the first carers did
care for him and considered him to be important. He explained that his
first foster carer:

*. . . seemed to sort of be, like, there whenever you needed her. Whatever
she was doing she'd always put it down and come straight to you.*

However, he subsequently had what he thought was consensual intercourse
with a girl he knew but was charged with indecent assault and placed
with different remand foster carers. These carers emphasised his
"abnormal" behaviour, which had a detrimental impact on the way Tom
saw himself:

*I thought some of the stuff he said was really out of order. . . like
'You've got to be in at this certain time because of the stuff you've done,
you're not normal', like rubbing it in. I felt like saying 'No, I'm not
normal, but that's no reason to rub it in'.*

Whilst Tom had allegedly committed a sexual offence it was personally
undermining to accuse him of being 'not normal'; such comments are
unprofessional and contrary to the fundamental presumption of innocent
until proven guilty.

Natalie, who prior to the previous week spent in secure accommodation
had never lived away from home, felt particularly uncomfortable in her
foster placement and thought that she was intruding into others' lives:

*. . . sort of just invading someone else's life . . . they were doing their
own thing and it didn't feel right . . . It wasn't the same as what my mum
does so it felt different, living with someone in their own house.*

Sleeping there was horrible . . . I didn't like really feel comfortable in someone else's house.

Natalie seemed very insecure which was either not recognised or not addressed by the foster carers with whom she was placed.

Unsurprisingly, being welcomed, made to feel worthy of attention, consideration and care, and being trusted were important factors in making the young people feel settled and secure in the placement. Conversely, not being trusted or respected, being treated differently to other children in the family or neighbourhood, and having to wait for the carers' time and attention could add to young people's feelings of discomfort or of being "in the way".

Matching young people's needs with foster carers' skills and caring style

One of the difficulties faced by remand foster care schemes is that the current scheduling of court hearings allows very little time for "matching" the child's needs with the skills and abilities of the carer (see Triseliotis *et al*, 1995). Farmer and colleagues (2004) found that mainstream foster placements made in an emergency, with limited time for matching, planning or preparation, were significantly more likely to disrupt than those in which there had been more time for matching and preparation. Remand decisions, by their very nature, are made with little notice and limited access to information about the child's needs makes planning and preparation for the placement difficult. In addition, the relative scarcity of remand foster carers will often mean that there is no choice of placement and thus no opportunity for "matching" the child's needs with the carer's abilities.

However, as the comments from the young people indicate, the success of the placements was influenced by the relationship they had with the foster carer and the way in which the carer approached the task of looking after the young person, and it is important to achieve a match between what a particular child needs and what the carer can offer. For some young people, such as Tom, caring for the young person as a parent would care for their own child was appropriate. He enjoyed being praised by the carers:

I felt more proud, having people to say 'That's brilliant', like when you bring home a picture from school or something.

However, other young people resented this style of "parenting" as they felt they were not children and should not be treated as such. For example, Paul was placed with a family that encouraged his involvement with the carers' own children, but he felt that he was more mature than this:

They wanted me to go to the pond and feed the ducks with their daughters but I was 16, 17, I didn't want to do that.

Similarly, Trevor believed that he had to relinquish his independence and adapt to rules within a family that curtailed his freedom and self-determination. It might be that Paul and Trevor would have appreciated being placed with a foster carer who did not try to "parent" them so much but who encouraged and promoted more independence. The foster carers' approaches to their role are discussed further in Chapter 11.

Additionally, the geographical surroundings of the placement could influence the young person's attitude towards it. For example, one young person remanded to a rural location thought that 'it was crap as there was nothing to do', yet another young person remanded to a similar placement enjoyed being there:

I used to love it, walking in the morning and that, hearing the birds singing and out in the country air, the fresh air, do you know what I mean? It's just lovely. I used to go running and that.

However, as mentioned above, the current scarcity of remand foster carers often means that there is no choice of placement and, until a wider pool of remand foster carers can be recruited, such factors cannot be taken into consideration, even though they might affect the outcome of the placement.

What makes a good foster carer?

The young people talked about the characteristics of the foster carers and what skills they considered necessary to be a good foster carer. One important issue was that the carers did not see fostering as just a source of income but that they truly wanted to help the young people. Lawrence and Chantalle both explained that mainstream foster carers with whom they had been placed previously 'were in it for the money', but that the remand foster carers wanted to help them as individuals. Other capacities that the young people valued were honesty and fairness, being loving and caring, respecting the young people, being non-judgemental, listening to them and understanding their backgrounds.

For Darren, the most important characteristic was the ability to listen to the foster child:

Listening and talking. 'Cos if you won't listen to your, whatever you want to call him, your boy, you ain't going to listen to what his problems are and you ain't going to do anything about them.

Some young people also talked about what they did not want from foster carers, which may be a reflection of the type of parenting they had received from their parents or other carers. For example, Pete, who had a difficult relationship with his step-father, had previously experienced an unhappy foster care placement and had lived in a number of hostels as well as on the streets, said:

They couldn't hire someone who would like hit 'em, or someone who goes out drinking in the pub all the time or something like that. You've got to hire someone who's kind . . . helpful, like someone who would actually want to, like, pick someone up and put them back, show them the right path and that. You couldn't hire someone that was just, like, 'Bugger off, you just live here, I'm not doing anything for you'.

The young people's comments encapsulated the principle of normalisation outlined by the Swedish Royal Commission in 1974 (cited by Hazel, 1993b) and adopted by the Kent Family Placement Project (Hazel, 1980; 1981a; see Chapter 4). Paul said that a good remand foster carer would be 'someone who treats you as normal, nothing else, nothing extra'. Simon believed that, in foster care 'you feel part of a family, it helps you, you feel normal'. Similarly, Mikey felt that remand foster care allowed a child to 'live normally and naturally, instead of when you are in a prison'. Feeling "normal" was crucial to the young people's sense of security and stability and could potentially reduce the young people's inclination to offend, by counteracting their sense of criminal identity and of being socially excluded.

Impact of the placement on the young people and their offending behaviour

The prevalence of offending by young people whilst they are in remand foster care is obviously a key factor in assessing the success of remand foster schemes. The young people were asked whether or not they had offended whilst they were in the placement, and if not, why not. Excluding taking drugs and breaching conditions (discussed later), six of the 18 young people admitted to having committed offences whilst they were in the placement, principally shoplifting and car theft or vehicle interference. The foster carers were not always aware of the offending, and their responses to it, when they did know, varied. One young person explained that he was arrested for stealing and his foster carers confiscated his television as a punishment. Another said that after his third arrest (for car theft) the foster carer refused to continue the placement.

Steven, who committed a series of robberies during the placement, described how he had previously stolen goods for his "uncle". The police confiscated these goods when Steven was first arrested and he was forced, by his uncle, to steal money whilst he was in the remand foster placement to replace the stolen goods. He said that it would have been better for him to have remained on remand in secure accommodation, rather than be moved to remand foster care, because he would not have been able to continue offending if he had been incarcerated.

Twelve of the young people said that they had not committed any offences whilst they were in the remand foster care placement. Some were pragmatic about the change in their behaviour, explaining that they had not offended because of their lack of familiarity with the geographical area, difficulties in realising or disposing of stolen goods, or the increased risk of being caught because '[the foster carers] know all the people'. Alfie said:

I didn't do any robbing when I was there . . . I didn't really know where to rob . . . and I wouldn't know where to sell it so I would end up piling it all up in my room so I didn't rob nothing . . . I didn't do any other offending.

Similarly, Luke felt that:

There's nothing to do up there, there's nothing to get into trouble with. There's no shops to thieve, it's like a little village, there's nothing worth having in there anyway.

Others believed that there was a deeper reason for the change in their behaviour, related to the way they perceived themselves and the offences that they had committed:

It made me think about my offending a lot. It made me think, 'Well, I was out of order, I was bang out of order, the things that I've done'. I dunno really, it does . . . it just makes you think. You're there [in the foster placement] and there's nothing really else to do except think, do you know what I mean? You've just got so much time on your hands and just thinking, thinking.

It gave me a bit of perspective on life, made me think about things. Before I was like, I thought life owed me, now I know that everything ain't going to come to me.

Again, these comments are indicative of the potential of remand foster carers to reinforce the young people's respect for human rights and the fundamental freedoms of others and to promote their reintegration into society (Article 40, UNCRC).

Friends and peer relationships
Being away from the influence of friends and peers was also instrumental in reducing the likelihood of the young people offending whilst they were in the foster placement. Luke, Tom and Paul all said they did not offend because they were not in contact with the friends with whom they had previously offended. Paul explained that his parents had tried to discourage him from being friends with particular people and that being in remand foster care had helped him to appreciate this:

Mum and dad have always said about my mates but I didn't listen. Now I know they were right all along. You can think about it more as you are away from your mates.

There was a very fine line between remanding the young people far enough away from their home area to help them dissociate from negative influences and remanding them too far from friends and family networks and it could be difficult to achieve this balance. Craig found it hard to meet new people in the area and wanted to be able to return home more easily. He thought that his condition of non-association was:

> . . . not fair really because they can't expect to just put us in these places and expect us to sit in all day long.

Three of the young people who absconded[34] from their remand foster placements said that they did so because they were too far from their friends or family or they were bored. Making friends in the placement appeared to be difficult for many of the young people, particularly those who appeared to have low self-esteem. Paul said:

> They [foster carers] would say I should make new mates there but you can't just do that, go up to people and make friends.

Some foster carers made a point of explaining to the young people that they would not tell anyone else that the young person was on remand so that they were not judged or stigmatised by the neighbours. However, the need to attend court hearings and appointments with YOTs and having curfew restrictions meant that the young people could easily be identified as offenders by their peers. Tom, in particular, found it very difficult to deal with the restrictions placed on him by the foster carers when he was on remand for alleged indecent assault. The carers stipulated that, if he was out playing with friends, he had to go back to the house every 15 minutes, which was embarrassing for Tom. He said that he had to make excuses to his friends to hide the true situation, but that he 'couldn't go to the toilet every 15 minutes' as his friends would become suspicious. He also felt that the level of surveillance he was under was invasive:

> I was different from all my friends. I was watched to go down the road to school. And I couldn't go round any of my mates to call for them. I had to walk there on my own and walk back on my own.

---

[34] See Chapter 6 for more details about absconding from placements.

Natalie made friends with a boy who lived in the neighbourhood but broke off the friendship when her foster carer began asking questions about him:

He sort of came over one day but Sue was sort of all nosy . . . trying to find out what he was like and that, and I didn't like it so I told him to not bother coming round.

It was apparent that these foster carers were in a very difficult situation: Natalie seemed to be a vulnerable girl who was easily led by others; Tom potentially could have placed other children at risk. Mirroring the wider tensions between care and control that are apparent within welfare and justice systems, these carers had to reach a balance between protection and intrusion into the young people's lives.

Being in remand foster care thus could be a very lonely time for some young people. It is important for children on remand to maintain their existing friendships or to make new friendships, partly to limit the likelihood of absconding, but also to offer support throughout the remand period. Young people need the companionship of others to maintain psychological and emotional well-being (Argyle, 1988), particularly in times of stress or disruption.

Some foster carers introduced the remanded young person to their family and friends as a way of keeping them occupied and involving them in local community networks. Simon and Lawrence both appreciated being taken out to restaurants with their carers' friends and family or to family parties because it made them feel included and involved and decreased feelings of loneliness and isolation. This is an area of good practice that should be encouraged and supported by remand foster care projects.

Birth family relationships

Being separated from their parents caused some young people distress but others, with the support of foster carers, were able to re-negotiate their relationships with their families whilst they were in remand foster care. This is something that is generally not possible for a young person remanded to residential or custodial institutions as dealing with family relationships is not part of the staff's remit and even if it was, staff would be unlikely to have the time to focus upon one individual's needs to such an extent.

Luke believed that the time he had spent on remand in foster care led to an improvement in his relationship with his mother, partly due to the enforced separation from her which allowed Luke to 'sort my head out' but also because his mother developed a good relationship with the foster carer. The foster carer was able to offer advice to Luke's mother when she and Luke were experiencing difficulties. He said that at the start of the placement he and his mother 'couldn't even stay in the house for half an hour without arguing' but by the end of the placement, through the foster carer's involvement, they could sit down together and actually 'speak to each other'. In contrast, Mark felt that his parents 'hated' his foster carer because she made it clear that she did not trust any members of his family and she disagreed with any suggestions or comments his mother made. Clearly, dealing with family relationships could be problematic. These issues are considered further in Chapter 11.

Stewart had a court-ordered condition of non-association with his mother and said that this period of separation from her enabled him to think about their relationship and he began to appreciate his mother more:

It helped me realise how much I needed my mum, that I missed her and I needed her.

After a couple of weeks, however, missing his mother became too much and Stewart breached his condition of non-association. He began to meet with her although he 'kept it quiet' from the foster carers and criminal justice agencies.

Both Craig and Darren said that they did not have close relationships with their families and did not miss them whilst they were in foster care, but acknowledged that regular contact might be important for other young people. Corey did find it difficult to be apart from his family and said that his foster placement was 'too far away . . . I always wanted to be around my family'. Pete also felt that the distance between his foster care placement and his family was too great and he resented the condition of non-association with his brother that the court had ordered. However, as Alfie and Stewart both pointed out, maintaining contact with family members was much less difficult in remand foster care than it would be if they had been remanded to custody.

Providing proactive help to children to maintain or rebuild their family relationships whilst they are in remand foster care is important and contact with family members should be facilitated. A number of the young people said that being given a travel pass so that they could visit their family would be beneficial or, alternatively, transport arrangements should be established to enable their parents to visit the foster placement.

Court-ordered conditions attached to the remand period

Six of the young people had court-ordered conditions of non-association with friends or family members and nine had court-ordered curfews. In all but two of the cases where the court had not imposed a curfew, the foster carers set their own curfew for the young people. Four young people were also banned from certain areas, for example, shopping malls, town centres or their home estates, in an attempt to prevent them from committing offences in these areas.[35]

As discussed above, non-association with family members was resented and the young people similarly found non-association with friends difficult to manage. Tom felt that it had not been properly explained to him why he should not see his friends or what would happen to him if he did choose to see them. Some also found it hard to comprehend why they could not return to their home areas. For example, Paul was critical of the conditions placed on him, which he believed the foster carers had requested:

> *They said they would only take me if I agreed to certain things like the curfew and that. It was like blackmail. I didn't like them as they asked for the ban from [Xtown]. I was only 16. How can you ban someone from their own area? You get seen, you get nicked.*

Paul's comments reflect the lack of understanding some young people had about the reasons for court-ordered conditions. He knew that breaching the

---

[35] At the time of the research, electronic monitoring ("tagging") was not being used for young people placed within the scheme, although discussions as to the feasibility of this were being held.

conditions could lead to his arrest but saw this as an unjust infringement of his liberty rather than as a way of keeping him out of trouble.

Curfews were also seen as unfair by some of the young people, including Paul, Craig and Trevor, especially as they were not considered by the young people themselves to be effective in preventing offending. Trevor thought that younger children would be more accepting of rules and restrictions but that those who were older or who had lived independently would dislike the regulations:

I was doing alright for a couple of weeks but then I met this really nice girl and I wanted to see her and her kid, and stay over with her, not every night, but some nights, but I had to be in by 10.30, so I couldn't stay over. I was 17 and used to having my own place, doing what I want. I get on alright with rules, but not with stupid rules. Should have your own key and just say when you are going to be in . . . For kids under 16 it would be fine, they're more adaptable, but I had spent two years living in my own place.

Of the 16 young people who had either a court-ordered or carer-enforced curfew, seven admitted that they breached the curfew on at least one occasion. Those who did not breach the curfew said that they did not do so either because there was nothing to do or nowhere to go, or because they were afraid of being arrested and returned to prison. However, the latter reason was dismissed by other young people who thought that the courts would not take action even if they did breach the conditions:

I got arrested and taken to court and let go the next morning. I thought it was pretty sad actually, 'cos you waste all that time, all the police's money and stuff, just to be told 'Oh bad boy, Tom, don't do it again please. Off you go.'

If you don't like a condition, really the best thing you can do it just breach it and breach it and breach it until they stop and say, 'Well, that's not working. Let's try something new.'

This reflects the magistrates' views (Chapter 7) that young people who breached their conditions were likely to be given numerous "second chances". Many foster carers were also thought to be quite lenient in how they dealt with breached curfews. Most of the young people said that they were allowed some leeway before the carers called either the project or the police to report the breach.

Five of the six who had conditions of non-association breached those conditions, as did one of the four who had a geographical restriction placed upon them. One of the young people with a geographical restriction said that he avoided breaching the ban by arranging to meet his friends on the edge of the area from which he was barred.

Pre-sentence reports

In most instances, the remand foster carers wrote reports about the young people that were included in the pre-sentence reports submitted to the court, which, as discussed in Chapter 7, could influence the sentence passed by the court. For a few young people this increased their determination not to offend or breach their conditions whilst they were in the placement. Natalie said she was told that if she was to cause trouble in the foster placement, she would be given a heavier sentence. Stewart also felt that he 'ought to be good' as he had a court case pending. However, other young people said that the report that the foster carer would be writing and the potential effect it could have on their sentence did not affect their behaviour. Mikey said that he was not behaving in order to achieve a good pre-sentence report but that:

I was behaving myself for the simple fact that Beryl was good enough to keep me in her house. Beryl was like good enough to take me into her house so I was good enough to behave for her . . . I didn't want to misbehave and that, I didn't want to be like a bastard 'cos she was good and she didn't deserve it.

Lawrence admitted that, to begin with, getting a good pre-sentence report did motivate him to stay out of trouble but that after the first week he forgot about it yet continued to behave well and not offend.

As the above quotations from Paul, Luke, Lawrence and Mikey demonstrate, being away from peer influences, having time to think about their behaviour and being shown respect by non-judgemental adults helped some of the young people re-assess themselves and their offending identity. Mikey continued his narrative, saying:

It's good for your self-esteem and that, 'cos I realised that I was a bastard for what I done and I realised that there is people like Beryl . . . that are willing to give you a chance, so you can't be all bad. They're willing to give you a chance and get you away from that life.

The young people who did offend during the placement were asked if there was anything that they felt could have been done to help them stop offending. Simon felt strongly that being employed would have helped to reduce his involvement in criminal activity but no other young people felt anything else could have been implemented that would have affected their behaviour. There was a pronounced feeling of individual determinism amongst the young people who believed that they were the only people who could change their behaviour. For instance, Chantalle said:

If you don't want to change, you won't. It's alright people going to you 'You've got to change, you've got to do this, you've got to do that' but you ain't listening to them, you ain't taking in what they're saying, you're just, like, 'I'm right, everyone else is wrong'.

Craig echoed this, saying 'I've just got to decide for myself that I don't want to do it'.

Education and employment

Education and employment were related to reduced offending for some young people. Lawrence was emphatic about the positive impact that going to college and starting a part-time job had had on his offending behaviour and thought it was something that should be promoted more actively by the foster carers for all young people. He believed that the project should have a policy:

. . . so people also had to go out and . . . they gotta do something, they just can't laze around all day and do nothing . . . It gives them some-thing to do, keeps things off their mind, keeps them busy . . . I think if [the project] . . . pressured them in a good way to get on to a college course or work or something like that, just nudged them in the right direction, I think that would help a lot. Like Dave and Paula, they just

got me straight into work and that was good. I ended up going on a college course and got myself a job in a building merchant, which was day release.

Other young people were encouraged to start life skills courses or to find part-time or voluntary work. Two young people helped carers with their work, one in a shop and one as a lorry driver's "mate". Although it was harder for him than when he lived at home, Stewart continued attending college throughout his foster placement.

The young people on remand and their foster carers face particular difficulties in obtaining employment or accessing education as the available time is limited. Although the Department of Health (2000)[36] issued guidance on the education of looked after children, which placed a requirement on local authorities to secure an educational placement within 20 school days, some remand placements may not last this long. Furthermore, as the length of the remand placement is not known at the outset, it can be difficult to make suitable arrangements. In addition, having to attend court, deal with adjournments and delays can make it very difficult for young people to attend school or work regularly. Pete was unemployed at the start of his remand placement and said:

They [foster carers] were trying to find out other stuff, and we went down to Careers in town and that . . . but before I could, like, sort out what I was doing the court had, like, sentenced me.

Some foster carers themselves provided the young people with access to computer-based educational packages or additional educational support at home as little other provision was available. Luke had weekly home tuition, with his foster carer working in partnership with the tutor:

I've done education up at Sarah and Bob's. I had a folder full of work, maths and that . . . she had to give it, like she knew it and that, and then the tutor would come round to see me once a week.

---

[36] in conjunction with the Department for Education and Employment, now the Department for Education and Skills.

The problems experienced by remand foster carers in their attempts to access educational provision for the young people are discussed further in Chapter 11.

Drugs and alcohol use

One area in which the foster carers appeared to be less involved was dealing with issues of drug and alcohol use. As mentioned earlier, many of these young people had frequently misused drugs and alcohol, with all the concomitant risks. However, the majority of the young people said that the foster carers had not talked to them about their substance use other than to say, for example, 'just don't ever bring them in the house'. Some of the young people continued to take drugs, mainly smoking cannabis, whilst they were on remand but others said they did not, largely because they did not know where to obtain drugs in the area:

> You can't really get it up there, can you? Not when you don't know no one.

Those who did use cannabis when they were on remand tended to smoke it away from the house when they were visiting friends. The carers might comment on the young people's state when they returned home but generally did not take any further action. For instance, Chantalle said:

> I used to go back there stoned . . . after I had a joint or something. She'd see it in my eyes, [that] I'd had a joint, you know? 'You been smoking?' That's what she'd come out with.

Similarly, Stewart said that he did not get into trouble with the carer when he returned home "stoned" but that his carer asked him to respect her wishes not to have drugs in the house. Chantalle and Stewart both said that their carers did not discuss the drug use further, the implications of which are discussed in Chapter 12.

Some carers would talk to the young people about the physical dangers of taking drugs but again there was a feeling of self-determination, with the young people believing that using or not using drugs was a choice they had to make themselves:

We talked about the effects it has on your health and that, but I knew that anyway. Other people had already said it. I used to just ignore most people. I'd pretend to be listening but in the end it's up to me.

It was also apparent from the young people's comments that they did not always feel comfortable talking to the foster carers about drugs and appreciated support from adults outside the placement. For example, Lawrence was given additional support through the bail support team. He felt that this was particularly advantageous because he could talk to his bail officer about his drug use, whereas he did not feel at ease talking to the foster carers about it:

I could sit down and talk to her about my drug problem 'cos I didn't really want Dave and Paula to know the full extent of it, because, they probably did but I just couldn't talk to them about it, do you know what I mean? . . . It's just hard to talk about it to someone who you're living with, 'cos it would make me feel that they're always . . . if you come in a bit pissed, what are they thinking, I'm on crack? And then I'd have to say 'I'm not on crack' and then it sounds like I am on crack and then, and then I'd . . . it's just weird so the less said about it the better, for me.

However, only one of the young people said that he saw a drugs counsellor whilst he was in the remand foster placement, and this was a continuation of his existing involvement with the service rather than something that was arranged whilst he was on remand. Other young people said that they did not need to see a counsellor as they were not "addicted" or did not have a "drugs problem" although they reported relatively high levels of drug use. Two young people had previously seen a drugs counsellor but felt that they were lectured rather than helped and so did not want to see another counsellor. As previously mentioned, Trevor felt that his foster carers did not like him because of his drug use and he felt that they were constantly 'sniffing around' him to see if he had been smoking cannabis. He clearly did not feel able to talk to his carers about his substance misuse but was not given alternative support to deal with his problem.

It was similarly difficult for the foster carers to influence the young people's alcohol use. For example, Darren (aged 17) said that his foster carer 'got a bit touchy' when he said that he was going to the pub. He felt that she was less concerned after about a week when she knew him better but that there was nothing that she could have done to stop him drinking. However, the strategy adopted by Mikey's carer appeared to work for him. She allowed Mikey to have one bottle of beer a night which he felt was:

> ... alright, 'cos she weren't saying you can get pissed up, but she was saying you could have a beer, watch the telly and have a drink ... It was good 'cos she was treating me like an adult and not a kid, and I appreciated it.

Again, this appears to be related to the young person's self-esteem and their positive response to being treated with respect and trust by the foster carers.

Summary

This chapter has discussed the young people's initial feelings about being remanded to foster care, how being remanded to foster care affected their peer and family relationships and the impact that the placements could have on their sense of identity and their behaviour. It was apparent that the relationship between an individual young person and his/her foster carer was a key factor in the quality or "success" of the placement; this is discussed further in Chapter 12. The following chapter investigates how remand foster care differs from other forms of care and custody the young people had experienced, the role of other professionals in supporting the young people during placements and placement endings.

10 Young people's experiences of remand foster care (Part 2)

Introduction

This chapter compares the young people's experiences of being in remand foster care with other forms of care and/or custody, discusses their involvement with other professionals during the remand placement, explores how the placements ended and what happened to the young people afterwards, and provides an overview of the placements.

Comparisons with local authority accommodation and custody

Whilst this was not a comparative study, all but two of the young people had prior experience of either a remand or sentence in local authority accommodation or prison service custody (Chapter 8). Many young people drew comparisons between these forms of provision and remand foster care.

As already indicated, the young people felt that there were few restrictions within residential units and some believed that the lax discipline was preferable to being in foster care. Corey explained that when he was in a children's home he was never asked where he was going or when he was coming back. He said that he had more freedom to do what he wanted when he was on remand in the children's home than he did when he was in the remand foster care placement. However, as much as the young people may have enjoyed the freedom allowed by the residential staff, it clearly placed them at risk of harm and of offending. Of his placement in a children's home, Tom said:

> . . . there was loads of people coming in drunk, stealing and stuff, being sick everywhere . . . I saw again a different side of life which was go to bed at night, wake up in the morning, go out, come back in for lunch, go out, come back in for dinner, go out, go back in and go to bed. And . . . in between eating dinner and going out, commit offences.

Although there were more restrictions in remand foster care than there had been in children's homes, many young people enjoyed the additional opportunities they had in remand foster care, which they knew they would not have in custody or secure accommodation. For example, they appreciated being able to go for walks (particularly if the carers had a dog), go shopping or just spend time outdoors. Ashley, however, found his placement 'boring' and absconded from it. He thought that it was better being in a YOI as there was more for him to do there. He said that having a bike, a computer or a TV in his room would have made the foster placement better and could have stopped him absconding.

The problems of bullying and difficulties with peers encountered by some young people in residential or custodial accommodation were described in Chapter 8. Although they did encounter some difficulties with making and sustaining peer relationships whilst they were in remand foster care, none had experienced the same level of bullying or intimidation in foster care that they had in secure accommodation or custody. Lawrence explained that it was easier in foster care not to become involved in fights:

. . . you can walk away from stuff like that when you're in foster care; in [secure] you can't walk away from it, it's like stand there and punch them or get punched.

Similarly, Tom thought it was easier not to be held with other children because of the influence their emotional state could have on him:

It's like one day you get on with them and the next they'd come in in a bad mood and you'd be in a bad mood and that would be it. If one person in the secure unit was in a bad mood, you all were.

Tom also resented the lack of privacy and confidentiality he was afforded in the secure unit where he believed that the staff had told other children about the nature of his alleged offences. Young people in O'Neill's (2001) study of secure accommodation also found the lack of privacy and confidentiality oppressive and intrusive. In contrast, as earlier comments demonstrate, the young people in remand foster care were granted privacy by the carers: they all had their own bedrooms which the carers would generally not enter without the young person's permission. The carers also made it clear that they would not tell their friends or neighbours any personal details about the young people, thus preserving confidentiality and the young person's trust.

The individual attention that foster carers were able to give was appreciated by many of those interviewed who noted that this was not possible in other residential or custodial institutions:

I think the best thing is you've just got people there for you, not people that have got to look after other people as well; you've got one-to-one attention.

You've got someone there who can give you attention, like look after you, sort you out and that, and it's better than if you're being in a jail with hundreds of other inmates.

In contrast, Steven thought it was easier being in a secure unit than it was being on remand in foster care. Moving into yet another family environment was complicated for him and he found it too difficult not to offend because of the external pressure he faced from his uncle. In addition, he believed that he had to take responsibility for his own medication (for ADHD) which was problematic:

It was settling in to another family which, when you leave it's a lot, bloody horrible . . . It's a lot easier to be in here [secure], 'cos in foster placements you go and get in trouble; in here all you can do is get a bloody sanction. It was alright to be there, they were quite nice people. And another thing, I had to look after my own tablets and that was hard to do. I missed a couple of days off my tablets. Some mornings I get up, think I've taken them but then you can't remember and then you're like, 'Oh God,' but in here you have a nurse come in the morning and at night and they check that you've taken them; there's no way you can miss tablets in here.

The National Minimum Standards and Fostering Services Regulations (Department of Health, 2002) make explicit the foster carer's responsibility (as delegated by the social worker) for ensuring that the fostered child has access to appropriate health care. In this instance, that should have included monitoring and, if necessary, administering Ritalin to Steven. However, it is not clear whether the foster carer knew that Steven was taking Ritalin; it might be that she was not informed by Steven's social worker or the project staff (who themselves might not have been aware) of his need for regular medication. Obviously, it is vital that this basic information about a young person and his or her medical requirements is shared with remand foster carers.

A number of young people said that remand foster care had given them 'a chance' that they would not have had on remand in custody:

It gives you a chance to express yourself in like a home environment . . . when you are in prison you've got more chance of having a fight, you've got more chance of being offered heroin or like anything else, you've got more chance of screwing up . . . You've got less chance of screwing up [in foster care]. You're on a one-to-one basis and it's good, it's good for you.

Paul talked about being given the opportunity to prove to the YOT staff and the court that he could learn from his mistakes and make improvements, which he would not have been able to do if he had been remanded in custody. Darren emphasised the importance of being able to demonstrate to the court that he had found employment and had not been involved in offending behaviour and felt that sentencing might be more lenient as a result. This reflects the magistrates' comments (Chapter 7), which suggested that witnessing an improvement in the behaviour and circumstances of a young person would influence their sentencing decision.

Comparisons with being remanded on bail at home

A few of the young people also drew comparisons between being on remand in foster care and being remanded on bail at home. Generally, young people said that they would have preferred to be at home but that remand foster care was a preferable alternative to children's homes, secure units and custody. However, Mikey thought that being remanded to foster care also had advantages over being bailed to return home:

When you get bailed to go home you get all the comforts of home but then you've also got the risks of going out and getting into trouble. When you are in remand foster care in the middle of nowhere, then you haven't really got any chance of getting into trouble, have you?

Stewart thought that being remanded to foster care was like being at home, but that it was more stable. He appreciated the quieter, more relaxed atmosphere in the foster family and enjoyed not having to listen to his mother shouting at him and his siblings.

Involvement with other professionals during the placement

Aside from the foster carers, the young people had contact with other professionals during the placement, such as YOT officers and social workers. However, as noted previously, very few were seeing substance abuse counsellors and none had any mental health support from psychologists or psychotherapists, despite many having experienced traumatic situations or exhibiting signs of mental health problems. For example, Natalie had experienced hallucinations in the week prior to moving to the foster placement, yet she had neither a psychiatric assessment nor was she offered any counselling. Mikey had been on suicide watch whilst he was remanded in custody and concerns about his mental health had instigated his transfer to remand foster care but he was not given any counselling in the placement. It appears that the reluctance to address the mental health needs of young people in custody is replicated in community placements (Birmingham et al, 1996; NACRO, 1999b). Whilst the UNCRC does not specifically mention mental health, Article 24 stipulates that children have the right to the highest attainable standard of health and to facilities for the treatment of illness and the rehabilitation of health, and it should be presumed that this mandate encompasses mental health as well as physical health. The Fostering Service Regulations (Department of Health, 2002) state that it is the responsibility of the fostering service provider to ensure that each child has access to psychological and psychiatric advice and treatment yet this was not being achieved.

All of the young people had an allocated YOT officer and some also had a social worker,[37] probation officer or bail support worker. Their

---

[37] Whilst all young people remanded to local authority accommodation become "looked after children" and therefore should have a social worker, staff shortages in the area meant that many did not. Young people bailed to reside with remand foster carers do not necessarily have a social worker.

views of these professionals were mixed, with some young people feeling supported and respected but others feeling undermined by the practitioners. Although Steven's social worker had a statutory responsibility to visit, Steven said that 'there was no telling when he would come'. Tom and Stewart both disliked their YOT officers for similar reasons. Stewart said that his YOT officer always believed that she was right and would not listen to his point of view. Tom said that his officer tried to dictate to him how he should live his life, which he resented. He also disliked the manner in which she would avoid addressing concerns or issues that he had:

If I want to get something changed, it's sort of like, 'Yes, we'll think about it at the meeting,' and . . . the meeting is always two or three months away, so it's her way of saying 'Forget about it'.

The young people were expected to attend frequent meetings during the course of the placement and, again, had mixed opinions of their involvement in them. Usually the others involved would be the foster carer, the remand fostering officer, the YOT officer and their social worker, bail support officer or probation officer (where applicable). Four of the young people spoke very positively about their participation in the meetings, explaining that they were listened to and allowed to join in the discussions. Darren said that he was never excluded from meetings:

I was always there. It wasn't like they were speaking about me behind my back, they always let me be there, listening.

Pete explained that minutes were taken during his meetings, which were later reviewed:

It all gets written down in minutes and that, and then it all gets typed up and then we actually go through it again properly, like pick out the subjects which are most important.

Again, these comments reflect the positive response the young people had to being treated with respect and courtesy.

Unfortunately, three young people spoke particularly harshly of their involvement in meetings. Their comments suggested that, although the professionals had accepted the spirit of the Children Act 1989 and the

UNCRC and were attempting to include the young people in discussions, in practice their involvement was restricted or ineffective. For example, Paul did not like attending meetings as he thought that the professionals were thinking of themselves rather than considering his needs. He found the language used difficult to comprehend and it was therefore impossible for him to contribute:

> *I don't usually want to be there . . . You don't want to hear it, them talking about what's best for them not what's best for you. They're talking for ten minutes, using all complicated words and then suddenly are asking, 'What do you think of that, Paul?'.*

Chantalle also found meetings upsetting because she was not listened to and she felt that the professionals involved were making judgements about her that she was not able to contest:

> *They all used to come round and sit there and write. I never used to like it . . . I'd come down all nice and calm and one of them would have to say something to annoy me and that's it, that would start me off . . . like the one thing that used to really annoy me was they never listen . . . It's just like, it's all written down, like 'You're Chantalle, you're violent, you're this, you're that' . . . You don't get a choice whether it's right or wrong, or they're right or they're wrong. 'Cos they don't care . . . they don't listen, you just got to sit there. I just had to sit there and just listen to it all basically, 'cos it didn't matter what I would have said . . . They all had their little thing, by the time it got round to me it was time to end it, so no, I wasn't involved. I broke down in the middle of it, started crying. Let them get on with it.*

These comments are suggestive of the token nature of some young people's involvement in discussions about their welfare. Merely being allowed to attend the meeting is not enough to ensure the young person's right to be heard in proceedings that affect them (Murray and Hallett, 2000). Young people must also be given the opportunity to speak and be heard throughout any meetings, not just when the session is being concluded. Furthermore, professionals need to ensure that the young people understand the terminology being used. This is particularly an issue for young people like those in this study, who have had little formal secondary education and who might have a somewhat limited vocabulary.

The written reports about the young people were also contentious for the young people themselves. As Chantalle explained above, what was written about her in her files was believed by all of the professionals with whom she had involvement, even though Chantalle felt that she had changed. Luke also debated what was written about him and his mother in his case records and felt that his mother was being unfairly held responsible for his behaviour:

> She's writ things in there like his mum didn't care and his mum threw him out and all that, never used to feed him, used to reject him and all that like. That's a load of bollocks . . . She used to take care of me, it's me that fucked up. But they, basically they twisted it the other way.

The role of remand fostering officers

The young people would meet the remand fostering officers from the project, usually when they were first remanded to the placement and subsequently at all of the meetings. The project stipulates that the remand fostering officer's role is to support the foster carer and that the young person would receive support from their YOT officer and social worker. However, this was not made explicit to the young people who were not sure what the remand fostering officer's role was. For instance, Paul said:

> I'm not sure what he did. I don't know if he was in charge of me or of the people who worked for him.

This could cause difficulties for the young person, particularly if there were issues within the foster placement that they wanted resolved, as they were not always aware of whom they could talk to. The problem was exacerbated for young people who did not have a good relationship or had unreliable contact with their YOT officer. For example, Tom wanted to be moved from his second remand foster placement but he felt that, because she avoided dealing with his concerns, he could not talk to his YOT officer. He wanted to be able to talk to another adult, such as the remand fostering officer, but could not do so:

> I think it would be good if someone come round, like every fortnight or three weeks, to see if you've got problems, 'cos sometimes it's hard to

say in front of the foster carers [and] the foster carers are always there. At Lee and Fiona's I really wanted to say, like, 'Get me out of here'.

The end of the placement

To reiterate, ten (43 per cent) of the 23 placements described by the young people lasted until the completion of the court hearings and 13 (57 per cent) broke down before then. The shortest placement experienced by this group of young people was only two days but the longest was 144 days, with a mean length of 35 days.[38] Obviously, placements that ended before the young person was sentenced gave rise to considerable concern but difficulties were also encountered by those whose placements lasted until the week after the final court hearing.

Breakdowns

The majority of young people whose placements ended prematurely implied that, rather than being a decision made by the project or the foster carer, they themselves "decided" to end the placement by not returning to it at the appointed time. The reasons they gave for this choice included boredom, missing their friends and disliking the rules and restrictions enforced by foster carers. Difficulties in the relationship between the young person and the foster carer were sometimes reported as influential in occasioning the placement's end.

As already indicated, Ashley thought his placement was 'boring'. He said that he 'just decided it wasn't going to work out and just went off'. Similarly, Chantalle left the placement after only a few days because she missed her friends and did not like the regulations placed upon her:[39]

I suppose it's 'cos there were restrictions. I weren't allowed to smoke in the house, just didn't really take none of my friends up there. I did like it [but] I love my friends that much that I couldn't be away from them.

---

[38] The median length of these placements was 23 days. NB. To find the "mean", each number in the group is added together to give a total. This total is then divided by the amount of numbers in the group. To find the "median", numbers are set out sequentially and the middle number in the sequence is the median.

[39] However, unusually for the project, Chantalle was then placed back with the foster carers as a specialist foster placement and remained there for a number of months.

Corey also absconded from his placement because he missed his family and simply chose to leave; likewise Craig suddenly decided that he had had enough and did not return to the placement.

It is difficult to predict these situations as the young people were not visibly unhappy in the placement, had not shown difficult behaviour nor developed a negative relationship with the carers but, almost on the spur of the moment, they decided that it was not what they wanted. The breakdown of other placements was less unanticipated, however, being the culmination of a series of minor events or problems. For example, Paul had a difficult relationship with his carers and felt that they neither trusted nor liked him. He had regular disagreements with both carers, which ultimately led to him deciding to leave the placement:

[The foster carer's] watch was all coming apart with the battery all come out and they accused me of taking the battery . . . they said I'd put fag butts in the plant pots and silly things like that, accusing me of stuff. So I said to their face, 'I'm going,' and packed my bags . . . Social services said that I could go back to that placement, that they would have me back, but I didn't want to if they were accusing me of things, like saying I had taken a bar of chocolate even though on the first day they said I could help myself to food, tea and all that.

It was clear that Paul felt very unjustly treated by the foster carers and unfairly accused of things that he said he had not done. Similarly, Mark felt that he was treated very differently to his carer's own children which caused him to feel resentful. The end of his placement occurred after a series of arguments with the foster carer's children, in which she had always supported her children. Eventually he had a 'big argument' with the foster carer who requested that he be moved.

In other instances the end of the placement was triggered by a single event. For example, Darren's placement had been progressing very well but ended abruptly when he returned to the placement drunk and acting aggressively:

I went down the pub and . . . I'd had quite a skinful . . . Then I went back to Jacqui's house and I got in a right stress and I threw a bottle or something and one of the next-door neighbours thought that I was kicking up and called the police. And I cut my hand, ended up in [Xtown

Hospital] . . . but she come and visit me in hospital. She said that she wished that I was still there, 'cos you can't live with someone for that amount of time, can you, and not get attached to her. 'Cos it wasn't her choice to end the placement, it was her boss's choice . . . She said she wanted me back; she said she argued it.

Whilst it appeared that the foster carer would have continued the placement, the project decided that, in the light of Darren's history of violent offences, it was better not to continue the placement. Darren returned to court the next day to have his remand status reviewed but was actually sentenced by the court.

Three placements ended because the young person was arrested during the placement. As already explained, Steven was placed under immense pressure from his uncle to replace the stolen goods confiscated by the police. He believed that returning to secure accommodation was appropriate in such circumstances and felt that it was the only way he could keep out of trouble. Another young person was arrested for stealing a neighbour's van. He returned to court and was remanded to another foster carer within the project with whom he stayed until his court hearing. Although this was the only occasion within the study that a young person was remanded to a second foster carer, it is an intention of the scheme to be able to offer an alternative placement to someone whose initial placement was unsuccessful.

Simon was repeatedly arrested during his placement, principally for offences he had allegedly committed prior to its starting. Although he said he could understand the foster carer's decision not to continue the placement, he was upset by it:

I got arrested twice, then got arrested again and she wouldn't have me back . . . I wasn't bothered as I was going to Portland and I knew what that was like . . . I could see what she was saying about me not going back but I was quite annoyed.

Simon had established a good relationship with the carer and possibly felt rejected by her, as he had been by his mother when she felt unable to control his behaviour.

Tom's first placement had similarly been very successful and he had developed a very positive relationship with the foster carer. However, in the few days before his final court hearing, his behaviour deteriorated rapidly and the foster carer asked for him to be moved immediately after he had been sentenced, rather than after the following week as was customary. Tom knew that he could not return home because of his mother's continuing substance abuse difficulties and that another foster placement had not been found for him. It is possible that Tom felt threatened by the prospect of moving from a placement where he was settled to a children's home or secure unit (of which he had previous negative experiences) and that his difficult behaviour was a defence mechanism that helped him deal with the uncertainty of moving (see also Farmer *et al*, 2004). He was determined to 'stick out' his second foster placement, even though he disliked it, because he thought that he would be placed in secure accommodation otherwise.

One of the concerns for young people whose placements have ended prematurely is that they will be "up-tariffed" by the court, that is, they will be remanded to a secure unit or YOI because their remand foster placement has been unsuccessful. Paul acknowledged this, saying, 'You can't go back if you muck up so you end up in a secure unit.'

Planned endings

Some of the young people whose placements did continue for a week after their final court hearing also experienced trouble moving on from the placement, both dealing with the emotional separation but also practical problems such as finding and maintaining accommodation. For some, the positive achievements that they had made during the placement were negated by a lack of support after the placement and the difficulties that they experienced re-adjusting to living back at home.

Tom believed that he had benefited from his foster placements, particularly the first, but realised that moving home could then be a disillusionment. He said that remand foster care:

> . . . *gives you some self-esteem and gives you an idea of what love is, 'cos when you've known no different and, it's like, being with your mum that's what you're going to get. When you come in here you get a lot more and then when you go back you realise how different things are. So that's good and bad.*

Similarly, Pete was happy that the court hearing had been concluded and that he could return home, but he found it distressing to leave the foster carer:

I was pleased at, like, one point and then I was unhappy as well. I was pleased that it was all over, that all, like, the court and sentencing and that was over. I went back to Sarah's . . . and when I left it was like, I was upset. I was disappointed but I was happy at the same time. It's like, while you've been there, like for two, two-and-a-half months, it's like I've quite got attached and, like, that week it's like a coming apart sort of thing.

His comments highlight the importance of the additional week spent with foster carers post-sentence in helping the young people come to terms with their sentence and move forwards. Some did maintain contact with the foster carer, sometimes for a considerable time after the end of the placement, which was widely appreciated by the young people. The obvious emotional upset caused by the ending of some placements, both for the young people and carers (see Chapter 11), does raise the question of how appropriate it is to expect young people and carers to form positive relationships for very short periods of time, only to then disrupt the relationship on the basis of remand requirements rather than the young person's needs and wishes.

Lawrence was disappointed by social services after both of his remand foster placements because they were not able to provide him with appropriate move-on accommodation or support. He felt that the project should work more closely with social services to find accommodation:

They [social services] just didn't look [for anywhere]. They didn't look until the last week of the thing, which wasn't directly the project's fault at all, 'cos they do do their best, I find, but they don't have enough involvement with the aftercare and social; they don't liaise as well as they could with social services . . . If social services say 'We're going to look for a move-on place', they take their word for it. They don't really help pester 'em to give you something better, something suitable, 'cos these people know what your problems are, what you need, and they should get more involved in that way.

Likewise, when his placement ended, Mikey was not provided with appropriate accommodation so he moved into a hostel for the homeless. He was unable to stay there and started shoplifting food and stealing money in order to survive.

Pete also ended up on the streets after he moved back home and his relationship with his mother deteriorated again:

At first I went back to my mum's, spent a little while there, but . . . things were getting on top of me, so I moved out one day . . . I went down to my mate's, stayed there and that for a while . . . then went to a night shelter, then I went from there to a night shelter in [Xtown]. I was there for a while, and then I got kicked out of there and I was staying in a car.

Stewart's relationship with his mother, which had undergone such an improvement whilst he was in remand foster care, also deteriorated once he returned home. Providing these young people with additional practical and emotional support once they had left the remand foster placement might have prevented the relapses in their family relationships and might have helped them maintain the improvements they had achieved during the placement.

These difficulties are similar to those faced by young people leaving institutions and mainstream foster care (Stein and Carey, 1986; Lyon *et al*, 2000; Pinkerton, 2002). However, some young people in remand foster care did experience a much more co-ordinated and successful move from placements. For example, Darren discussed the help his foster carer gave him:

Everything I wanted got done. I got drove back down here, go to look for a job for when I moved back, go to look for places to live.

In addition, Darren maintained regular contact with his remand foster carer after he left the placement and believed that the support she was able to offer continued to assist him. His experience demonstrates that it is possible for an integrated service to be provided for young people and also emphasises the importance of continued support from somebody with whom they have developed a positive relationship.

After the placement

It is not possible to conclude definitively whether or not the experience of being on remand in foster care had a long-term impact on the young people's behaviour, particularly their offending behaviour. Six of the young people were sentenced to custody immediately after their remand foster placement, either for the offence that had led to the placement or for offences committed before or during it (of these, four young people were still serving this sentence at the time of the interview). Being incarcerated would prevent the young people from committing further offences[40] and this experience would also influence their involvement in offending once they had been released. Furthermore, some of the benefits of remand foster care may not be realised until later. Alfie articulated both of these points:

> It didn't change me. Not that I know of now . . . I dunno if it helped 'cos I went straight from there to here.

However, young people did talk about their behaviour since the placement had concluded, including whether they had offended and the factors that influenced this. Eight young people said that they had committed offences, citing either a return to their "old ways" or, as indicated above, the need to offend to survive because of their homelessness. Luke explained that, after the remand foster care placement and a short custodial sentence, he returned to his home area and became involved in criminal behaviour again:

> I come back down here after I got out of prison and started getting back in trouble . . . getting all the habits back in my head of thieving cars and thieving.

---

[40] At least within the community. Minor offences committed within a prison would be dealt with through the prison disciplinary procedures; more serious offences committed whilst in prison would be dealt with through the usual court process. Only one of the young people admitted to having been involved in disciplinary procedures within the prison, and none admitted to having committed any serious offences since they had been incarcerated.

Six young people said that they had not committed any further offences, either because they were scared of the consequences or because their experiences in the remand foster care placement had helped them change their attitude and their identity in more fundamental ways.

Natalie thought that her previous involvement in the criminal justice system had not deterred her from offending, but that being separated from her mother through being remanded both to secure accommodation and foster care was an effective deterrent. She said that she had not, and would not, commit any further offences:

. . . in case I get put in foster care again, or secure. Thing is, it's not that I didn't like it, just don't want to be there 'cos I like to be at home with my mum and that . . . That's what I think stopped me from doing it, 'cos anything else, like put in a cell or going to court or getting supervision, didn't scare me but the last straw, I think, was when I got put in secure and taken into foster care.

Ten young people said that they had changed because of the remand foster care placement and the influence of foster carers. For example, Chantalle said:

I went up there and I calmed right down, chilled right out. Like I used to be a very angry person, the littlest thing I'd snap at . . . I went up there and I totally changed my issues on people, like I could have a joke and a laugh, it was the first time I'd laughed in ages . . . She taught me a lot as well . . . like not to let people get to me and stuff like that. She'd just sit down and we'd talk a lot, we'd communicate and I ain't good at communicating . . . I like the way I changed; I like the way I am now. 'Cos I knows I wouldn't be nowhere if I still had that attitude I had. Big chip on my shoulder.

Although Luke did admit to having committed criminal offences since the remand foster placement, he also said that being in remand foster care had helped him change his attitude and that he had learnt 'how to treat people with respect'.

Lawrence explained that he would reflect on his experiences in the remand foster placement to lift his mood and to motivate him to continue staying out of trouble, rather than reverting to his previous behaviour:

Sometimes, when I do feel depressed, sometimes I just think about that, about to when I was in Dave and Paula's . . . about the good times we had and how if I just get myself sorted out again I can have a life like that again and that's what I think about . . . Not to just give up and go out and steal a car or get into a fight or anything really, just, just gives you that sense of hope.

Overview of the placements

As the comments above demonstrate, the majority of young people felt that being in remand foster care was a generally beneficial experience and was certainly preferable to custodial or residential accommodation. Indeed, of the 18 young people, only one thought that remand foster care was not at all worthwhile. Ashley, whose placement broke down after three days when he absconded, said:

I don't think it's worth having; you should either go home or get put in prison . . . But I don't think nothing works really . . . Remand foster care isn't worth having at all and I don't think secure is any good either. If you're in secure you get used to being locked up and it's OK there, then you go to prison and you're already used to being locked up so it's alright.

However, even if their own experience had not been entirely positive, all of the others believed that remand foster care had either been advantageous for themselves or could be advantageous for other young people. Corey thought that remand foster care could be beneficial for vulnerable young people although his placement had broken down:

It's a good idea, it's good to start a new life but it didn't work for me, as I always wanted to be around my family . . . It would be better than prison for some people, 'cos there is a lot of bullying in prison.

Paul had experienced both a negative and a positive remand foster care placement yet still believed that it was a good idea:

There should be more carers. It's good for people who haven't got any-where to go, if they can't go back to their mum and dad's, or if it's a serious crime and they can't go back to their area 'cos of intimidation of witnesses, or if they are homeless . . . It's a good idea for people that need it, for people that need a chance, they can stay out of trouble. They can learn from their mistakes when they're there, like I did; otherwise they will just be at home stealing with their mates.

However, he added a caveat about the distance from home:
The bad thing is that it's far way from home, that's the only bad thing. There are none in my area; it would be better if you could be close to home.

Similarly, Trevor thought remand foster care was beneficial but added a warning: that having their own children in the household could be difficult for the carers:
It's a good idea to have remand foster carers but the way I see it is you put criminals like me in a family environment, where there could be children, and the carers are worrying that your ideas might rub off on them.

This was a concern expressed by some of the foster carers too, and is discussed further in the following chapter.

Summary

This chapter has considered the young people's views of the benefits and disadvantages of being remanded to foster care, both for themselves as individuals and for young people as a whole. The young people's involvement with other professionals during the foster placements was not always satisfactory, although there were some examples of more positive practice, and there was a particular lack of support regarding substance misuse and mental health concerns. The young people described how being remanded to foster care had affected their behaviour even after the foster placement itself, but how the achievements that they had made during the placement could be rapidly undermined by a lack of support and appropriate accommodation once they had left the placement.

11 Foster carers' experiences of providing care for young people on remand

Introduction

This chapter discusses the findings from interviews conducted with eight remand foster carers employed by the project. Three of the carers were single females and there were five couples. Within these couples, three female carers were mainly responsible for the remanded young person, one male carer had the main responsibility and one couple explained that they shared the caring role equally. This couple was interviewed together; the other interviews were conducted with the main foster carer.

Profile of the foster carers

The foster carers' demographic profile is presented in Table 11.1; all were of white British origin.[41] Five carers had their own children living in the household, two had adult children who were living independently and one carer had no children. Collectively, the carers had looked after 104 young people on remand, with placements lasting between 'a day or two' and six-and-a-half months. Five carers had experience of looking after both boys and girls, although the number of girls was small. However, many of the carers, including those who had not had girls placed with them, had strong views about caring for girls, which will be discussed later.

---

[41] Only two of the foster carers discussed ethnicity as a factor within the placements: one carer explained that she had some personal understanding of issues related to ethnicity as she had dual-heritage grandchildren; another carer had experienced racial abuse from one of the minority ethnic young people she had fostered. This is an area that warrants further research within a remand foster scheme that more frequently provides placements for black and minority ethnic children.

Table 11.1
Demographic characteristics of the remand foster carers

	Minimum	*Maximum*	*Mean*
Age of main foster carer	32.0	63.0	47.0
Years' experience of remand fostering	0.5	5.0	2.5
Number of own children	0	9.0	3.0
Number of remand foster placements	3.0	22.0	13.0
Number of boys cared for	3.0	22.0	12.0
Number of girls cared for	0	3.0	n/a*

* Three carers had looked after one girl; one carer had looked after two girls; one carer had looked after three girls.

Aside from raising their own children, fewer than half of the carers had experience of working with children, either in a professional capacity or voluntarily, and none had been involved in mainstream fostering prior to becoming a remand carer. One carer had previously worked in a residential unit for disabled children, one as a learning support assistant in a secondary school, and another had run a local youth group. Two carers mentioned having been in care themselves as children, which enabled them to understand and empathise with some of the issues with which the young people on remand were having to cope. Hazel (1978) found that carers joining the Kent Project tended not to have prior fostering experience, and less than half of the carers appointed by the CAPS scheme in Scotland had previously fostered children (Walker *et al*, 2002). This suggests that people attracted to remand foster care may have different characteristics to, or be motivated by different factors from, those who undertake mainstream foster care, rather than being existing mainstream foster carers who are seeking a change in their role.

Becoming a remand foster carer

The carers had varied reasons for beginning to foster but, for each, their decision to become a carer was underpinned by a desire to help children in some way. Two of the carers said that fostering was something they had always wanted to do. One had initially chosen to become a mainstream foster carer but was so disillusioned by the delay in receiving a response from social services, he turned to the remand fostering project instead:

We phoned up to apply for mainstream and they said that the person we wanted was on holiday for a couple of days and they'd get back to us, and sort of three months later we phoned up again and yeah, yeah, the person was there but she was actually busy on the other line so would get back to us. And this went on I suppose about nine months and we hadn't heard anything so we phoned them up one more time and . . . I said, '. . . you've got 24 hours and if nobody knocks on our door in that time we won't be interested'. So we phoned [the remand scheme] up and the next day someone was here.

Another carer was motivated by her own unhappy experience of being in a residential unit as a teenager, an experience which led her to think, 'That's all I ever want to do, I want to be a foster parent for teenagers'. She decided to become a remand foster carer for the challenge and for the chance to:

. . . try to make that difference, make them open their eyes and see something different, to stop them going to prison and going down the criminal route.

Two of the foster carers knew other remand foster carers and were aware of some of the implications of the role but others knew nothing about remand fostering until they saw the scheme's advertisement. Two carers were looking for a way of combining work with their own childcare responsibilities; one was intending to take a lodger but was tempted by the advertisement to find out more about the scheme; and another was uninspired by other vacancies advertised in the job centre:

Because of my age, it was difficult to find a job. I had no qualifications of any sort, left school at 15, nothing, never done anything, always been a mum . . . I saw [the project] advertised . . . and I thought, 'Well, it's something I can do' . . . I can deal with kids, it's the only thing I can do.

Financial remuneration was essential for most, although not all, carers but none seemed primarily motivated by the money offered. As mentioned in Chapter 9, this was important to the young people who resented carers who appeared to be 'in it for the money'. Almost all of the carers said that there were easier ways of making money than being a remand carer, yet many expressed concern that attempting to improve the recruitment and retention of foster carers by increasing the financial incentive would encourage applications from people who wanted to 'make a quick buck' rather than those who wanted to help the young people themselves. However, financial difficulties could result if a placement was unoccupied, as a "retainer" was not paid to the carers.

Training

Whilst all of the carers were impressed with the initial response from the scheme, usually within a few days of their original enquiry, many did express dissatisfaction with the length of time the training and approval process took. They understood that the approval process had to be thorough but thought that there might be ways of increasing the carers' involvement with the scheme during this time:

... they sent somebody out to speak to you and it's all great, you know. I mean you get told all of the good parts and a few of the bad parts, and then, ten months later you're still waiting to qualify, you know. You sort of start questioning yourself, don't you, after the first month or two ... I know F forms take a while to do and I know it's important that it's done properly and everything else, but ... they should be able to either have you shadowing people to pick up experience or you could do sessional work with people. I mean there's got to be ways round speeding the process up.

Respondents in Hucklesby and Goodwin's (2002) survey of pre-trial accommodation for young people also believed that the lengthy approval process could hinder the recruitment of remand foster carers.

The amount and intensity of pre-service[42] and annual training under-

---

[42] The carers received training, both pre- and post-approval, on a wide range of issues relating to fostering (including child development, communication skills, safe caring, substance misuse, mental health, dealing with aggressive behaviour, self-harm and suicide ideation), plus topics relating to the criminal justice system, such as relevant legislation, the role of an appropriate adult and interagency working. The amount and type of training provided in other schemes, however, varies considerably (Hucklesby and Goodwin, 2002).

taken by the carers was considerable and equates more to the amount of training that specialist foster carers in the USA receive than that provided by mainstream fostering schemes in England (Hill *et al*, 1993). Furthermore, the amount of child welfare training the foster carers received clearly was much more intensive than many prison officers and staff within secure and residential units would have (O'Neill, 2001; Paton, 2003; Chapter 4). The training was not grounded within any one theoretical basis, but incorporated different elements from, for example, cognitive-behavioural therapy, attachment theory, solution-focused therapy and so forth, so that the carers were equipped with a "toolbox" of different approaches that they could use as appropriate.

The training provided during the approval process, and subsequently at monthly training sessions, was generally considered to be of a high standard and was valued. Specific sessions that were appreciated included hearing ex-fostered children talking about their experiences of remand foster care, and developing listening skills:

The training was superb . . . the listening technique. Are you listening? Because children quite often don't tell you they've got a problem, they don't tell you anything's wrong. You have to read between the lines and then address whatever it is that you pick up between those lines. They're frightened, they're vulnerable and they just don't know how to say things to you . . . so it's quite a juggling act and we were trained in how to do that.

The carers were made aware of the likelihood of the young people having low self-esteem and of ways that they could avoid reinforcing this image:

. . . like you don't say 'Don't be stupid' because it just reinforces your own view of yourself and if you haven't got a good opinion of yourself, or if you didn't do well at school, then it just reinforces that.

Many of the training sessions took place at an activity centre so that the young people on remand and the carers' own children could participate in sports and outdoor activities whilst the carers undertook training and were involved in meetings. There are clear benefits in doing this: the young people and children felt more included in the placements and the scheme itself and the carers did not have to find alternative childcare provision for the training days.

There were some criticisms of the training, for example, that it did not relate to the problems carers were having to deal with at the current time. Some of the carers were dismissive of training provided by professionals, such as social workers, who were perceived to have limited experience of direct work with children:

A lot of it is sort of social workery type stuff which, to be honest, goes in one ear and out the other because, yeah, they're all extremely qualified people, but anybody can be a monkey and do a job from a book . . . I think the best people for things are the ones that have actually done the job.

Training provided by other foster carers or by professionals actually working with the children was seen as more insightful and beneficial for the remand foster carers and, in turn, the young people on remand.

There was also considerable confusion about whether the training was compulsory. Whilst the scheme was insistent that the training was obligatory, many of the carers believed that it was not, or that they were allowed to miss, for example, two sessions a year. Some carers appeared to have received contradictory instructions from the project staff. For instance, one carer agreed that attendance at the training sessions was a requirement of the scheme but then said:

. . . actually, I don't think it can be compulsory because, like sometimes I've been going to go and then got a new client, whatever you wish to call them, come in and they [the project staff] say, 'Well, you can't come because he's not settled, he's just moved in the day before,' so it can't be.

As another carer noted, criminal legislation, both substantive and procedural, changes rapidly and it is important that carers are made aware of any changes that might affect the young people in their care, as well as continuously developing their skills in working with young people. Furthermore, attending training sessions can be an important source of support for the carers; this issue is discussed later.

Parenting styles and carer strategies

As documented in Chapter 9, the style of "parenting" the carers adopted appeared to have an influence on the success of the placements. The carers were expected to seek to achieve goals in their own ways, with general guidance from the project, rather than being taught a specific intervention technique, such as behaviour modification, psychodynamic therapy or family therapy, as is the more usual procedure in treatment foster care schemes (Hill *et al*, 1993). It was apparent that some carers would be reluctant to follow a standard model of working with the young people. For example, one carer explained that 'Everyone's got their own way and every child is an individual anyway... The rule books can go out the window.' The carers acknowledged how they had developed different ways of dealing with the young people since they had become carers. For instance, one woman admitted that, when she first started fostering, she would 'smother' the young people but that she had learnt to relax and realised that the young people had to maintain their independence whilst they were in the placement.

The flexible approach adopted by most carers meant that they could address the very diverse needs of the children they cared for, which may not be possible in custodial or residential institutions. However, it was apparent that there was considerable confusion in terms of what was expected from the foster carers, what their role incorporated and where their loyalty lay – with the young people or with the criminal justice system – which could lead to some questionable attitudes and practices. These issues are addressed throughout this chapter and in Chapter 12.

"Regulatory" carers and "nurturing" carers

As Walker and colleagues (2002) found,[43] the carers' attitude towards their role and the fostering strategies they utilised could be broadly categorised into two approaches, although the distinction between these categories was blurred and some carers adopted strategies from each stance. Several carers took a nurturing approach, which encompassed providing a

---

[43] Walker *et al* (2002) defined the CAPS carers as either task-oriented or process-oriented. Those described as task-oriented saw their role as experts helping the young people effect change and adopt a different lifestyle; those described as process-oriented aimed to work alongside the young people to make the placement work, thus enhancing the quality of their present experience and extending the time that could be spent in placement.

generally affectionate, supportive atmosphere in which the young people were permitted relative freedom and encouraged to learn from their mistakes. These carers took a developmental approach to youth crime, tending to view difficult behaviour, such as breaching curfews and other conditions, as "normal" for teenagers. Other carers took a more regulatory approach towards the fostering role and, whilst still obviously caring for the young people, were more control-oriented and were less accepting of difficult behaviour. These carers perhaps had a less sympathetic view of the children they cared for:

> *I mean the ones we get normally are the worst of the worst because . . . you know, if they're going to be paying £1,000 a week to keep you here, then it's not going to be the nice chappies that really shouldn't be here, is it? You know, I mean it's just, you know, that 90 per cent of what you get are going to be the worst.*

Whilst the nurturing carers tended to see the young people they had looked after as essentially good, describing them as 'brilliant', 'a little sweetie', 'a loveable lad' or 'really excellent kids', the regulatory carers were more likely to say that a child was 'a total nightmare' or 'one of the nastiest bits of work I've ever met'. One nurturing carer described a young person's behaviour, which suggested that he was a blatant liar, then said mildly that 'He was a bit of a story teller, I think,' whereas a regulatory carer described a similar young person as 'absolutely awful . . . sly'. Such statements are clearly problematic, but are a reflection of the different views the carers had of their roles. Some perceived themselves as law-enforcement professionals, whilst others were more childcare oriented, which in itself is indicative of the burgeoning policy and practice fracture between child care and youth justice systems previously acknowledged.

Neither approach was consistently more successful than the other, although each could be more or less suitable for specific children. As discussed in the preceding chapters, some children wanted to be nurtured whilst others resented it and saw it as being mollycoddled. There were advantages and disadvantages to both stances, for example, the nurturing approach could be more productive in helping children improve their self-esteem or develop life skills but did not always prevent the children from participating in unwanted behaviour, such as drug use or offending, and was therefore less likely to meet the requirements of the criminal justice system. Contrastingly, the regulatory approach was more able to ensure that the young people adhered to the conditions of their remand, through the imposition of more stringent discipline, but was less likely to address issues of self-esteem or self-care. The latter approach potentially was more expansionist, due to the carers' increased willingness to report breached conditions, which could result in the young person being remanded in custody.

Dealing with difficult behaviour

Correspondingly, the carers had varied ways of dealing with the young people's behavioural problems. Most foster carers, whether they took a nurturing or regulatory approach, attempted to influence the young people's behaviour through subtle measures that were built into everyday life, rather than through explicit tasks (see also Walker *et al*, 2002). Many of the carers, particularly those who could be categorised as nurturers, minimised the difficult behaviour they encountered and said that the problems that they did have to deal with, such as being argumentative, were typical of adolescents and not specific to young people on remand. They acknowledged that some children would push the boundaries but that they did so because it proved to them that someone cared.

One carer explained that, eventually, all of the children would appreciate having the opportunity to talk to an adult about their problems. The nurturing carers recognised the importance of responding to the child when s/he wanted, even if it was at an inconvenient time for the carer:

Sometimes they need to talk about things . . . I will leave everything, I'll switch a dinner off in the middle of cooking and say, 'Right, let's talk about it now. I'll finish dinner later, to hell if it's ruined' . . . I think they haven't had attention, not the right sort of attention. If you want to talk to somebody and they say, 'Well, give me a minute, I've just got to finish this,' then no. No, you leave it. 'OK, let's talk about it now, we'll go for a walk and talk about it.'

Conversely, some of the regulatory carers thought that the young people should wait to talk about their problems at a more appropriate time of day, encouraging them to be more respectful of other people's needs. For example, one young person breached his curfew, eventually arriving home at 2.45 am. He wanted to talk to the carer then, but she felt he should be more considerate: 'Like I'm interested at the moment? . . . Go to bed, we'll talk about this in the morning.'

The typical difficulties foster carers encountered included getting the young people to come in on time, particularly if they did not have a court-ordered curfew (this is returned to later), managing children under the influence of excessive alcohol or drugs, dealing with thefts of food or toiletries, plus dealing with the young people's verbal aggression and "attitude". Different sanctions used to deal with these kinds of behaviour included regulating access to the television, or emphasising the negative implications of non-co-operation. The latter approach was more empowering for the young people but the former could be more effective:

I say to them, 'You help me do the chores, that gives us time to go out and do something. If you don't help me, you don't get to go out because I've got to do double the chores, so the choice is yours.' And they laugh and I laugh. And they do it, they do it.

The rule was the telly goes off in your bedroom at midnight . . . Quarter past three, by this time I'm losing my temper . . . and I said, 'Will you please turn this off?', and he said 'No'. Right, so I went and got some scissors and I cut through the wire. 'Telly's off now.' And he went absolutely mental, of course, but I was so tired. So anyway, we talked about this in the morning and decided the telly was coming out for four days. Now within that time, if they misbehave again, the stereo will come out, but it never got that far.

A more structured approach was reported as being successful with some young people. For example, several children responded well to star charts, where they were given a reward if they had been awarded a specified number of gold stars in a week. Whilst some foster carers thought that older young people would find this approach derogatory, it could also work with 16- and 17-year-olds. Most of the carers recognised the importance of finding ways to increase the young people's self-esteem, through praise and positive reinforcement, which in turn could promote their resilience (Gilligan, 2002).

Within both approaches, being consistent was seen as key to developing a trusting relationship with the young people, as they had generally experienced so much inconsistency in their lives. Some problems did arise if the young person was permitted to do things the carers' own children were not, for example being allowed to smoke or to stay in bed. It is interesting to note that this is the reverse of what some of the young people felt, who thought that the carers' children were treated preferentially. Arguments between the carers' own children and the fostered child could be problematic for the carers as their loyalty was divided:

They clashed and one night it did go to blows and they really were screaming at each other. That was hard 'cos I could see both points of view here and I've got my own child looking at me saying, 'You should be siding with me' and of course Eddie looking at me saying, 'You're going to side with them, aren't you?' . . . He was so scared that I was going to say, 'Right, that's it, you're out' and I had to reassure him that whatever it was, it could be sorted, 'Let's not worry about it', you know . . . But it was all over and done with in one evening, you know. Couple of hours later they were, 'Come on, shake hands, let's get it over with'.

Being open and straightforward with the young people was something that the young people appreciated (Chapter 9) and was an effective way of developing a relationship with the young person. For example, one carer talked about the arrival of a teenage girl:

She didn't want to be here, it was crystal clear . . . I said, 'You don't want to be here, do you?' and she said, 'No, I don't'. I said, 'I'm sorry, I'm going to do my best . . . I'm not going to tell you what to do, let's just be friends. If you want a friend I'll be here, that's all I want to do.' She just looked at me and said, 'That's fair enough, let's get on with it,' and she has. No one can actually believe the change in her, and they said to me, 'If she ever smiles you'll never believe it' but she laughs and smiles all the time.

Both the regulatory and the nurturing carers emphasised to the young people that they were responsible for their own choices. For instance, one nurturing carer said:

We don't put any pressure on any of them. We say, 'There's no locks on the doors, no bars . . . If you want to walk, you walk. We won't run after you, but you face the consequences of your actions.'

Similarly, the more regulatory carers explained that they could not stop the children from leaving, but were more authoritarian in their attitude:

You can't stop them but on the way out you just got to point out that, whatever time their curfew is, is the time you phone the police and their next place isn't as pleasant.

There were examples of very serious difficulties within some placements. One young person was suspected of physically assaulting a small child within the household, others were physically and verbally abusive towards the foster carers, with one carer effectively being "held hostage" within her house for a number of hours. The more nurturing foster carers often held themselves equally responsible for problems that occurred. For example, one carer called herself 'stupid' for leaving alcohol on display when she knew that the young person had a problem with alcohol and became aggressive when he was drunk. Most of the carers explained that they trusted the young people, but were conscious of not putting temptation in their paths by leaving wallets or purses lying around or having alcohol in the house. One of the more regulatory carers suggested that the courts should be able to impose a condition of abstinence on the young people:

I think there ought to be a ban on drinking for them, because that's where they get into trouble . . . it should be the case if they come back and if they've been drinking, they've broke their conditions . . . If they were locked up they wouldn't have drink, they wouldn't have any freedom, and I know we're not there to lock them up and that's not what I'm about, but we're there to keep them out of trouble.

Some carers felt that being away from their home environment went some way to helping the young people control their aggression:

Half the time they don't get violent. It's because you're taking them out of the situation that's making them violent . . . here . . . there's nothing to make them violent. I don't wind them up because I've been trained not to, so what have they got to be violent about?

The carers acknowledged the importance of communicating with the young people in a manner that would not encourage a negative or aggressive response:

You can't say 'Don't', 'You don't', 'You won't'. You have to say something like 'I think it's a good idea if you stay in'. You have to be so careful how you word it.

I never tell them to do anything. I always ask them. I don't say, 'Go and clean your room'. I'll say to them, 'Have you done your room yet, love?' 'No.' 'Oh, do it in the next few minutes, will you? Then we can get on and . . .'. Don't talk down to them. They're growing up, they don't want it . . . I don't like being talked down to. If somebody bullies me and says, 'You get and do this' it puts my back up, so yeah, I always ask them, not tell them.

Remaining calm and 'refusing to rise to the bait' was essential in dealing with young people's moods and attitudes. Saying nothing at all or speaking quietly were other techniques that helped defuse difficult situations with some young people:

We find silent works very well because they're used to being shouted at . . . Silence really, really does affect them, because if you start they shout at you and then you shout back and then she shouts higher or he shouts higher and then in the end you're both screaming at each other and you're getting nowhere, so we found now that the lower the voice . . . the better response you get.

The foster carers acknowledged that the young people themselves had to be at least partly committed to the placement and to addressing some of their problems for the placements to be beneficial. They also recognised that there might be some children with whom they could not work or for whom the particular placement was unsuitable:

A lot of the time you can iron the problems out, a lot of the time you can say, 'OK, well do you understand why I'm not happy, why you did this?' and we can work things out. If, on the other hand, they're completely adamant that this placement isn't going to work then there's very little, it's not going to be successful, so unfortunately we have to change, and quite often what we try to do is keep young people still within the project.

Ideally, the young people would move to live with another foster family within the project. However, the research indicated that this rarely happened and the primary placement usually broke down, with the young person absconding or being remanded to custody before an alternative placement became available.

Curfews and conditions

Placement agreements, established at the outset of the placement, helped prevent some disputes, particularly when the house rules were negotiated between the carers and the young person. The carers also valued court-ordered conditions, such as curfews, as it gave them an additional control mechanism over the young people. If the court had not ordered a curfew, the carers would generally impose their own. One regulatory foster carer believed that the court should automatically impose a curfew for all children in remand foster care placements and resented the defence solicitors who argued against the imposition of curfews:

I would normally ask for a curfew time, but then sometimes the judges won't set a curfew, you know, because there's not a reason to do it. The solicitors, right, who, bless them, act for their clients, don't they, in the best interests of their clients, will turn around and say, 'But Your Honour, this person hasn't actually been in trouble at night'. Bless them, they are wonderful, solicitors, aren't they?

However, the courts are, and should remain, under obligation to impose the least restrictive requirements necessary to limit offending whilst on remand and conditions must only be applied where they are directly related to the commission of offences. Extending the power of the court to impose unwarranted conditions, such as curfews or abstention from alcohol, could lead to increased incarceration if defendants breached those conditions.

Offending in placement

The carers also had different attitudes towards addressing the young people's previous or current offending behaviour, which again reflects the confusion about their roles and responsibilities. One carer said that she did not encourage the young people to talk about their offending behaviour at all because she did not want them to gain attention through 'bragging' about their offences. The majority of carers said that only a very few young people committed offences whilst they were in the placements but acknowledged that offending did occur. One experienced carer said: 'Very, very few have actually offended on placement, really. It's occasional.'

One particularly nurturing carer described a placement she had when she first became a remand carer and the continued pattern of offending of the young person whilst he was in her care:

Regular as clockwork . . . Wednesday he'd always say to me . . . 'I'm just going up the road to make a phone call' . . . I'd say 'OK, but just make sure you're in before your curfew.' 'Yeah, alright.' That was it, he'd be gone . . . he's straight back to [Xtown] and by Friday, Saturday we'd get the phone call, 'He's been arrested, can you come down?', so we'd go straight down to [Xtown] police station, do the appropriate adult, and bring him back. That would be okay, until Wednesday again, you know, and it was really, you know, it was almost comical.

Whilst the carer was clearly aware of the offending behaviour, she did little to try to prevent it occurring. She was perhaps unwilling to jeopardise the placement for the young person because, she said, 'While he was in our home he was brilliant.' Another young person admitted to his carer that he had stolen items from a car but the carer chose not to report the theft to the police or project staff:

I couldn't. Because Jack had put so much trust in me, and I felt he'd put a hell of a lot of trust in me to tell me that. I mean, obviously if I saw a child in danger I would report, there's no two ways about that . . . [but] he begged me not to tell anyone 'cos he could obviously tell by the look on my face that I wasn't amused by this . . . So what I said to him was 'If I am questioned about this at any time I am not going to deny that I know. If nobody ever questions me, I won't say anything.'

Other carers seemed similarly reluctant formally to acknowledge offending behaviour, particularly relatively minor offending, either because they did not want to endanger the continuation of the placement or because they saw the offending as a normal part of teenage behaviour. One carer denied that the young people offended, saying that they would threaten to but not actually do so, yet talked about a young man who had stolen a bottle of vodka. Another said she had no doubt that a few of the children were shoplifting because they would come home with sweets when they had no money, but she was not overly concerned by this behaviour. A number of the foster carers said that they would feel guilty about letting the young person down if they reported them to the police. They did not like having to end a placement but knew that it was not always a realistic option to allow it to continue.

There is a clear conflict here that has implications for both the success of the placements and for the protection of the public from offending by young people on remand. Placing the foster carers under an obligation to report any suspected offending behaviour would influence the relationships they are able to develop with the young people, yet not informing the police effectively condones the young people's behaviour and undermines the effectiveness of remand foster care as an alternative to institutional remands. These tensions and incongruities are discussed in more detail in Chapter 12.

One carer described a more serious offence committed by a child in her care. Due to the nature of the offence the police were involved and the young person was identified from CCTV footage. The carer was completely unaware of the young person's involvement in the offence until the police arrived at her house; she said she had:

. . . no idea whatsoever. He was absolutely wonderful, he was one of the family . . . And there is nothing that I can say, honestly, that would have ever suspected it was him.

The carer was clearly upset by the allegations and the young person's subsequent arrest, which occurred in a dramatic and aggressive way. Although the carer herself did not complain, it was of concern to note that none of the project staff were able to be with the carer to support her during this time.

This was, however, a unique situation and the majority of the young people were not involved in offending whilst they were in the placements.[44] Few of the foster carers were able to explain why this was so, but providing support and security was seen as vital:

What is it that we give that, as soon as they leave, they're back doing it [offending] again? It's got to be the support that they get from someone . . . they must feel secure.

I haven't got a clue . . . I'd like to say because we're excellent carers and we're worth every penny we get paid, and because we give them support and they have everything they want . . . within reason. They get clean clothes, they get food, they get pocket money, you know, so it would be nice to say because we give them all the support they need, but I don't know whether that is the reason.

The foster carers also echoed the young people's own belief that taking them away from their home areas, and especially moving them away from specific friends, was influential in reducing offending behaviour:

You've taken them out of their area, for starters. You've taken them away from the peer pressure, haven't you?

None of the carers underestimated the influence that peers had on the young people but acknowledged that separating them from their friends could mean that they could become lonely or isolated, particularly if there were no other children in the placement.

Education, employment and activities

Establishing a routine for the young people was seen as an important element in preventing offending, in developing skills and in reducing isolation and loneliness. Arranging morning appointments with YOT staff or other professionals was one mechanism used by the carers to ensure that the young people got up in the mornings, rather than in the

---

[44] The case-file analysis (Chapter 6) indicated that 24 per cent of the young people offended in placement; the interviews suggested that this figure was slightly higher at 33 per cent (Chapter 9).

afternoons. The regulatory carers thought that providing this kind of structure kept the young people occupied so that they could not get into trouble:

I try to get appointments in the morning . . . And they think you're just being awkward, which you are, but if you've got appointments, at least they are about, you know. Otherwise when they sort of go walkaround, normally they'll end up getting something, getting drunk or doing whatever.

The nurturing carers believed that facilitating such a routine helped the young people improve the way they felt about themselves:

Quite often you will find that they want to make you happy so they watch and they try to copy you in some ways, the things you do. They know that I have my rules and expect certain standards . . . I expect them to get up and have a bath and wash their hair, and make their bed and tidy their room and do their washing and keep themselves clean . . . and by the time they leave here they want to have a bath in the morning and they want to have clean clothes, you know. They take it with them.

Developing basic life skills, including telling the time, making purchases in a shop and dealing with money, washing regularly, learning to iron or cook and improving table manners were also ways of helping the young people improve their self-esteem and ability to care for themselves in the future. Whilst developing self-efficacy is not an explicit aim of any remand placements, it is clearly a valuable "by-product" and may promote resilience, possibly helping the young people to desist from offending in the future.

Many of the carers were proactive in finding educational provision or employment for the young people, or in helping them develop hobbies and leisure activities that could also be educational. For example, a few of the carers would take the young people fishing which kept them occupied but also taught them a number of new skills:

He'd never fished before and he caught his first fish and it's 'Wow, I could do this', and from there he learnt so much. He learnt patience, he learnt all about the tides and the times, he learnt the different baits. He learnt all the different fish, he used to make charts . . . He then went to books and read about it, where he'd never been bothered before.

Whilst one of the perceived advantages of remand foster care is the provision of education or employment in the community, accessing educational provision was never easy, and one carer described it as their 'biggest bugbear'. The carers explained that the education officer in the YOT would rarely come to the placement meetings, even though getting the young people back into education was seen as key to preventing offending. Part of the problem was the limited time available to the carers and educational authorities to arrange provision, but there was also evidence of an apathetic attitude on the part of the latter towards young people on remand:

Within five, six weeks you can't set anything up, it doesn't happen. It's too quick, and a lot of the time their excuse would be, 'Well, we don't know, he might be going to prison, so what's the point in setting anything up? Let's just wait and see what happens after sentencing.'

If it's a problem child they just seem to wash their hands of him and be glad he's out of the way.

Some of the carers arranged to have work sent home by the young person's school but were generally frustrated by the difficulties in getting the work marked or getting any feedback for the young people. If the young people were older, the carers were able to enrol them on training courses or with employment agencies. A few colleges had induction courses that began every two weeks that could be utilised for young people on remand, but again the limited length and the unpredictability of the remand period could be problematic:

Sometimes they can't go to work 'cos they're not going to be here long enough so we go to Careers and the job centre. They sign on and then when they go back home it can all be transferred to their local job centres or Careers office, so we start setting everything up so that they've got move-on when they leave here.

A few carers also established relationships with local organisations, such as riding stables or businesses where the young people could work as a volunteer or on an *ad hoc* basis. For example, one carer was able to arrange work cleaning cars at a local garage:

> *This was actually teaching him how to look after an engine; he'd watch how to do it, how to clean the car up . . . see the owners' faces when they come to pick it up and they would praise him, 'You've done a brilliant job.' They'd give him a couple of quid for a tip. So it's actually giving him some self-esteem.*

Helping the young people find a job also allowed them to experience earning and spending money legitimately:

> *I got him a job working at Burger King . . . he was chuffed. 'I've got some money in my pocket at the end of each week . . . and I can go out, legally. I don't have to steal anything to go and buy anything, I've got my own money.'*

Keeping the young people occupied was clearly beneficial for them but was also considered necessary for the carers, to have some respite from caring for the young people all day.

The nurturing carers enjoyed playing games, such as scrabble or snakes and ladders, with the young people and participating in activities like swimming or shopping together. Whilst some of these games and activities had an educational element, the carers were also aware of the importance of making the children feel part of a family. One carer explained that a boy in her care was particularly appreciative of the time the carers spent playing with him, because no one had had time to do so whilst he was in a children's home. Another carer talked about the difficulty of maintaining a balance between encouraging the young people to play games and sports and spoiling them:

> *You do try to do activities with them . . . I don't feel that I could do more in the activity line 'cos it's not real life, is it? You know, that's what you've got to think about. You're not here on holiday. You can try to over-compensate.*

"Street" age and emotional age

Several carers recognised the importance of allowing the young people to play and act as younger children would. Whilst many appeared very streetwise and experienced, much of their behaviour was seen as bravado to hide their emotions. Some of these young people had taken on adult responsibilities and attitudes at an early age:

They've never been children as such . . . they've had to go straight up to being almost adults. The childhood bit's gone, missing.

None of them have had a proper childhood; they all have had to fend for themselves from such an early age. But inside they are all still children.

Encouraging the young people to have fun without having to "prove themselves" to their peers could enable them to reveal their emotional age rather than their "street" age:

And they're paddling in the little rivers and what have you, and at the beach, they're setting a can up and they're throwing stones at it to see who can knock it off. It's just boys' things, you know, there was no pressure there to be tough.

This is an extension of Farmer and colleagues' (2004) findings that many children in foster care have a much younger emotional age than chronological age; the young people on remand had a much older "street" age than their chronological and emotional age.

The foster carers held different views as to which age children were easier or more difficult to work with. It was considered, by one carer, easier to occupy 16- and 17-year-olds because they could be enrolled on training courses, but another carer felt that 17-year-olds were 'more set in their ways' and therefore harder to influence. One carer felt that younger children stood 'a chance of being helped' but another said that 'there's something about these 14-year-olds, they're not ready to work with us'. This preference for working with children of a particular age has implications for any potential matching between the young people and carers.

Related to their age was the amount of involvement the young people had previously had in the criminal justice process. One carer felt that it was easier to work with children who had less experience of the system: *I mean we get the kids when they're pretty much down the line and they're really facing a good chance of being locked up, but when you're lucky and you get them early on in the system, I think you stand a chance of changing them.*

However, another carer thought that the shock of having spent a few days on remand in a YOI prior to arriving at the foster placement made the young people more willing to co-operate.

Girls

Some of the carers similarly expressed a preference for working with boys, rather than girls. Another perceived advantage of remand foster care is the ability to cater for the specific needs of girls, who are often marginalised in residential and custodial institutions, but half of the carers said that they were reluctant, or indeed would refuse, to care for girls (see also O'Neill, 2001). One male carer explained that he would like to work with girls but that the risk of an allegation was too great: *I have recommended that I don't look after girls . . . And it's a shame 'cos . . . I think I could probably work better with girls than I do boys, but I wouldn't risk it. I really would like to work with girls . . . but it's just not worth the risk.*

In the light of difficulties in recruiting sufficient foster carers and the particular needs of girls within the criminal justice system, it is unfortunate that the prevailing image of all men as potential abusers is deterring men from working with girls.

Of the three female carers who said they would prefer not to work with girls, two had not had girls placed with them but were daunted by what they had heard from other carers: *I haven't had any girls . . . but I've heard horror stories from the other carers, and I know what I was like as a child and what my own girls can be like. They are more lippy, there's more mouth . . . Boys may be nasty but at least they just do it to your face. Girls can be very sly.*

I haven't had a girl and I'm dreading it . . . They are worse . . . I have been told, and [another carer] has had girls and I've been in the company, you know . . . They're more mouthy.

The third carer had had two negative experiences of caring for girls, which had made her consider her ability to work with them:

Girls are horrible . . . more needy than the boys . . . The boys appreciate there's a problem, boys are actually easier. They're more happy-go-lucky, they're more laid back than girls . . . It did put me off . . . In fact, even now, if I had a choice I don't think I would have a girl here . . . I don't know why, I just find, maybe it's a case of discipline, maybe I find I cannot discipline young women. Maybe I can't communicate with them half as well.

There are a number of reasons why carers may be reluctant to care for girls, some of which may be related to gender stereotypes, limited experience or gender bias within the training provided.[45] As girls are much less frequently involved with the criminal justice system, training is likely to concentrate on the needs of boys, rather than girls, and carers are less likely to have experience of caring for girls. They might thus feel less able to deal with the specific needs of girls and might feel more capable of working with boys. The case-file analysis (Chapter 6) indicated that girls may have more difficulties that the carers have to contend with, being more likely than boys to have been physically and emotionally abused, to have self-harmed or attempted suicide, and to have experienced a greater number of background adversities. Farmer and colleagues (2004) also found that foster carers were less sensitive to the needs and anxieties of girls than boys.

Whilst some carers were equally happy to work with girls and boys, none said they would prefer to care for girls. Carers who felt confident

---

[45] Dealing with issues of female sexuality, particularly prostitution or indiscriminate sexual activity, is often cited as another reason why women are hesitant to work with girls (Cain, 1989; Aymer, 1992; Farmer and Pollock, 1998; O'Neill, 2001). The possibility of girls becoming pregnant poses an additional risk and some carers might feel unable to deal with this in addition to other issues the young person presents.

working with both girls and boys said they judged each as an individual and that gender did not make a difference. This is clearly an area where further research is necessary.

Additional needs and vulnerability

Foster carers were able to deal with a wide range of problems that are unlikely to be managed effectively in custodial or residential institutions. Whilst all of the children required emotional and physical care, some had additional, specific needs and could be particularly vulnerable. For example, one young person would have been vulnerable to bullying in custody because he had a congenital abnormality and another because he was a transvestite, but both were successfully cared for in remand foster placements. A number of the young people placed in remand foster placements self-harmed or were at risk of attempting suicide which could be managed more individually than in residential or custodial placements (Howard League, 1995b, 1999b, 2001d; O'Neill, 2001; Goldson, 2002a). The carers were aware of inherently risky times when the young people were likely to be more upset or prone to self-harming, for example, on family members' birthdays or the night before court hearings.

Whilst not all carers were able to offer placements to children charged with sex offences, due to the risk to their own children or grandchildren, others could. Again, such children would be particularly vulnerable in custodial and residential units and might present risks to other children within the unit. One carer was concerned that, if it were known publicly that she did look after young sex offenders, both she and the young person could be at risk from vigilantism from people who were '. . . ignorant, [who] don't understand what young people go through, [who] don't appreciate the court process'. However, her anxieties had never been realised and she had not experienced any criticism or hostility from her neighbours.

Several carers had been able to access psychiatric services or counselling for young people whilst they were in the placements, including drug and alcohol support, although all admitted it was difficult to do so: 'We battle, we battle . . . You have to battle for everything.' Again, the length of time it took to arrange appointments could be problematic, with the young person being sentenced before services could be utilised. Some felt that additional training in counselling skills and more information about other youth services in the area would be beneficial so that they could access further support for the young people.

Carers were also able to address physical health needs. Girls were seen as particularly likely to need treatment for venereal disease or to need contraceptive advice, which the foster carers could facilitate. Many of the young people were underweight when they first moved into the placements and the carers took pride in helping them improve the way they looked and felt about themselves:

They come and they're so, like, deprived. They're so thin and pale and, you know, so me, I just feed. 'Anything you want to eat, you can eat.'

Although they come in here very underweight sometimes, no self-esteem whatsoever, don't give a damn whether they live or die, unloved, 'Nobody wants me', you know, when they leave here they're usually one hundred per cent fit and healthy.

Helping the young people in this way could increase their self-esteem and confidence, and could also influence the courts by proving to the judiciary that, with support and direction, the young people were able to change. These benefits are unlikely to be achieved in YOIs where a young person's diet, personal hygiene and access to fresh air may be restricted by the regime of the institution (HMIP, 2000b; Hodgkin, 2002).

Management of family relationships

Whilst promoting or facilitating contact with family members was not a specified role for the carers, they all discussed the significance of helping the young people rebuild their family relationships. Contact is not unproblematic (Sinclair *et al*, 2000; Farmer *et al*, 2004), and several of these children had valid reasons for not wanting to have contact with their parents. For example, one foster carer explained that a remanded child resented contact with his parents because 'of the flak from them because they were dragged into court' and another carer witnessed a child being verbally and physically abused by his mother. However, as discussed in

Chapter 8, difficulties at home contributed to offending for many of the young people, and improving their family relationships could help limit their offending behaviour and provide them with emotional support. As one foster carer said:

With most of them it is all to do with their home life. I mean, you sort their home life out, you've sorted them out ... At the end of the day, right, if you can build their family relationship up, even if the whole scheme goes belly-up and they get locked up or they get into trouble again, they've always got somebody to turn to.

The foster carers recognised the young people's need for emotional support from family members or previous carers and encouraged contact, either by telephone or by facilitating face-to-face meetings.

Several carers talked about being a 'peace-keeper in the middle', neither on the parents' nor the child's side, but maintaining a neutral position whilst actively helping them to re-negotiate their relationship. Some children would try to play the foster carer off against their parents, testing the carer's loyalty to them, and several parents begrudged the carer's involvement. A number of parents resented the foster carers because the carers appeared to have fewer difficulties with the young person, or because they were more able to access support from social services or other agencies:

I remember seeing [his mother] in court and 'Oh, how many times have you found him drunk?'. 'Never', you know, and I almost wished I had because I felt so awkward, you know. 'Oh well, how comes he can bloody well do it for you and not for me?'

You get the resentment from the parents because they say, 'Well, you can get this, why couldn't I get this from the social? If I could have only had the help that you get, then I probably would not have been in the position I'm in now.'

Some parents were wary of the foster carers, viewing them as part of "the system" that could potentially remove their children from the family. It was important for the carers to reassure the parents that they were trying to keep the children out of custody, rather than trying to disrupt the family.

The foster carers also described situations where they had to manage parents whom, they thought, negatively influenced the young people, for instance by encouraging them to drink excessively or praising them for 'following in the family footsteps' by getting into trouble with the police. Other parents were extremely rejecting of their children and did not want to have contact with them, which was particularly difficult for the young people. Examples were given of parents moving house, and in one case moving abroad, whilst the young person was on remand, without telling them. A number of carers expressed dismay at the small proportion of parents willing to support their children during the remand period or at court hearings, and acknowledged the importance of being in court themselves to support the young people.

Inter-agency working

As well as working with the young people's parents, the foster carers had to manage relationships with other professionals associated with the young people. Whilst in principle the foster carers appreciated the inter-agency approach to working with the young people, many explained that, in practice, it did not work. It appeared that, not infrequently, no one would take full responsibility for the young person:

When we got to court it was an absolute farce because . . . her YOT officer wasn't there so it was another YOT officer that didn't know the case . . . The social worker was late . . . She was on a full care order, her solicitor knew nothing about the care plan . . .

The foster carers explained that they were increasingly being called upon in court to provide the judiciary with information about the young person because it was not forthcoming from other sources. The carers' comments about their role as professionals within the criminal justice system echo issues discussed by Walker and colleagues (2002): Is the role of a remand foster carer expected to include tasks previously undertaken by social workers or YOT officers or are they "expert" carers with distinct duties, clearly differentiated from social work and criminal justice workers?

As already noted, it was difficult to engage educationalists and the lack of inter-agency working was exacerbated by a shortage of social workers and YOT officers in the area. The carers felt that the young people were repeatedly let down by professionals who were meant to be working with them but who would not turn up or would not fulfil their promises. The carers appreciated the heavy caseloads of many social workers and YOT officers, but were disappointed by the attitude some professionals had towards the young people. For example, one carer said that the social worker 'liked Shaun as long as he doesn't have to do anything for him'.

The foster carers were aware of the lack of involvement the young people had in their review meetings and how this could affect their behaviour after the meetings:

> ... a lot of the children, after the professional people had left the house, they were a mess ... because they didn't understand basically what the people were talking about ... I know the social worker would say, 'Do you understand what I am talking about, Johnny?', 'Yeah, whatever.' So yeah, you'd have a bit of a behavioural problem after these people had left. They would rant and rave under their breath, but they're trying to tell me. I'd be putting the kettle on, 'Oh, bloody hell, that was boring, pointless, blah, blah, blah' ... and then after a while, [I'd say] 'Did you understand what the hell they were talking about this afternoon?', 'No, not really, did you?'. 'Well, I think they meant ...'

As with the young people's parents, the foster carers also acknowledged the need to remain neutral and not support the professionals more than the child.

Support

Support for foster carers

The foster carers were generally satisfied with the support that they received from the project, their friends and family, but several expressed a desire to see other agencies fulfilling their statutory requirements to support the young people, which would provide indirect support for the carers. In addition to the monthly training sessions, there was a support meeting each month for the foster carers. Some commented on the difficulty of attending regularly because of the timing of the meeting (a weekday evening), particularly if they were reliant on their partner to be driven to the meeting or if they had other children. Most of the carers were friends with other carers whom they could call for advice or to 'have a moan', although these friendships had developed on an *ad hoc* basis and one relatively new carer had not yet had the opportunity to meet many other carers.

Although some had initial concerns, the carers' own children and parents were generally supportive of the placements and would sometimes be involved in activities with the young people. For example, the father of one of the carers would take the young people fishing or to his allotment. As mentioned earlier, it could be problematic for the carers if their own children did not get on with the fostered child, but this was a rare occurrence and the fostered child was generally well integrated into the family. Whilst most of the carers' neighbours knew that they fostered children, few were actually aware that the children were on remand. The foster carers were, as already indicated, concerned about the possibility of vigilantism and strove to protect the children from unwarranted hostility by not telling their neighbours that they were on remand. One carer said that she felt 'embarrassed' when she had to face her neighbours after a young person had offended in the area, but none had experienced any overt criticism from their neighbours. A few carers had developed good relationships with local police officers who could be called upon to give them additional support.

The out-of-hours support involved phoning the local bail hostel which would page a specified remand fostering officer (RFO). Usually the RFO would return the call within a few minutes but there were instances when the foster carers were waiting for over two hours before anybody called, and on one occasion the RFO did not call back at all. One of the carers was critical of the limited help the duty RFO was able to offer:

But the problem is . . . they're either going to turn round and say, 'Well, no, don't put up with that, phone the police,' or they're going to say, 'Well, try to put them to bed and we'll talk tomorrow,' you know. So half the time you don't even bother 'cos you know what it is. I mean it's not a case of somebody's going to come out there and then. It's always, 'Well, we'll sort it out the next day' because that's all they're there for, they're only there to talk, you know. I mean it's nice to have somebody to talk to sometimes but, basically, after you've been doing it for a little while you just weigh the situation up and you just go ahead and do what you've got to do.

Several carers discussed the need for a "panic button" that they could use if a young person was being particularly aggressive or violent which would be linked with the local police station so that the police could be summoned instantly. The carers gave examples of situations where the young person had physically prevented a carer from reaching a telephone and felt that a panic button would increase the safety of the carers.

Pre-placement

The flexibility of the project was appreciated by the carers, most of whom felt they could take a break from fostering when they needed to, and that they were not put under pressure to accept any placements with which they did not feel comfortable. One area of weakness, which could undermine the carers' ability to decide whether to offer a placement to a particular child and to manage the child once in the placement, was the lack of information about the child obtainable at the outset. The carers generally acknowledged that the project staff themselves made available all of the details that they had about the child, but said that the project was not always fully aware of the facts. One carer felt that information could be deliberately withheld by social services or the YOT (although not by the project itself):

You only get told what they want to tell you, don't you? At the end of the day, they're desperate to find a placement for 'em so they tell you what they think you want to know and you find the rest out afterwards.

It was suggested by another carer that obtaining information about the young people had become more problematic recently, possibly due to difficulties in inter-agency working:

Initially . . . you wouldn't take the placement unless you had all the relevant information [but] we've found that's got a bit lax over the last year. It's not altogether [the project's] fault but the social workers will sometimes say, 'I can't get hold of the file' or 'I can't get you the relevant information for a couple of days'.

A few carers were willing to accept such placements and hope that the information would be forthcoming but others would refuse to take a child without background details being provided. There are obvious implications for the safety of the child and the foster carers if a placement is made without the carers being aware of, for instance, any medical needs or the fact that the child had previously been involved in arson (both situations foster carers had faced). Moreover, there are implications for children who are refused foster placements because other agencies have not provided sufficient information about them; these children are likely to be remanded into custody, possibly unnecessarily.

Occasionally, foster carers were able to meet the young people before the initial court hearing, which was considered beneficial by the carers, as it was by the young people themselves (Chapter 9). However, carers explained that the typical situation involved a telephone call in the morning and the arrival of the young person in the afternoon, and it was not uncommon for this time-frame to be considerably less, which prevented any meetings prior to the placement.

Conversely, one carer described a problematic occasion when she met a young person before the court hearing only to have the placement rejected by the judiciary who remanded the young person into custody. The benefits of meeting the carer and allaying concerns therefore must be balanced against the disadvantages of raising a young person's hopes. In a similar vein, another carer said:

> *The lovely thing is if you do make a mistake on that referral and the placement is unworkable, for everybody's sake, it's endable.*

But she did not appear to recognise that this could be construed by the young person as a form of rejection.

Ending placements

The end of a placement, whether it occurred prematurely or as planned after the conclusion of the court hearings, could also be difficult for the carers and young people, and was a time when additional support might be advantageous. Even if the placement thus far had been successful, some children displayed increased difficulties in the week prior to moving on because they were scared, upset or resentful of being "rejected" by the carers. One carer described a fostered girl as turning into 'Jekyll and Hyde' towards the end of the placement because she was so distressed about having to leave the foster carer's home. In the event, her behaviour became so violent and dangerous that the placement had to be ended abruptly, ahead of the planned move. Extra assistance to the carers and increased reassurance for the young people might limit this kind of occurrence.

As already indicated, some of the carers felt guilty about reporting a young person to the police when they knew it would precipitate the closure of the placement or asking the project to close a placement that they felt was unsustainable. Generally, the carers were in agreement that the project would not expect them to continue with a placement that was experiencing prolonged difficulties but one carer felt that pressure could be placed on them to persist:

They normally try to get you to give them another chance but . . . we will discuss it amongst ourselves and we will make a decision and if we decide that we're not doing anything to help this person and he's giving us more trouble than it's worth, then we will make up our mind and that's the end of it, you know. So they'll come out and have a meeting with us, but we've made up our minds and that's the bottom line.

The conclusion of a placement could be emotionally distressing and a time at which the carers might question whether they were going to withdraw from fostering, either if the placement had been successful or if it had broken down:

Quite often when, if it's been a good placement and we've had a great time and we feel that we've achieved . . . then I don't want them to move and I go upstairs and I think, 'I don't, I don't like this job, I'm packing this up'. If it's been a bad placement, it has exactly the same effect because I go up there and I think, 'That's it, I'm not having any more'.

As mentioned in the previous chapter, the emotional upset caused by the ending of some placements, particularly those that the carer deemed to be positive, illustrates the discrepancy between the welfare system and the criminal justice process – remand foster carers are expected to build close, supportive relationships with the young people for very short periods of

time, only to then disrupt the relationship on the basis of legal requirements rather than the young person's needs and wishes. As previously
acknowledged, recruiting and retaining foster carers can be problematic;
providing additional support at the end of a placement might prevent the
"retirement" of some carers.

Move-on

One of the elements that made ending placements distressing for both the
young people and the foster carers was the dire shortage of appropriate
move-on accommodation or support for the young people after the
conclusion of the placement.[46] The majority of the carers said that move-
on was the most problematic part of the process and the area in which
they would most like to see improvement. There were two main issues:
firstly, carers were reluctant to see children return to the environment that
they had come from with limited, if any, support to help the child maintain
the improvements s/he had made:

> *Sometimes we feel we're being cruel. You think, 'We're giving them all
> this and then we're snatching it way again', you know? Chucking them
> back again. Someone's chucked them in the river up there, we've fished
> them out and then we chuck 'em back in the river again.*

> *Move-on is always the most . . . difficult part of the placement. Quite
> often you're putting somebody back into the environment that they were
> in when they offended initially . . . and there's nobody there to pick
> them up.*

The carers hoped that the young people had learnt enough during the
placements to be able to stay out of trouble afterwards, but realised how
difficult this could be for young people if other factors in their environment had not changed.

The second issue of concern was the lack of suitable move-on accommodation for those who could not return home:

---

[46] Obviously some young people would receive custodial sentences and not need move-on
accommodation at that specific time (although clearly would need it on release from
custody) but many do not receive custodial sentences.

There was no move-on for him . . . He ended up . . . in a hostel. We knew he wouldn't stay there but there was nowhere else. He needed continuous support.

The problem is, with the older ones, there's nowhere for them to go. I mean, this is where the scheme falls apart. You finish with the court system with them and you say goodbye. Basically you open the door, kick them out and close the door behind them. Where do they go? There's nowhere available to them . . . Occasionally you can get them into a hostel but that hasn't really got the support they want or it's full of people that are drinking and drugs and that, all the time anyway, but they leave here, everything falls apart for them.

The carers were aware that moving on could be a very traumatic and distressing time for the young people. One carer said that 'You can see the panic in them' when the children had to move on. Another gave an example of a young person physically refusing to leave the placement, and two carers gave anecdotal evidence of a young person who committed suicide within a week of moving on from a successful placement.

Obviously young people remanded to custody or residential institutions would face similar difficulties and this is not an issue specific to remand foster care, but it was one that caused considerable, and clearly warranted, concern for the carers. Many offered the young people informal support after the end of the placement, through meetings, telephone calls and letters. A few carers maintained a relationship with the young people's parents after the placement and were willing to offer support to the parents in times of crisis. The consensus, however, was that the support needed by the young people and their parents should be provided on a more formal basis, complemented by suitable housing.

Summary

This chapter has explored the experience of caring for young people on remand, including the motivation to become a remand foster carer, the support and training available and the reality of inter-agency working. The different approaches taken towards the fostering role have been discussed, including the management of difficult behaviour, highlighting the apparent lack of clarity about the carers' roles and responsibilities. The carers acknowledged a number of areas of concern, for example, the difficulties in obtaining mental health support and educational provision for young people on remand and the lack of suitable accommodation after the remand placement had been concluded. These issues are discussed further in the next chapter, which aims to draw together the key findings from the case-file analysis and interviews with all participants.

12 Research summary, conclusions and policy implications

Introduction

This chapter summarises the key findings from the empirical research, locating them within a penal reductionist framework. It begins with a discussion of the difficulties of evaluating the outcomes of youth justice interventions, before examining specific issues within each stage of the remand process – making the remand decision and instigating the placement, during the placement, ending the placement and post-placement. Consideration is given to the implications for policy and practice, both for remand foster care schemes themselves and also for wider remand policy, although it is acknowledged that, due to the relatively small-scale nature of this research, these conclusions will need further corroboration.

Research summary

Evaluating outcomes

Evaluating the outcomes of any intervention is always a complicated process: the "success" or "failure" (themselves both value-laden terms) of a placement will depend upon which criteria are used to assess the placement and whose perspective is being considered (Miller, 1991; Triseliotis *et al*, 1995; Quinton *et al*, 1998; Walker *et al*, 2002). Magistrates, the police, the general public, foster carers, parents and the young person may all have different expectations of a remand foster placement and their opinion of the relative success of the placement will vary according to those expectations. For example, taken in isolation, the high rate of placement breakdown (50 per cent) could be interpreted by criminal justice professionals as demonstrating that remand foster placements are not a "successful" alternative to institutional remands. However, foster care professionals might be less critical of the breakdown rate as it is not dissimilar to that found in other teenage foster placements (Berridge and Cleaver, 1987; Triseliotis *et al*, 1995; Farmer *et al*, 2004), and might appreciate the potential welfare benefits of foster care more so than criminal justice professionals.

The outcomes of any intervention for a young person are usually multi-dimensional, being neither wholly positive nor entirely negative, and it is often a matter of balancing the "benefits" and "losses" across a number of elements (Whitaker *et al*, 1985). Within the criminal justice arena, this equation is particularly complex as the potential benefits of remand foster care for a young person need to be weighed against the possible losses for members of the public who, for example, may become victim of an offence committed by a young person remanded to foster care. An evaluation simply based on whether the placement lasted until the young person was sentenced exercises a very narrow interpretation of the term "success" and a broader appraisal is perhaps more prudent. For example, a placement might end before sentencing, but might have been a positive experience for the young person that resulted in improved family relationships, or a re-engagement with education or employment.

Similarly, the relative frequency with which young people offend whilst in the remand foster placement (between a quarter and a third, depending on the source of the information; Chapters 6 and 9) initially appears to be of concern. However, when the rate of offending in placement is compared with the levels of offending in other remand situations, remand foster care can be seen as a much more successful option than children's homes, and as equivalent to remands on bail (Brown, 1998; Morgan and Henderson, 1998; Youth Justice Board, 2002). Moreover, in evaluating outcomes, the severity of initial difficulties and the subsequent degree of change need to be considered (Triseliotis *et al*, 1995). For instance, a young person who was previously involved in persistent offending may not cease offending completely, but the placement could be considered beneficial if the frequency or severity of his/her offending behaviour decreased during the placement.[47]

Outcome judgements will also vary depending on the time at which the assessment was made, for example, during the placement, at its

---

[47] Although, as acknowledged above, a victim of an offence committed by such a young person would be highly unlikely to feel that the placement had been beneficial.

conclusion or at a point in time after the placement has ended (Parker, *et al*, 1991; Quinton *et al*, 1998; Walker *et al*, 2002). The young people in this study indicated that they believed that the quality of care provided during the remand foster placements was generally considerably higher than that which they had received in custodial, secure and residential institutions (see also Walker *et al*, 2002). Many of the foster carers supported this view but the opinions of the magistrates varied, with most arguing that children's homes were unsuitable for remand placements but some believing that prison service custody could be appropriate.

As discussed above, an evaluation of the success of the placements at the point in time at which they ended could be somewhat biased due to the relatively high number of placement breakdowns. Furthermore, the true influence of the placements on the young people's behaviour may not be apparent until later in their lives (Triseliotis *et al*, 1995). It was apparent that, for some young people, the improvements that they had made during the placement were not sustained beyond the end of the placement, particularly where appropriate support and/or accommodation was not available. However, in some instances, the experiences the young person had whilst they were remanded to foster care appeared to continue to influence their behaviour for a considerable time after the placement had ended.

Moreover, as Miller argues, the benefits of any particular intervention may extend further than preventing offending by an individual during a specific period of time. By helping to develop an insight into young people's behaviour, the experience of providing an alternative to custody can assist youth justice professionals, practitioners and academics in reaching a greater understanding of the possible causes of, and effective responses to, youth offending:

Though I recognized the need to control the youth's crime or violence, I wanted to give due consideration to and respect for each one's life history, with the hope that we, the definers, would occasionally reconsider the ways in which we dealt with delinquents . . . In this sense the question of whether our alternatives worked was not primary. Solutions in this field are inevitably dangerous. Programs which "work" by some standards can cause more problems for the larger

211

society than those which "fail" but tell us more about an offender and his world. (Miller 1991, p. 183)

The particular standpoint taken will therefore affect the judgement of whether remand foster care is a viable alternative to residential and custodial remands. The rate of breakdown is problematic, and the level of offending whilst on remand is of concern, particularly to potential victims, but in terms of promoting a young person's welfare and meeting their rights whilst they are on remand, foster care has distinct advantages over custodial institutions and residential accommodation. These benefits are now considered alongside specific issues that were significant or contentious, at each stage of the process.

Making the remand decision and the initial placement

It was clear that there were few differences between the demographic characteristics or offending histories of those placed with the scheme and those not (Chapter 6). The principal difference was that young people with more disadvantaged backgrounds were more likely to be RLAA and placed in remand foster care than those with less disrupted backgrounds, possibly due to concern for their welfare. It is feasible that these young people were already known to social services, which may have affected the information presented to the courts, but further research would be needed to explore this supposition. There were no significant differences in the current offence, the offending history, the age, gender or ethnicity of the young people, nor their propensity to self-harm, between those remanded to foster care and those not. This suggests that the scheme could be appropriate for more children who are currently being remanded to children's homes, secure accommodation or custody. It is also disturbing that factors such as the risk of a child self-harming or attempting suicide are not being given due consideration within the court hearing.

The lack of identifiable characteristics of those placed in remand foster care implies that the magistracy, in conjunction with the YOTs and the remand foster care scheme, did not make consistent decisions about whether or not to place a young person in remand foster care. This inconsistency was evident in the interviews with magistrates who made irregular use of the available written guidance, which itself was open to varied interpretation (Chapter 7). The lack of recent training for magistrates, particularly in the remand stage of the criminal justice system, was of concern, although it must be recognised that lay magistrates are volunteers and some would consider it unreasonable to expect a lay magistracy to be completely *au fait* with penal legislation and provision (Parker *et al*, 1989), particularly as legal advisers are present within a court to advise the bench. However, the National Remand Review Initiative suggested that some court staff, typically those based in small courts, could be unfamiliar with remand procedures, which could occasionally lead to a remand not being lawful (Moore and Peters, 2003). Furthermore, a third of young people remanded to custody were remanded from courts other than youth courts (Goldson and Peters, 2002) where the legal advisers may not be fully conversant with remand legislation and procedures for young people. The training and guidance available to all court professionals, including legal advisers, magistrates and judges, should perhaps be reviewed.

There are some courts in inner London that have specialist panels of magistrates who sit only in the youth court (Vernon, 2000). The magistrates in this research sat, on average, 24 times per year, but many of these hearings would be uncontested bail applications or trials; their experience of making complex remand decisions might therefore be limited. Developing dedicated youth court magistrates could reduce some of the discrepancies in knowledge and interpretation that were apparent, by easing the difficulties with training (outlined in Chapter 7) and encouraging the development of expertise in dealing with young people.

The magistrates were less aware of the remand foster care project than they were of the bail support scheme and less often saw representations from the remand fostering officers or YOT staff in court. The White Paper, *Respect and Responsibility* (Home Office, 2003), outlined a new power for courts to require local authorities to undertake an initial investigation of the young person's circumstances and to advise the court on how it would exercise its responsibilities if a remand to local authority accommodation was imposed. It is thought that this will increase the use of remand foster care, by facilitating a dialogue between courts and local authorities. However, it is not clear how this will differ from the current expectation that YOTs will provide such information to the courts. Moreover, the magistrates still need to be persuaded of the efficacy of remand foster care and both YOTs and the magistracy need to be given guidance about those for whom remand foster care is most appropriate. For example, young people who had previously been in care were particularly likely to abscond from the placements, and those who were charged with theft and/or multiple offences were more likely to experience a placement breakdown.[48] Consideration needs to be given to the most efficient way of training and informing magistrates, taking into account the knowledge that the judiciary are not easily influenced by government guidance (Parker et al, 1989; Hudson, 1993).

The majority of the magistrates were frustrated by their inability to impose a remand directly to foster care, due to their dissatisfaction with the alternatives (namely, an inappropriate return home or placement in a children's home). Legislation could be amended to enable the direct imposition of a remand to foster care if, in light of the YOT's investigation and recommendations, it is considered appropriate. Clearly, a sufficient number of foster placements would need to be provided, although it is apparent that magistrates are not deterred from ordering a secure or custodial remand, assuming that a placement will always be found (see also Hough et al, 2003). Implicitly, it has been considered easier to build new prisons than to recruit and support new remand foster carers, particularly in light of the dire shortage of mainstream carers (Fostering Network, 2006). However, active recruitment policies and the promotion of remand foster care in adherence with a reductionist policy framework could help reverse the current expansionist tendencies.

Conversely, whilst it is vital that foster care is actively promoted as a viable option for young people on remand, it is important to resist any potential net-widening, especially in light of the government's recent emphasis on remand foster care and the proposals for "intensive" fostering (Home Office, 2002a, 2003; see also Austin and Krisberg, 2002). It is imperative to implement sufficient safeguards to prevent children being placed with foster carers inappropriately, when they could justifiably be

---

[48] This is not to say, however, that these young people should not be placed with foster carers, but additional consideration of the young person's needs and behaviour may be necessary before a placement is made.

granted bail, and to ensure that remand foster care is seen as an alternative to secure or custodial accommodation rather than as a supplementary resource. If not carefully managed, both remand foster care and intensive fostering could potentially be at variance with the underlying philosophy of the Children Act 1989 and the UNCRC[49] by unnecessarily removing children from their families.

The continued erosion of the presumption in favour of bail and the judicial practice of taking the prosecution's case "at its highest" should also be moderated. At present, the balance of the judicial process is weighted against the defendant from the outset, and the outcome of any decision may depend largely on the advocacy of the defence solicitors, the ability of the YOT to inform the solicitor of potential alternatives, and the availability of such provision. In accordance with the right to be considered innocent until proven otherwise, the criminal justice process needs to be re-adjusted and the defendant's right to bail re-asserted. It is obviously difficult to achieve equilibrium between protecting the public and justifiably restricting a defendant's liberty, but it is imperative that the rights of the defendant are maintained.

On a practical level, the court schedule needs to be re-arranged to allow the young person an opportunity to meet the carers prior to moving to a placement, as this was appreciated by both the young people and the carers. Meeting the carers beforehand helped to allay some of the fears and anxieties that the young people had and it should be encouraged for the benefit of the young people, particularly those who are reluctant to live with another family. There is, conversely, the difficulty of raising a young person's hopes which may be dashed if a remand foster placement is rejected by the magistrates and it is important that there is clear, open communication with the young person so that they are not overly disappointed should a secure or custodial remand ensue.

---

[49] It is argued within the Children Act that children are best brought up in their own families and that supportive measures should be implemented to obviate children being unnecessarily removed from their families (Department of Health, 1989, 1990). Articles 5, 9, and 18 of the UNCRC refer to the importance of respecting the responsibilities, rights and duties of parents to care and provide for their child, and promoting the maintenance of the child within the family.

"Matching" the young person with the placement

The findings of this research also suggested that the caretaking style of the foster carers influenced the young person's satisfaction with the placement and its ultimate "success" (Chapters 9 and 11; Sinclair and Wilson, 2003; Farmer *et al*, 2004). Whilst it is acknowledged that the time and capacity for "matching" will always be restricted due to the pressure of court schedules and the current shortage of remand foster carers, it would be advantageous to match the characteristics and requirements of the child with the approach of the carers, for instance, not placing a particularly independent young person with regulatory carers, or placing a young person who does not want to live with a family with a single carer. Similarly, some carers expressed a preference for working with children of a particular age or gender and it would be prudent to place such children with them. Although it was not possible to demonstrate it in this research, Farmer and colleagues' study (2004) found that placing children who did not match the carers' preferences in terms of age or gender increased the likelihood of placement breakdown. However, as noted above, the lack of remand carers presently limits the amount of placement choice for any individual young person, regardless of their needs or their or the carers' preferences.

Although not prohibitive, there were suggestions of particular difficulties in finding placements for children who were accused of violent or sexual offences. The ability to care for such children depends on the attitude of the carer, the training and support they receive and their own family situations, but is also contingent upon the magistrates' awareness that remand foster carers *could* provide placements for children charged with serious or sexual offences. Ensuring that magistrates are cognisant of this is therefore essential. The scheme was, however, reluctant to provide placements for those with a history of mental health problems; this is understandable in light of the persistent difficulty reported by the foster carers in obtaining psychiatric or psychological support for the young people whilst in the placement. Increasing the provision of therapeutic services is important to support both the young people and, indirectly, the foster carers.

Regrettably, the perceived benefits for girls of remand foster care, for example, the provision of individualised care, were not always achieved.

In some instances, carers expressed a reluctance to care for girls, although this was not always grounded in personal experience and could be fuelled by comments made by other foster carers. Carers need to be trained and supported to meet the needs of girls and it is essential to ensure that training is not specific to working with boys but also focuses on the particular needs of girls so that they do not become marginalised within remand foster care, as they have been in other care settings (Gabbidon, 1994; Hodgkin, 1995; Howard League, 1997b; O'Neill, 2001). Whilst it is understandable that some men may not want to work with girls due to the inherent risk of allegations, further research needs to be undertaken to determine why working with girls is considered problematic by some female carers (see also Aymer, 1992; O'Neill, 2001).

The relatively limited availability of placements meant that young people could be placed a considerable distance from their home, which was of concern to some of the magistrates and young people. One foster carer acknowledged that being placed away from home could result in the young person becoming isolated, but most did not see this as a problem. Support networks could also be disrupted if children were not placed near their home area, and there could be a lack of continuity of support once they returned home (see also Walker *et al*, 2002). However, it must be recognised that the young people were significantly closer to their home area than they would have been had they been remanded to a custodial institution (Farrant, 2001), and the carers were generally willing to facilitate contact with friends and family where appropriate. The scheme and foster carers could be encouraged to promote this further, and to help the young people make new friends in the area.

Maintaining sufficient placements for young people on remand is problematic; whilst the scheme studied had an active recruitment policy and provides extensive support to its carers, it did not always have a full complement of carers. Obviously if a placement is not available for a child, he or she may be remanded to less suitable accommodation to the detriment of the child. Although the majority of YOTs are either developing or have established remand fostering schemes, many are small-scale and the lack of availability of remand foster care placements has been cited as contributing to the high use of custodial remands in some areas of the country (Moore, 1999; Hucklesby and Goodwin, 2002).

Consideration clearly needs to be given to maximising the number of remand foster placements available for young people to ensure that, wherever possible, an appropriate placement can be found for a child on remand.

A challenging issue for the carers in the scheme studied was that a retainer fee was not paid if the placement was unoccupied (see also Hucklesby and Goodwin, 2002). Fluctuations in the patterns of remand decisions meant that there could be considerable periods when the foster carers were not utilised by the courts and YOTs. To combat this, the scheme had begun to offer placements to children released on licence after serving the custodial part of a Detention and Training Order (DTO). Whilst such initiatives are beneficial for children sentenced to a DTO, and for the carers who are fully employed, there is a concern that placements for children on remand may be occupied by those serving a DTO. Specialist remand foster care schemes have previously been pressured into providing placements for children outside the core criterion, such as children needing mainstream foster placements (Hazel, 1981b; Fry, 1994; Walker *et al*, 2002), and this is clearly still problematic. An increasing proportion of looked after children are fostered rather than placed in residential care, with 68 per cent of those in the care system now being fostered (Department for Education and Skills, 2005). However, as previously acknowledged, recruiting and retaining foster carers is difficult and it has been estimated that currently there is a shortage of 8,000 foster carers (McVeigh, 2001; Fostering Network, 2006). In the current political climate, it is unlikely that children on remand will be seen as a priority for foster care, with non-remanded children taking precedence.

The Youth Justice Board hopes to reduce the number of custodial remands imposed, and to lower the rate of offending whilst on bail or RLAA, by encouraging the use of bail with an intensive supervision and surveillance programme (ISSP), and associated measures such as electronic monitoring (NACRO, 2002b). In turn, this could reduce the demand for remand foster care placements. However, a lack of appropriate accommodation has already been shown to restrict the granting of bail with bail support or an ISSP as an alternative to custody, for example, where social services are reluctant to find accommodation for young people who are not already accommodated, or where the only available placements are in bed and breakfast accommodation (NACRO Cymru, 2002; Hucklesby and Goodwin, 2002). Furthermore, it has been argued that bail support schemes do not consistently reach the most "challenging" and "difficult" young people (Goldson and Peters, 2002) who are perceived to need additional support that is not forthcoming within other forms of accommodation. Remand foster care might be the most appropriate option for these young people. Bail support schemes, ISSPs and electronic monitoring can also be imposed on a young person remanded to foster care, thereby providing additional safeguards for the protection of the public (NACRO, 2002b).

During placements

Moving into a placement was a time of considerable anxiety for the young people, as it is for those remanded to custody, but the young people's comments suggested that remand foster carers are more able to deal with these anxieties than are staff in secure or custodial institutions (Chapter 9; O'Neill, 2001; Goldson, 2002a). Children arriving at a foster placement can have a bath, a meal,[50] telephone their families and spend time (privately, if they so choose) reflecting on their situation. Conversely, children arriving in a YOI are expected to participate in an inflexible institutionalised regime, are unlikely to be able to shower[51] or to have access to telephones and whilst food is provided, it may be re-heated rather than freshly prepared (HMIP, 2000a, 2002b). Young people remanded to a YOI are typically given written induction material, but this is not always appropriate or reassuring (HMIP, 2002b), and induction talks do not always occur on the day of arrival (HMIP, 2002b), even though it is recognised that the first night on remand is particularly difficult for children to manage (Goldson, 2002a).

The reception at a secure unit may be more flexible and sympathetic to

---

[50] Basic nurturing tasks, such as providing a meal, were successful in "breaking the ice" when the young person first arrived at the placement, and appeared to demonstrate to the young people that they were welcome in the foster carers' home.

[51] This is of particular concern when children have spent prolonged time in prison vans, or "sweat boxes", on their way from court to the YOI (Howard League, 2001e; Goldson, 2002a; HMIP, 2002a).

the needs of the child than the reception in a YOI, but children arriving there may still feel intimidated by the perimeter fences and security systems, and the ability of staff to respond to individual needs is curtailed by the institutional regime and demands of other children (O'Neill personal communication, Goldson, 2002a). Foster carers are able to respond immediately to the young person's apprehension, individual needs, concerns and insecurities, in a relatively unthreatening environment, to which the child can adjust at his/her own pace. Although some young people were reluctant to move to a new family, the welcome offered by foster carers was clearly preferable to the induction procedure in a residential or custodial institution. This may contribute to a diminution in feelings of isolation, depression and anxiety, with a related reduction of self-harm and suicide attempts in the early stages of a remand period.

Once settled into the placement, the overwhelming majority of young people felt that it was preferable to living in a children's home or custodial institution (Chapter 10). A few also noted the benefits of living in foster care as opposed to being remanded on bail at home, such as increased support, material comforts and having someone to help them renegotiate difficult family relationships. The young people and the magistrates talked about the lack of control within children's homes and the inability of staff to contain difficult or disruptive behaviour, including bullying and offending (see also Cawson et al, 2002; Hucklesby and Goodwin, 2002). Young people in the remand foster care placements were the only child placed and therefore were not subject to the forms of bullying, violence and intimidation that occur in residential and custodial institutions, and were not encouraged to offend by other young people. They were also not exposed to other people self-harming and the distress that it causes, and their own self-harm could be managed more appropriately in remand foster care than in children's homes and custodial institutions.

The young people had the opportunity to develop an individual relationship with the carer, who could provide physical care, emotional support and advocacy. The carers were able to help young people negotiate their relationships with their family and with the other professionals with whom they were involved. This continuity and level of support and encouragement are frequently not possible in institutional accommodation: the staff–child ratio and the shift system mean that different staff will be on duty at different times. The young people and foster carers recognised the importance of living "normally" in the community, reflecting the developmental approach to youth offending, so that the young people could grow and mature without being exposed to the negative influences of institutionalisation (Zimring, 1978; Rutherford, 1986, 1992; Stein and Carey, 1986; Hoare, 1992; Malek, 1993). Whilst problems were sometimes apparent, it was evident that the foster carers were able to work much more flexibly with the young people than would be possible in many institutions where the demands of surveillance, control and discipline take precedence over meeting the needs of individual children (Kelly, 1992; Littlewood, 1996; O'Neill, 2001).

Although the sample size was small, it was possible to distinguish two approaches to caring for the young people on remand, defined in this study as nurturing or regulatory (Chapter 11; see also Walker *et al*, 2002). These different parenting styles signify a deeper confusion and lack of clarity regarding the role and responsibility of remand foster carers. For example, the nurturing carers' ethos was influenced more by child welfare concerns than notions of crime control, with the result that they were relatively lax in enforcing conditions such as curfews. Their reluctance to report the young people to the police if they committed offences, however, could potentially undermine public and judicial confidence in remand foster care. Conversely, the regulatory carers' disciplinary stance was more in adherence with the demands of criminal justice agencies but was resented and defied by a few of the young people, who generally seemed more accepting of the nurturing approach. Nonetheless, "turning a blind eye" to the young people's offending behaviour and drug use raises concerns about child safety and protection because, by effectively condoning the young people's behaviour, the carers could potentially prolong their involvement in offending or drug misuse, albeit unintentionally. In these situations, the foster carers' nurturing instincts might have to be subordinate to the need for professionalism.

This is a key tension within the provision of remand foster care: to whom does the foster carer have more responsibility and loyalty – the criminal justice agencies through which they are employed and the wider public, or the young person for whom they are caring? Whilst it could be argued that all infringements should be reported to ensure the protection of the public and to achieve the interests of the criminal justice system, it was apparent that not reporting the young people to the police could extend the length of the placements, thereby benefiting the young people (see also Walker *et al*, 2002). Ideally, foster carers should make a judgement as a "reasonable parent", for example, involving the police in more serious instances but dealing with minor offending behaviour within the family. However, the role of a remand foster carer is not the same as a parent and the foster carer also has a duty to the project, the public and the criminal justice system. There is a tension between allowing the young person to mature within a family environment and involving other criminal justice agencies – the former places the public at risk but the latter could lead to the expansion of incarceration.

These incongruities are a microcosmic example of the wider tensions evident in the fracture between child welfare and youth justice strategies and are testament to the difficulties in reconciling child welfare and youth justice demands (Goldson, 2002c). Remands to foster care implicitly have a restrictive dimension, but it is important that this does not become punitive or overly authoritarian, as the aim of remand placements are not to punish but to provide a safe and secure "holding placement" whilst the young person awaits trial or sentencing (Cliffe and Berridge, 1991, p. 204). Some flexibility in reporting suspected offending behaviour or breached conditions should be facilitated and the suggestions made by some of the foster carers regarding the automatic imposition of more stringent conditions and sanctions should not be endorsed.

Whilst overall the foster carers were extremely committed to the young people and provided high quality care, there were a few examples of questionable attitudes towards the young people, for example, referring to an individual as '*one of the nastiest bits of work*' (Chapter 11). It is not clear whether these problematic attitudes, revealed during the interviews, were replicated in the carers' relationships with the young people themselves, but that they were shared with the author of this book creates ethical concerns. Whilst it could be argued that the demands of criminal justice process perhaps make it harder to achieve best welfare practice as evidenced within civil childcare planning, remand foster carers have a duty to the young people to maintain professional and ethical standards of care.

The carers' ability to meet the young people's needs could be undermined by the inaccessibility of education, mental health provision and substance misuse services. The carers said that they had to 'battle' for services and were often confronted by apathy and indifference from other professionals; both the young people and foster carers acknowledged that the professionals could be reluctant to take responsibility for the young person and that some young people appeared to be at risk of 'slipping through the gap' between the care and criminal justice systems. One of the central tenets of the development of YOTs was that it would incorporate a multi-agency approach, yet this research suggests that the responsibility for meeting the needs of young people involved in offending behaviour is being devolved to youth justice professionals, with other agencies neglecting their statutory duties to the young people (see also Goldson, 2000a; Muncie and Hughes, 2002).

The young people emphasised the need for additional support from professionals, such as a drugs worker or an independent advocate, with whom they could talk about issues they did not wish to or felt they could not share with the foster carers or their YOT officers. However, the contact the young people did have with professionals was not always satisfactory; the young people and foster carers discussed the lack of real involvement of the young people in meetings during their remand period, acknowledging that, whilst the young people could attend the meetings, they did not always understand the discussions held or the consequences of any decisions made.

There was also only limited time available to instigate any service provision, a problem that has been exacerbated by the "fast-tracking" process for persistent young offenders. Whilst the average time young people spend on remand has been reduced, the inference appears to be that children on remand do not need to be provided with services during this time because it is not meant to be a lengthy period. The intention may be that the remand period is "only" to be a few weeks, but this is a considerable length of time for a child to be without education or therapeutic services and unexpected delays can also increase the length of the remand period far beyond the initial expectation.

Ending placements

The ideal situation for the scheme is that the foster placement will last for a week after the young person has been sentenced and the young person will then move to a form of accommodation appropriate to his/her needs, but it was apparent that this rarely occurred. The case-file analysis (Chapter 6) indicated that half of the placements broke down before the young person had been sentenced, which is an area of significant concern. The interviews with the foster carers and young people also demonstrated that, even when the placements did not break down, ending the placement could be traumatic and that appropriate move-on accommodation was rarely forthcoming (discussed below).

Few factors appeared to be associated with the disruption of placements prior to the final court hearing and placement breakdowns tended to be either the result of a culmination of interacting negative factors or a specific, unexpected incident. Children who had previously been in care seemed particularly vulnerable to placement breakdown, largely due to their heightened propensity to abscond from the placements. Conversely, prior experience of being in custody was not related to breakdown or to absconding: children in custody cannot run away and so they have to develop other coping strategies that may be of benefit in the foster placements, and they also know that the alternative available to them is custody, which may deter them from absconding. As previous research has suggested (Melvin and Didcott, 1976), young people who had been charged with theft and/or multiple offences[52] were more likely to experience a placement breakdown, although it is not clear why.

The reasons for any foster placement disruption are often highly complex (Berridge and Cleaver, 1987; Fenyo et al, 1989; Farmer et al, 2004) and further investigation would be necessary to identify measures that may limit placement breakdown. One specific area of concern is discovering ways to reduce the temptation to abscond, particularly for children who have previously been looked after who may need assistance in developing alternative coping strategies. A very simple but potentially successful remedy was suggested by some of the young people

---

[52] In this instance, five or more offences.

interviewed who recommended that the provision of additional resources, such as computers or televisions, might help relieve boredom and in turn reduce the desire to abscond.

Increased support for the foster carers and children towards the end of the placement would be beneficial, for example, more contact with the remand fostering officers and YOT staff. The trial itself increases the level of stress and anxiety for both the young person and the carer, and the young person is also likely to be concerned about where s/he is going to live after the trial has concluded. The anxiety could be manifest in the young person's behaviour, for example, through increased difficult behaviour, absconding or unhappiness and depression. Many young people had made clear attachments to the foster carers and were sad to leave them; a few maintained contact with the foster carers after the end of the placement and seemed to gain support and reassurance from this. Providing additional support at this time and immediately after the placement has ended may also increase the retention of foster carers. The foster carers' comments suggested that this is a time when they may question their role and, as they are not committed to a particular young person at that stage, consider withdrawing from remand fostering.

After placements

Difficulties in finding appropriate move-on accommodation were identi-fied by all of the research participants (see also Walker *et al*, 2002), but it must be acknowledged that these problems would be equally apparent for children remanded to secure or custodial institutions (Howard League, 1998; O'Neill, 2001). Whilst a minority of remand fostering schemes allow the young person to remain in the placement after conclusion of the trial (Hucklesby and Goodwin, 2002) this could lead to "bed-blocking" and the unavailability of placements for young people on remand. Social services and other housing providers are often reluctant to provide accommodation for young people who have been involved in offending behaviour (Hucklesby and Goodwin, 2002; NACRO Cymru, 2002; Social Exclusion Unit, 2002). Although the Children (Leaving Care) Act 2000 and the Homelessness Act 2002 hope to reduce this problem, historically it has been particularly difficult for 15-, 16- and 17-year-olds to find suitable accommodation due to the withdrawal of their right to receive state benefits and social services' prioritisation of other, more "deserving" young people.

It was a matter of considerable frustration for the foster carers and young people that the achievements made during the foster placements could so easily be reversed if no support or appropriate accommodation was forthcoming after the placement. As mentioned above, some foster carers maintained contact with the young people (and their families) after the placement had concluded, but this contact and support were offered voluntarily. It could be of assistance to establish further contact more formally to help maintain some continuity of support to the young people, whether they are incarcerated after the placement, receive a community sentence or are acquitted. Furthermore, the young people, carers and magistrates all recognised the incongruity of expecting young people and their carers to form close, positive relationships, only then to artificially bring the relationship to an end in accordance with the demands of the criminal justice process. A more welfare-based approach would advocate a graduated approach to ending the placements, based on an under-standing of the young person's needs, wishes and abilities.

Being on remand in a foster care placement appeared to have an impact on the sentence that the young person ultimately received; although it was not possible to demonstrate this statistically in this study, the young people, foster carers and magistrates all believed that giving a young person the opportunity to prove that they could respond positively to community-based alternatives increased the likelihood of them receiving a community sentence[53] (see also Hough *et al*, 2003). The magistrates were reluctant to incarcerate a child who had a successful remand foster placement, arguing that a custodial sentence would not benefit a child who had already begun to "change their ways". The converse may, however, also be true and a negative remand foster placement could result in a custodial sentence being passed. Information about the subsequent sentence received by young people whose placements had broken down

---

[53] It has been argued (see, for example NACRO, 2000) that the quality and clarity of pre-sentence reports affect the likelihood of a custodial sentence being passed; however, it is not yet clear how influential are reports of a young person's response to pre-trial interventions.

was not available in this study, but the potential of unsuccessful remand foster placements to contribute to expansionist tendencies needs to be monitored carefully. This is perhaps an area for further research and investigation.

Although tempered by the lack of appropriate accommodation and support after the placement, the benefits of remand foster care went beyond the remand period itself. In light of the extent and persistence of the young people's previous offending histories, and the relatively short-term nature of the foster placements, it is necessary to have realistic expectations of the amount of change that can be achieved (Rutter *et al*, 1998). However, six of the young people said that they had not committed any offences since the end of the placement,[54] and ten believed that they had changed for the better due to their experience of foster care. These young people's previous involvement in criminal justice system had clearly been ineffective in preventing further offending behaviour. For some of these young people, remand foster care had contributed towards a turning point in their lives, even if the placement itself had broken down. Some of the young people added a caveat, in that they recognised the effect of their own maturation and the influence of girlfriends or families in "growing out" of crime, but still believed that the foster placements had been beneficial for them.

It was clear that remand foster care could help the young people develop their confidence and self-esteem which could help them to re-

---

[54] Drawing comparisons with the rate of offending by young people subject to other forms of remand is highly complex (and beyond the remit of this research) for two inter-related reasons: firstly, figures regarding re-offending after remand are rarely available, with most statistics reporting recidivism after the conclusion of the young person's sentence; and secondly, the numerous compounding variables that may also simultaneously affect a young person's behaviour (such as the sentence received, the appropriateness of subse-quent accommodation, the availability of education or employment opportunities, further support and the multitude of other influences on their lives) are not generally considered. For example, NACRO Cymru (2002) reported that 76 per cent of those who completed a bail supervision programme did not re-offend, but none of the factors above or indeed other influences were documented, nor were offences committed by young people who did not complete their bail programme recorded. Furthermore, the timescale for measuring the incidence of subsequent offending varies across studies.

assess and perhaps change their lifestyle and offending behaviour (Eaton, 1993). This suggests that, if successfully managed, the remand period can be an important transitional phase that can "redirect" the young person's life course trajectory (Sampson and Laub, 1993) and help young people move away from offending. The remand period thus has significance in and of itself, and is more than just a stage within the criminal justice process.

Remand foster care as a rehabilitative intervention with young offenders

The skills of foster carers echo the characteristics of successful interventions with young offenders identified through the meta-analyses summarised by Pitts (2003; Chapter 4). The specific scheme studied is managed outside the justice system, although this is not true for all remand foster care schemes, some of which are managed by YOTs (see, for example, Hucklesby and Goodwin, 2002). The majority of the carers dealt with the young people holistically, taking into consideration their educational and employment needs, their physical and mental health, and their relationships with family members and peers. Most of the carers appeared to be influenced by an underlying developmental rationale, which recognised difficult and offending behaviour as part of a young person's development. They sought opportunities to build on the young people's strengths, to increase their confidence and self-esteem, and to facilitate reintegration into the community, rather than focusing on their weaknesses. Remand foster care is clearly an intensive approach, with the young people spending the majority of their time with the carers, which facilitated the supervision of the young people, but also meant they were given opportunities to talk about themselves and their backgrounds, and helped the development of links between the young people and pro-social adults.

The areas in which the foster care placements did not fulfil the criteria outlined by Pitts (2003) included the relative inability to provide educational and vocational opportunities and professional counselling; as noted, although these were desired by the foster carers, the apathy demonstrated by educationalists meant that the facilitation of schooling was rare and psychiatric and therapeutic resources were limited. Another comparative weakness was the lack of involvement the young people had in the remand decision itself, prior to the onset of the placement, although most were more fully involved in decisions and planning once the placement had begun. In addition, although within a placement, clear and consistent boundaries were enforced, different foster carers did vary in their attitude towards what was or was not acceptable behaviour. The police were also perceived to be inconsistent in their response to breached conditions and the young people felt that the magistrates were similarly ineffective in sanctioning breached conditions.

It was not within the scope of this study to undertake any kind of cost-benefit analysis, but the cost of a remand foster placement clearly has political and practical implications. Remand foster care is more expensive than mainstream foster care and can be as expensive as residential accommodation, but is considerably less than the cost of secure or custodial accommodation (see Moore and Smith, 2001). Any decrease in offending after the conclusion of the remand placement could further reduce the financial costs incurred by the criminal justice system, and there are, potentially, also other financial benefits, for example, the reduction of substance abuse, fewer unplanned teenage pregnancies, and increased involvement in education or employment (Aos *et al*, 2001).

The reductionist agenda

This research has demonstrated that remand foster care has the potential to be an important resource within a reductionist criminal justice system (Chapter 2; Rutherford, 1980, 1984; Mathiesen, 1990; Miller, 1991). Clearly, remanding children to foster care rather than custodial or secure accommodation has an immediate impact upon the size of the prison population. Furthermore, within a systems management approach, the impact remand foster care can have on the imposition of custodial sentences suggests that remanding children to foster care could reduce the number of children ultimately spending time in prison (Bottomley, 1970; Thorpe *et al*, 1980; Thorpe, 1983; Tutt and Giller, 1987; Haines and Drakeford, 1998). However, this research also indicates that the remand period is an important stage in and of itself, in that a young person's life can be quite radically influenced whilst s/he is on remand. It is important, therefore, to recognise the remand decision as a crucial juncture within the criminal justice process that can have a considerable impact on a young person's life. In this respect, remand foster care has marked advantages over institutional remands in terms of rehabilitation, reintegration and social inclusion (Hodgkin, 1995, 2002; Lyon et al, 2000; Goldson, 2002a). In addition, remand foster care accords with the principles of the UNCRC by dealing with children in a manner appropriate to their age, which promotes their sense of dignity and self-worth and their respect for others, and which emphasises reintegration into the community rather than exclusion from it. However, the achievements of remand foster care are currently marred by the relatively high rate of placement breakdown, although this rate of breakdown is not unusual within teenage foster placements (Rowe et al, 1989; Walker et al, 2002; Farmer et al, 2004).

In addition, in order to become a viable alternative to custodial and secure remands, public, political and judicial attitudes should be directed away from "punitive populism" to an approach that respects young defendants' rights and needs. Government politics and penal policy should be separated to restrain and reverse the growth of incarceration (Zimring, 2001). The need to appear "tough" has long debased public discourse about criminal justice (Tonry, 1994; Newburn, 2002) and it is necessary to return to a rational debate that considers effective strategies to deal with young offenders. These strategies must be founded on rationality and effectiveness, balancing the needs and rights of young offenders with the protection of the public, rather than on the over-dramatic demands of the media and the reactions of an often ill-informed public (Weijers, 1999; Tonry, 2001; Cohen, 2002; Goldson, 2002a). The decarceration of young offenders in Massachusetts was accompanied by widespread television and radio publicity, aimed at improving the public's understanding of youth offending and their acceptance of alternatives to custody (Rutherford, 1978, 1986; Mathiesen, 1990). Similar publicity is required to challenge the ideology of prison and to explain the philosophy of community-based remands.

As discussed in Chapter 2, the invisibility of prisoners contributes to the continued belief in imprisonment; children's experiences of being involved with the criminal justice system need to be made visible, and young offenders need to be recognised primarily as children. Through the narratives of young people on remand, this study has begun to develop an understanding of what it means to be a child in a remand foster care placement and how this period can be managed successfully. Although there are a number of difficulties that need to be addressed, this research has demonstrated that remand foster care can bridge the gap between the demands of welfare and criminal justice agencies, facilitating positive outcomes for many young people whilst maintaining an unequivocal commitment to children's rights.

References

ACOP/NACRO (1993) *Awaiting Trial: Final report*, London: NACRO.

Alanen L. (1994) 'Gender and generation: feminism and the "child question" ', in Qvortrup J., Bardy M., Sgritta G. and Wintersberger H. (eds) (1994) *Childhood Matters: Social theory, practice and politics*, Aldershot: Avebury, pp. 27–42.

Allen R. and Maynard W. (1999) 'Bail supervision and support', *On Track*, 4, February, special insert.

Altschuler D. and Armstrong T. (1984) 'Intervening with serious juvenile offenders', in Mathias R. and DeMuro P. (eds) *Violent Juvenile Offenders*, San Francisco: National Council on Crime and Delinquency, cited in Pitts J. (2001a) *The New Politics of Youth Crime: Discipline or solidarity?*, Lyme Regis: Russell House Publishing.

Anderson K. and Jack D. C. (1991) 'Learning to listen: interview techniques and analysis', in Gluck S. B. and Patai D. (eds) *Women's Words: The feminist practice of oral history*, London: Routledge, pp. 11–26.

Aos S., Phipps P., Barnoski R. and Lieb R. (2001) *The Comparative Costs and Benefits of Programs to Reduce Crime*, Washington: Washington State Institute for Public Policy.

Argyle M. (1988) 'Social relationships', in Hewstone M., Stroebe W., Codol J.-P. and Stephenson G. M. (eds), *Introduction to Social Psychology*, Oxford: Basil Blackwell, pp. 222–245.

Ashford M. and Chard A. (2000) *Defending Young People in the Criminal Justice System* (2nd edition), London: Legal Action Group.

Ashton J. and Grindrod M. (1999) 'Institutional troubleshooting: lessons for policy and practice', in Goldson B. (ed) *Youth Justice: Contemporary policy and practice*, Aldershot: Aldgate, pp. 170–190.

The Audit Commission (1996) *Misspent Youth*, Abingdon: Audit Commission Publications.

The Audit Commission (2004) *Youth Justice 2004*, London: Audit Commission

Austin J. and Krisberg B. (2002) 'Wider, stronger and different nets: the dialectics of criminal justice reform', in Muncie J., Hughes G. and McLaughlin E. (eds) *Youth Justice: Critical readings*, London: Sage, pp. 258–274.

Aymer C. (1992) 'Women in residential work: dilemmas and ambiguities', in Langan M. and Day L. (eds) *Women, Oppression and Social Work*, London: Routledge, pp. 186–200.

Bail (Amendment) Act 1993, London: The Stationery Office.

Bail Act 1976, London: The Stationery Office.

Bakal Y. (1973) 'Closing Massachusetts' institutions: a case study', in Bakal Y. (ed) *Closing Correctional Institutions*, Massachusetts: Lexington Books, pp. 151–180.

Beaulieu L. A. and Cesaroni C. (1999) 'The changing role of the youth court judge', *European Journal on Criminal Policy and Research*, 7, pp. 363–393.

Bebbington A. and Miles J. (1990) 'The supply of foster families for children in care', *British Journal of Social Work*, 20, pp. 197–220.

Becker H. S. (1963) *Outsiders: Studies in the sociology of deviance*, New York: Free Press.

Becker H. S. (1967) 'Whose side are we on?', *Social Problems*, 14:3, pp. 239–247.

Becker H. S. (2002) 'The life history and the scientific mosaic', in Weinberg D. (ed) *Qualitative Research Methods*, Oxford: Blackwell.

Berridge D. and Brodie I. (1996), 'Residential child care in England and Wales: the inquiries and after', in Hill M. and Aldgate J. (eds) *Child Welfare Services: Developments in law, policy, practice and research*, London: Jessica Kingsley, pp. 180–195.

Berridge D. and Cleaver H. (1987) *Foster Home Breakdown*, Oxford: Basil Blackwell.

Birmingham L., Mason D. and Grubin D. (1996) 'Prevalence of mental disorder in remand prisoners: consecutive case study', *British Medical Journal*, 313, pp. 1521–1524.

Boswell G. (1995) *Violent Victims: The prevalence of abuse and loss in the lives of Section 53 Offenders*, London: The Prince's Trust.

Bottomley A. K. (1970) *Prison Before Trial*, Occasional Papers on Social Administration No. 39, London: The Social Administration Research Trust.

Boyden J. and Ennew J. (1997) *Children in Focus: A manual for participatory research with children*, Stockholm: Radda Barnen.

Brown D. (1998) *Offending on Bail and Police Use of Conditional Bail*, Research

Findings 72, London: Home Office Research, Development and Statistics Directorate.

Burman M. J., Batchelor S. A. and Brown J. A. (2001) 'Researching girls and violence: facing the dilemmas of fieldwork', *British Journal of Criminology*, 41, pp. 443–459.

Burrows J., Tarling R., Mackie A., Lewis R. and Taylor G. (2001) *Review of Police Forces' Crime Recording Practices*, Home Office Research Study 204, London: Home Office Research, Development and Statistics Directorate.

Butler T. (2001) 'Remand in demand', *Foster Care Magazine*, 106, pp. 16–17.

Caddle D. and White S. (1994) *The Welfare Needs of Unconvicted Prisoners*, Research and Planning Unit Paper 81, London: Home Office.

Cain M. (1989) 'Feminists transgress criminology', in Cain M. (ed) *Growing Up Good: Policing the behaviour of girls in Europe*, London: Sage, pp. 1–18.

Carlen P. (1983) 'On rights and powers: notes on penal politics', in Garland D. and Young P. (eds) *The Power to Punish*, London: Heinemann, pp. 203–216.

Carlen P. (1996) *Jigsaw – A political criminology of youth homelessness*, Buckingham: Open University Press.

Cawson P., Berridge D., Barter C. and Renold E. (2002) *Physical and Sexual Violence Between Children Living in Residential Settings: Exploring perspectives and experiences*, Research Findings, Swindon: ESRC.

Chamberlain P. (1994) *Family Connections: Treatment foster care for adolescents with delinquency*, Eugene, OR: Castalia Publishing.

Chamberlain P. (1998) 'Treatment foster care', *Juvenile Justice Bulletin*, December, Office of Juvenile Justice and Delinquency Prevention, Office of Justice Programs, Washington: US Department of Justice, pp. 1–7.

Chamberlain P. and Reid J. B. (1998) 'Comparison of two community alternatives to incarceration for chronic juvenile offenders', *Journal of Consulting and Clinical Psychology*, 66, pp. 624–633.

Children Act 1975, London: The Stationery Office.

Children Act 1989, London: The Stationery Office.

Children (Leaving Care) Act 2000, London: The Stationery Office.

The Children's Society (1993) *A False Sense of Security: The Children's Society's Advisory Committee on Juvenile Custody and its Alternatives*, London: The Children's Society.

The Children's Society (2000a) *National Remand Rescue Initiative: Work at HMP and YOI Doncaster, 1st January 1999 to 30th November 1999*, London: The Children's Society.

The Children's Society (2000b) *National Remand Rescue Initiative: Work at HM YOI and RC Feltham, 1st January 1999 to 30th November 1999*, London: The Children's Society.

Cliffe D. with Berridge D. (1991) *Closing Children's Homes: an end to residential child care?*, London: National Children's Bureau.

Coates R. B., Miller A. D. and Ohlin L. E. (1973) 'A strategic innovation in the process of deinstitutionalization: The University of Massachusetts Conference', in Bakal Y. (ed) *Closing Correctional Institutions*, Massachusetts: Lexington Books, pp. 127–148.

Cohen S. (1972) *Folk Devils and Moral Panics*, London: MacGibbon & Kee.

Cohen S. (2002) *Folk Devils and Moral Panics* (3rd edition), London: Routledge.

Colton M. J. (1988) *Dimensions of Substitute Child Care*, Aldershot: Avebury.

Cornish D. B. and Clarke R. G. (1975) *Residential Treatment and its Effects on Delinquency*, Home Office Research Study 32, London: HMSO.

Councell R. and Simes J. (2002) *Projections of Long Term Trends in the Prison Population to 2009*, London: Office for National Statistics.

Crime and Disorder Act 1998, London: The Stationery Office.

Criminal Justice Act 1991, London: The Stationery Office.

Criminal Justice Act 1993, London: The Stationery Office.

Criminal Justice and Police Act 2001, London: The Stationery Office.

Criminal Justice and Public Order Act 1994, London: The Stationery Office.

Crowley A (1998) *A Criminal Waste*, London: The Children's Society.

Cullingford C and Morrison J (1997) 'The relationship between criminality and home background', *Children & Society*, 11, pp. 157–172.

Curtis P. A., Alexander G. and Lunghofer L. A. (2001) 'A literature review comparing the outcomes of residential group care and therapeutic foster care', *Child & Adolescent Social Work Journal*, 18, pp. 377–392.

Davies P. (2000) 'Doing interviews with female offenders', in Jupp V., Davies P. and Francis P. (eds) *Doing Criminological Research*, London: Sage, pp. 92–96.

Davis H. and Bourhill M. (1997) '"Crisis": The demonisation of children and young people', in Scraton P. (ed) *'Childhood' in Crisis*, London: UCL Press, pp. 28–57.

Department of Health (1989) *An Introduction to the Children Act 1989*, London: HMSO.

Department of Health (1990) *The Care of Children: Principles and practice in regulations and guidance*, London: HMSO.

Department of Health (2002) *Fostering Services: National minimum standards and fostering services regulations*, London: The Stationery Office.

Department of Health and Department for Education and Employment (2000) *Guidance on the Education of Children and Young People in Public Care*, London: The Stationery Office.

Department for Education and Skills (2005) *Children Looked After in England (including adoption and care leavers): 2004–2005*, London: DfES.

Dhami M. and Ayton P. (2001) 'Bailing and jailing the fast and frugal way', *Journal of Behavioural Decision Making*, 14, pp. 141–168.

Doherty M. and East R. (1985) 'Bail decisions in Magistrates' courts', *British Journal of Criminology*, 25, pp. 251–266.

Eaton M. (1993) *Women After Prison*, Buckingham: Open University Press.

East K. and Campbell S. (2000) *Aspects of Crime: Young offenders 1999*, www.homeoffice.gov.uk/rds/pdfs/aspects-youngoffs.pdf

Ely M., Anzul M., Friedman T., Gardner D., Steinmetz A. (1991) *Doing Qualitative Research: Circles within circles*, London: Falmer Press.

Farmer E. and Parker R. (1991) *Trials and Tribulations: Returning children from local authority care to their families*, London: HMSO.

Farmer E. and Pollock S. (1998) *Sexually Abused and Abusing Children in Substitute Care*, Chichester: Wiley.

Farmer E., Moyers S. and Lipscombe J. (2004) *Fostering Adolescents*, London: Jessica Kingsley.

Farrant F. (2001) *Troubled Inside: Responding to the mental health needs of young people in prison*, London: Prison Reform Trust.

Farrington D. P. (1996) *Understanding and Preventing Youth Crime*, York: Joseph Rowntree Foundation.

Farrington D. P. and West D. (1990) 'The Cambridge study in delinquent development', in Kaiser G. and Kerner H. (eds), *Criminality: Personality, behaviour, life history*, Berlin: Springer-Verlag, pp. 115–138.

Feenan D. (2002) 'Legal issues in acquiring information about illegal behaviour through criminological research', *British Journal of Criminology*, 42, pp. 762–781.

Fenyo A., Knapp M. and Baines B. (1989) *Foster Care Breakdown: A study of a special teenager fostering scheme*, Canterbury: University of Kent.

Fine G. A. and Sandström K. L. (1988) *Knowing Children*, Beverley Hills: Sage.

Fionda J. (2001) 'Legal concepts of childhood: an introduction', in Fionda J. (ed) *Legal Concepts of Childhood*, Oxford: Hart Publishing, pp. 3–18.

Firestone S. (1972) *The Dialectics of Sex*, London: Paladin.

Fisher M., Marsh P., Phillips D. and Sainsbury E. (1986) *In and Out of Care*, London: Batsford.

Fletcher G. (1992) 'Remands in context', in Bell C., Hill G., Crisp A., Fletcher G., Gibson P., Bell A., Hoare A. and Towler K. (eds) *Managing Remands in the New Youth Justice System*, London: NACRO, pp. 5–9.

Flood-Page C., Campbell S., Harrington V. and Miller J. (2000) *Youth Crime: Findings from the 1998/99 Youth Lifestyles Survey*, Home Office Research Study 209, London: London: Home Office Research, Development and Statistics Directorate.

Foster J. (2000) 'Social exclusion, crime and drugs', *Drugs: Education, prevention and policy*, 7:4, pp. 317–330.

Fostering Network (2006) '*Foster carers "let down" by government consultation*', www.fostering.net/news/?article=6090239.

Foucault M. (1977) *Discipline and Punish: The birth of the prison*, (translated by Sheridan A.), London: Allen Lane.

Friday P. C. (1983) 'Delinquency prevention and social policy', in Morris A. and Giller H. (eds) *Providing Criminal Justice for Children*, London: Edward Arnold.

Fry E. (1994) *On Remand – Foster Care and the Youth Justice System*, London: National Foster Care Association.

Gabbidon P. (1994) *Young Women in Secure and Intensive Care: Margins to mainstream*, Proceedings of Day Conference, November 1994.

Gee J. P. (1985) 'The narrativization of experience in the oral style', *Journal of Education*, 167, pp. 9–35.

Giller H. (1999) 'From centre stage to spear carrier: the repositioning of the English juvenile court', *European Journal on Criminal Policy and Research*, 7, pp. 395–403.

Gilligan R. (2002) 'Promoting resilience in children in foster care', in Kelly G. and Gilligan R. (eds) *Issues in Foster Care*, London: Jessica Kingsley, pp. 107–126.

Gittins D. (1979) 'Oral history, reliability and recollection', in Moss L. and Goldstein H. (eds), *The Recall Method in Social Surveys*, London: University of London Institute of Education, pp. 82–97.

Gluck S. B. and Patai D. (1991) 'Introduction', in Gluck S. B. and Patai D. (eds) *Women's Words: The feminist practice of oral history*, London: Routledge, pp. 1–5.

Godson D. and Mitchell C. (1991) *Bail Information Schemes in English Magistrates' Courts: A review of the data*, London: Inner London Probation Service.

Goldson B. (1997) 'Children, Crime, Policy and Practice: Neither welfare nor justice', *Children and Society*, 11, pp. 77–88.

Goldson B. (1998) *Children in Trouble: Backgrounds and outcomes*, Liverpool: Department of Sociology, Social Policy and Social Work Studies, University of Liverpool.

Goldson B. (1999) 'Youth (in)justice: Contemporary developments in policy and practice', in Goldson B. (ed) *Youth Justice: Contemporary policy and practice*, Aldershot: Aldgate, pp. 1–27.

Goldson B. (2000a) '"Children in need" or "young offenders"? Hardening ideology, organizational change and new challenges for social work with children in trouble', *Child & Family Social Work*, 5, pp. 255–265.

Goldson B. (2000b) 'Editor's Introduction: the New Youth Justice', in Goldson B. (ed) *The New Youth Justice*, Lyme Regis: Russell House Publishing, pp. vii–xi.

Goldson B. (2002a) *Vulnerable Inside: Children in secure and penal settings*, London: The Children's Society.

Goldson B. (2002b) 'New punitiveness: the politics of child incarceration', in Muncie J., Hughes G. and McLaughlin E. (eds) *Youth Justice: Critical readings*, London: Sage, pp. 386–400.

Goldson B. (2002c) 'New Labour, social justice and children: political calculation and the deserving-undeserving schism', *British Journal of Social Work*, 32, pp. 683–695.

Goldson B. and Peters E. (2000) *Tough Justice: Responding to children in trouble*, London: The Children's Society.

Goldson B. and Peters E. (2002) *The Children's Society National Remand Review Initiative*, Final Evaluation Report (December 1, 1999–November 30, 2001), unpublished.

Graham J. and Bowling B. (1995) *Young People and Crime*, Research Findings 24, London: Home Office Research and Statistics Directorate.

Grewcock M. (1995) 'STCs: locking up children for profit', *ChildRight*, 117, p. 2.

Hagell A. and Newburn T. (1994) *Persistent Young Offenders*, London: Policy Studies Institute.

Haines K. and Drakeford M. (1998) *Young People and Youth Justice*, Basingstoke: Macmillan.

Harris R. and Timms N. (1993) *Secure Accommodation in Child Care: Between hospital and prison or thereabouts?* London: Routledge.

Hayward K. (2002) 'The vilification and pleasures of youthful transgression', in Muncie J., Hughes G. and McLaughlin E. (eds) *Youth Justice: Critical readings*, London: Sage, pp. 80–94.

Hazel N. (1978) 'The use of family placements in the treatment of delinquency', in Tutt N. (ed) *Alternative Strategies for Coping with Crime*, Oxford: Basil Blackwell, pp. 82–102.

Hazel N. (1980) 'Normalisation or segregation in the case of adolescents', in Triseliotis J. (ed) *New Developments in Foster Care and Adoption*, London: Routledge & Kegan Paul, pp. 101–117.

Hazel N. (1981a) *A Bridge to Independence: The Kent Family Placement Project*, Oxford: Basil Blackwell.

Hazel N. (1981b) 'Community placements for adolescents in the United Kingdom: changes in policy and practice', *Children and Youth Services Review*, 3, pp. 85–97.

Hazel N. (1990) *Fostering Teenagers: Two innovative schemes in Kent*, London: National Foster Care Association.

Hazel N. (1993a) 'Towards the future', in Hazel N. and Fenyo A. (eds), *Free to be Myself: The development of teenage fostering*, Minnesota: Human Services Associates, pp. 51–53.

Hazel N. (1993b) 'The original phase: the Kent model and developments up to the mid-80s', in Hazel N. and Fenyo A. (eds), *Free to be Myself: The development of teenage fostering*, Minnesota: Human Services Associates, pp. 1–7.

Hazel N. (1993c) 'Theoretical background and the evaluation of teenage fostering', in Hazel N. and Fenyo A. (eds), *Free to be Myself: The development of teenage fostering*, Minnesota: Human Services Associates, pp. 8–14.

Her Majesty's Inspectorate of Prisons for England and Wales (1997) *Young Prisoners: A thematic review by HM Chief Inspector of Prisons for England and Wales*, London: HMSO.

Her Majesty's Inspectorate of Prisons for England and Wales (2000c) *Unjust Deserts. A thematic review by HM Chief Inspector of Prisons of the treatment and conditions for unsentenced prisoners in England and Wales*, London: HMSO.

Her Majesty's Inspectorate of Prisons for England and Wales (1999) *Suicide is Everyone's Concern: A thematic review by HM Chief Inspector of Prisons for England and Wales,* London: HMSO.

Her Majesty's Inspectorate of Prisons for England and Wales (2000a) *Report of an Announced Inspection of HM Young Offender Institution and Remand Centre Castington 15–19 May 2000,* London: HMSO.

Her Majesty's Inspectorate of Prisons for England and Wales (2000b) *Unjust Deserts: A thematic review by HM Chief Inspector of Prisons of the treatment and conditions for unsentenced prisoners in England and Wales,* London: HMSO

Her Majesty's Inspectorate of Prisons for England and Wales (2002a) *Annual Report of HM Chief Inspector or Prisons for England and Wales, 2001/2002,* London: HMSO.

Her Majesty's Inspectorate of Prisons for England and Wales (2002b) *Report of a Full Announced Inspection of HM Young Offender Institution and Remand Centre Onley, 9–13 July 2001,* London: HMSO.

Hester M., Pearson C. and Harwin N. (2000) *Making an Impact: Children and domestic violence*, London: Jessica Kingsley.

Higgins D. J. and McCabe M. P. (2001) 'Multiple forms of child abuse and neglect: adult retrospective reports', *Aggression and Violent Behaviour*, 6, pp. 547–578.

Hill M. (1997) 'Participatory research with children', *Child & Family Social Work*, 2:3, pp. 171–183.

Hill M., Nutter R., Giltinan D., Hudson J. and Galsway B. (1993) 'A comparative survey of specialist fostering schemes in the UK and North America', *Adoption & Fostering*, 17:2, pp. 17–22.

Hirschi T. (1969) *Causes of Delinquency*, Berkeley: University of California Press.

Hoare A. (1992) 'Remands as a system', in Bell C., Hill G., Crisp A., Fletcher G., Gibson P., Bell A., Hoare A. and Towler K. (eds) *Managing Remands in the New Youth Justice System*, London: NACRO, pp. 10–14.

Hodgkin R. (1995) *Safe to Let Out? The current and future use of secure accommodation for children and young people*, London: National Children's Bureau.

Hodgkin R. (2002) *Rethinking Child Imprisonment: A report on Young Offender Institutions*, London: Children's Rights Alliance for England.

Hollis V. and Cross I. (2003) *Prison Population Brief, England and Wales: April 2003*, London: Home Office Research, Development and Statistics Directorate.

Hollis V. and Goodman M. (2003) *Prison Population Brief, England and Wales: February 2003*, London: Home Office Research, Development and Statistics Directorate.

Homelessness Act 2002, London: The Stationery Office.

Home Office (2000) *Criminal Justice Statistics for England and Wales 1999*, London: Home Office Research, Development and Statistics Directorate.

Home Office (2001) *The Youth Court 2001: The changing culture of the Youth Court*, Good Practice Guide, London, Home Office, Lord Chancellor's Department.

Home Office (2002a) *Justice for All*, Cm 5563, London: The Stationery Office.

Home Office (2002b) *Statistics on Women and the Criminal Justice System*, www.homeoffice.gov.uk/rds/pdfs2/s95women02.pdf

Home Office (2003) *Respect and Responsibility – Taking a stand against anti-social behaviour*, Cm 5778, London: The Stationery Office.

Hough M, Jacobson J and Millie A (2003) *The Decision to Imprison: Sentencing and the prison population*, London: Prison Reform Trust.

House of Commons Home Affairs Committee (1993), *Juvenile Offenders: Memoranda of evidence*, London: HMSO.

The Howard League (1995a) *Troubleshooter: A project to rescue 15-year-olds from prison*, London: The Howard League for Penal Reform.

The Howard League (1995b) *Banged Up, Beaten Up, Cutting Up*, London: The Howard League for Penal Reform.

The Howard League (1997a) *The Howard League Troubleshooter Project*, London: The Howard League for Penal Reform.

The Howard League (1997b) *Lost Inside: The imprisonment of teenage girls*, London: The Howard League for Penal Reform.

The Howard League (1998) *Sentenced to Fail – Out of sight, out of mind*, London: The Howard League for Penal Reform.

The Howard League (1999a) *Child Jails: The case against secure training centres*, London: The Howard League for Penal Reform.

The Howard League (1999b) *Desperate Measures: Prison suicides and their prevention*, London: The Howard League for Penal Reform.

The Howard League (2001a) *Children in Prison: Provision and practice at Lancaster Farms*, London: The Howard League for Penal Reform.

The Howard League (2001b) *Children in Prison: Provision and practice at Castington*, London: The Howard League for Penal Reform.

The Howard League (2001c) *Missing the Grade: Education for children in prison*, London: The Howard League for Penal Reform.

The Howard League (2001d) *Suicide and Self-Harm Prevention: Repetitive self-harm among women and girls in prison*, London: The Howard League for Penal Reform

The Howard League (2001e) *Suicide and Self-Harm Prevention: Court cells and prison vans*, London: The Howard League for Penal Reform.

Howell J., Krisberg B., Hawkins D. and Wilson J. (eds) (1995) *Serious, Violent and Chronic Juvenile Offenders: A sourcebook*, London: Sage, cited in Pitts J (2001a) *The New Politics of Youth Crime: Discipline or solidarity?*, Lyme Regis: Russell House Publishing.

Hucklesby A. (1996) 'Bail or jail? The practical operation of the Bail Act 1976', *Journal of Law and Society*, 23, pp. 213–233.

Hucklesby A. (1997) 'Court culture: an explanation of variations in the use of bail by magistrates' courts', *The Howard Journal of Criminal Justice*, 36:2, pp. 129–145.

Hucklesby A. and Goodwin T. (2002) *Pre-Trial Accommodation for Young People*, Report to the Youth Justice Board, unpublished.

Hucklesby A. and Marshall E. (2000) 'Tackling offending on bail', *The Howard Journal of Criminal Justice*, 39:2, pp. 150–170.

Hudson B. A. (1993) *Penal Policy and Social Justice*, Toronto: University of Toronto Press.

Hughes G. (2000) 'Understanding the politics of criminological research', in Jupp V., Davies P. and Francis P. (eds) *Doing Criminological Research*, London: Sage, pp. 234–248.

Inquest (2006) *Youth Deaths in Prison*, www.inquest.org.uk/

Jackson S. and Martin P. Y. (1998) 'Surviving the care system: education and resilience', *Journal of Adolescence*, 21, pp. 569–583.

Judicial Studies Board (2001) *Youth Court Bench Book*, London: Judicial Studies Board.

Kagan J (1979) *The Growth of the Child: Reflections on human development*, Sussex: Harvester Press.

Katz K (1988) *Seductions of Crime: Moral and sensual attractions in doing evil*, New York: Basic Books.

Kearney P (2001) *Prison Medicine: A crisis waiting to break*, London: British Medical Association.

Kelly B. (1992) *Children Inside*, London: Routledge.

Kelly G. (2002) 'Outcome studies of foster care', in Kelly G. and Gilligan R. (eds) *Issues in Foster Care: Policy, practice and research*, London: Jessica Kingsley, pp. 59–84.

Kent G. (2000) 'Informed consent', in Burton D. (ed) *Research Training for Social Scientists*, London: Sage.

King M. (1971) *Bail or Custody?*, London: The Cobden Trust.

King R. D. and Morgan R. (1976) *A Taste of Prison: Custodial conditions for trial and remand prisoners*, London: Routledge & Kegan Paul.

King R. D. and Morgan R. (1980) *The Future of the Prison System*, Farnborough: Gower.

Kurtz Z., Thornes R. and Bailey S. (1998) 'Children in the criminal justice and secure care systems: how their mental health needs are met', *Journal of Adolescence*, 21, pp. 543–553.

Lemert E. (1967) *Human Deviance, Social Problems and Social Control*, New Jersey: Prentice-Hall.

Liebling A. (2001) 'Whose Side Are We On? Theory, practice and allegiances in prisons research', *British Journal of Criminology*, 41, pp. 472–484.

Lipscombe J. (2003) *Another Side of Life: Foster Care for Young People on Remand*, unpublished PhD thesis, Bristol: University of Bristol.

Lipsey M. W. (1995) 'What do we learn from 400 research studies on the effectiveness of treatment with juvenile delinquents?', in McGuire J. (ed) *What Works: Reducing re-offending*, Chichester: Wiley.

Littlewood P. (1996) 'Secure Units', in Asquith S. (ed) *Children and Young People in Conflict with the Law*, London: Jessica Kingsley, pp. 155–168.

Lord Carlile of Berriew QC (2006) *An Independent Inquiry into the Use of Physical Restraint, Solitary Confinement and Forcible Strip Searching of Children in Prisons, Secure Training Centres and Local Authority Secure Children's Homes*, London: The Howard League for Penal Reform.

Lyon J., Dennison C. and Wilson A. (2000) *'Tell Them so They Listen': Messages from young people in custody*, Home Office Research Study 201, London: Home Office.

Mackinnon C. (1987) 'Feminism, Marxism, method and the State: toward feminist jurisprudence', in Hardin S. (ed) *Feminism and Methodology*, Milton Keynes: Open University Press.

Magistrates' Association (2003), www.magistrates-association.org.uk/

Mahon A., Glendinning C., Clarke K. and Craig G. (1996) 'Researching children: Methods and ethics', *Children & Society*, 10:2, pp. 145–154.

Malek M. (1993) *Passing the Buck: Institutional responses to controlling children with difficult behaviour*, London: The Children's Society.

Mathiesen T. (1983) 'The future of control systems', in Garland D. and Young P. (eds) *The Power to Punish*, London: Heinemann, pp. 130–145.

Mathiesen T. (1990) *Prison on Trial*, London: Sage.

Mauthner M. (1997) 'Methodological aspects of collecting data from children: lessons from three research projects', *Children & Society*, 11, pp. 16–28.

Mayall B. (1994) 'Introduction', in Mayall B. (ed) *Children's Childhoods: Observed and experienced*, Bristol: The Falmer Press, pp. 1–12.

McVeigh T. (2001) 'Fostering in crisis as children are left at risk in unsafe homes', *The Observer*, 3 June.

Melvin M. and Didcott P. G. (1976) *Pre-Trial Bail and Custody in the Scottish Sheriff Courts*, Scottish Office Central Research Unit, Edinburgh: HMSO.

Miller J. G. (1973) 'The politics of change: correctional reform', in Bakal Y (ed) *Closing Correctional Institutions*, Massachusetts: Lexington Books, pp. 3–8.

Miller J. G. (1991) *Last One Over the Wall: The Massachusetts experiment in closing reform schools*, Ohio: Ohio State University Press.

Mishler E. (1986) 'The analysis of interview-narratives', in Sarbin T. (ed) *Narrative Psychology: The storied nature of human conduct*, London: Praeger.

Monaghan G. (2000) 'The courts and the new youth justice', in Goldson B. (ed) *The New Youth Justice*, Lyme Regis: Russell House Publishing, pp. 144–159.

Moore S. (1998) 'Children in prison: the work of the National Remand Rescue Initiative', *ChildRight*, 151, pp. 15–17.

Moore S. (1999) 'Children in prison', *The Magistrate*, January, pp. 8–9.

Moore S. (2000) 'Child incarceration and the new youth justice', in Goldson B. (ed) *The New Youth Justice*, Lyme Regis: Russell House Publishing, pp. 115–128.

Moore S. and Peters E. (2003) *A Beacon of Hope. Children and young people on remand*, Final Report of the National Remand Review Initiative, London: The Children's Society.

Moore S. and Smith R. (2001) *The Pre-Trial Guide: Working with young people from arrest to trial*, London: The Children's Society.

Morgan P. M. and Henderson P. F. (1998) *Remand Decisions and Offending on Bail: Evaluation of the Bail Process Project*, Home Office Research Study 184, London: Home Office.

Morgan R. and Russell N. (2000) *The Judiciary in the Magistrates' Courts*, London: Home Office, Research, Development and Statistics Directorate.

Morgan R. (2002) 'Magistrates: The future according to Auld', *Journal of Law and Society*, 29:2, pp. 308–323.

Morrows V. and Richards M. (1996) 'The ethics of social research with children: an overview', *Children & Society*, 10:2, pp. 90–105.

Muncie J. (1999) *Youth and Crime: A critical introduction*, London: Sage.

Muncie J. (2004) *Youth and Crime*, (2nd edition), London: Sage.

Muncie J. and Hughes G. (2002) 'Modes of youth governance: Political rationalities, criminalization and resistance', in Muncie J., Hughes G. and McLaughlin E. (eds) *Youth Justice: Critical Readings*, London: Sage, pp. 1–18.

Murray C. and Hallett C. (2000) 'Young people's participation in decisions affecting their welfare', *Childhood*, 7:1, pp. 11–25.

NACRO (1993) *Briefing: Juveniles remanded in custody*, London: NACRO.

NACRO (1996a) *Safe and Secure: Ending remands to prison for 15- and 16-year-old boys*, Report of the Juvenile Remand Group, London: NACRO.

NACRO (1996b) *Briefing: Remand fostering*, London: NACRO.

NACRO (1998) *Briefing: Bail support*, London: NACRO.

NACRO (1999a) *Briefing: Court ordered secure remands*, London: NACRO Youth Crime Section.

NACRO (1999b) *Briefing: Youth offending and health: the role of YOTs*, London: NACRO.

NACRO (1999c) *Briefing: Youth Offending Teams and education*, London: NACRO.

NACRO (2000) *Pre-Sentence Reports and Custodial Sentencing*, London: NACRO.

NACRO (2002a) *Youth Crime Section Update, June*, London: NACRO.

NACRO (2002b) *Youth Crime Briefing: Electronic monitoring of children remanded on bail or to local authority accommodation*, London: NACRO.

NACRO (2004) *Youth Crime Briefing: Remand fostering*, London: NACRO.

NACRO Cymru (2002) *Third National Evaluation Report: Bail supervision and support schemes*, Swansea: NACRO Cymru.

Neustatter A. (2002) *Locked In, Locked Out: The experience of young offenders out of society and in prison*, London: Calouste Gulbenkian Foundation.

Newburn T. (2002) 'Atlantic crossings: "policy transfer" and crime control in the USA and Britain', *Punishment and Society*, 4:2, pp. 165–194.

Oakley A. (1981) 'Interviewing women: a contradiction in terms', in Roberts H. (ed) *Doing Feminist Research*, London: Routledge & Kegan Paul, pp. 30–61.

Oakley A. (1994) 'Women and children first and last: Parallels and differences between children's and women's studies', in Mayall B. (ed) *Children's Childhoods: Observed and experienced*, London: Falmer Press, pp. 13–32.

Office for National Statistics (2003) www.statistics.gov.uk/

O'Neill T. (2001) *Children in Secure Accommodation: A gendered exploration of locked institutional care for children in trouble*, London: Jessica Kingsley.

Parker H., Sumner M. and Jarvis G. (1989) *Unmasking the Magistrates*, Milton Keynes: Open University Press.

Parker R., Ward H., Jackson S., Aldgate J. and Wedge P. (1991) *Assessing Outcomes in Child Care*, London: HMSO.

Paterson F. and Whittaker C. (1994) *Operating Bail: Decision making under the Bail etc. (Scotland) Act 1980*, London: HMSO.

Paton L. (2003) 'The ChildRight interview: Fran Russell', *ChildRight*, 194, pp. 14–16.

Penal Affairs Consortium (2000) *Juveniles on Remand*, cgi.www.penlex. org.uk/ pages/pacjuven.htm

Phillips C. and Bowling B. (2002) 'Racism, ethnicity, crime and criminal justice', in Maguire M., Morgan R. and Reiner R. (eds) *The Oxford Handbook of Criminology* (3rd edition), Oxford: Oxford University Press, pp. 579–619.

Pinkerton J. (2002) 'Leaving care and fostering', in Kelly G. and Gilligan R. (eds) *Issues in Foster Care*, London: Jessica Kingsley, pp. 85–106.

Pitts J. (2001) 'Korrectional Karaoke: New Labour and the zombification of youth justice', *Youth Justice*, 1:2, pp. 3–16.

Pitts J. (2003) *The New Politics of Youth Crime: Discipline or solidarity?*, Lyme Regis: Russell House Publishing.

Police and Criminal Evidence Act 1984, London: The Stationery Office.

Powis B., Griffiths P., Gossop M., Lloyd C. and Strang J. (1998) 'Drug use and offending behaviour among young people excluded from school', *Drugs: Education, Prevention and Policy*, 5:3, pp. 245–256.

Presdee M. (2000) *Cultural Criminology and the Carnival of Crime*, London: Routledge.

Prison Reform Trust (2002) *Press Release: Government draws go to jail card*, 9 December, www.prisonreformtrust.org.uk

Prison Reform Trust (2005) *Bromley Briefings: Prison factfile*, October, London: Prison Reform Trust.

Prisons Act 1865, London: HMSO.

Prisons Act 1877, London: HMSO.

Quinton D., Rushton A., Dance C. and Mayes D. (1998) *Joining New Families: A study of adoption and fostering in middle childhood*, Chichester: Wiley.

Qvortrup J. (1994) 'Childhood matters: an introduction', in Qvortrup J., Bardy M., Sgritta G. and Wintersberger H. (eds) *Childhood Matters: Social theory, practice and politics*, Aldershot: Avebury, pp. 1–23.

Reddy L. A. and Pfeiffer S. I. (1997) 'Effectiveness of treatment foster care with children and adolescents: a review of outcome studies', *Journal of the American Academy of Child and Adolescent Psychiatry*, 36:5, pp. 581–588.

Reiner R. (1994) 'Policing and the police', in Maguire M., Morgan R. and Reiner R. (eds) *The Oxford Handbook of Criminology*, Oxford: Oxford University Press, pp. 705–772.

Renold E. and Barter C. (2003) ' "Hi, I'm Ramon and I run this place": challenging the normalisation of violence in children's homes from young people's perspectives', in Stanko E. A. (ed) *The Meanings of Violence*, London: Routledge, pp. 90–111.

Riessman C. K. (1993) *Narrative Analysis*, London: Sage.

Roberts M. (2000) 'The ChildRight interview: Lord Warner, Chairman of the Youth Justice Board', *ChildRight*, June, 168, pp. 9–11.

Roche J. (1999) 'Children: rights, participation and citizenship', *Childhood*, 6:4, pp. 475–493.

Rowe J., Hundleby M. and Garnett L. (1989) *Child Care Now: A survey of placement patterns*, London: BAAF.

Rutherford A. (1978) 'Decarceration of young offenders in Massachusetts: the events and their aftermath', in Tutt N. (ed) *Alternative Strategies for Coping with Crime*, Oxford: Basil Blackwell, pp. 103–119.

Rutherford A. (1980) *A Statute Backfires: The escalation of youth incarceration in England during the 1970s*, London: Justice for Children.

Rutherford A. (1984) *Prisons and the Process of Justice*, London: Heinemann.

Rutherford A. (1986) *Growing out of Crime*, Harmondsworth: Penguin.

Rutherford A. (1992) *Growing out of Crime: The new era*, Winchester: Waterside Press.

Rutherford A. (1998) 'One year on', *Howard League Magazine*, 1, p. 8.

Rutter M. and Giller H. (1983) *Juvenile Delinquency: Trends and perspectives*, Harmondsworth: Penguin.

Rutter M., Giller H. and Hagell A. (1998) *Antisocial Behaviour by Young People*, Cambridge: Cambridge University Press.

Sampson R. J. and Laub J. H. (1993) *Crime in the Making: Pathways and turning points through life*, Massachusetts: Harvard University Press.

Sanders A. (2002) 'Core values, the Magistracy, and the Auld Report', *Journal of Law and Society*, 29:2, pp. 324–341.

Sanders A. and Young R. (2002) 'From suspect to trial', in Maguire M., Morgan R. and Reiner R. (eds) *The Oxford Handbook of Criminology* (3rd edition), Oxford: Oxford University Press, pp. 1034–1075.

Schur E. (1973) *Radical Non-intervention: Rethinking the delinquency problem*, New Jersey: Prentice-Hall.

Scott S. and the National Treatment Foster Care Team (2004) 'Multi-dimensional treatment foster care: implementation in England', Local Authority Social Services Letter LASSL (2004)5, Annex B, London: Department for Education and Skills/Department of Health.

Scully D. (1990) *Understanding Sexual Violence: A study of convicted rapists*, Boston: Unwin Hyman.

Shaw M. and Hipgrave T. (1983) *Specialist Fostering*, London: Batsford.

Sinclair I. and Gibbs I. (1998) *Children's Homes: A study in diversity*, Chichester: Wiley.

Sinclair I., Gibbs I. and Wilson K. (2000) *Supporting Foster Placements*, Report to the Department of Health, York: Social Work Research and Development Unit, University of York.

Sinclair I. and Wilson K. (2003) 'Matches and mismatches: the contribution of carers and children to the success of foster placements', *British Journal of Social Work*, 33, pp. 871–884.

Smith D. J. and McVie S. (2003) 'Theory and method in the Edinburgh study of youth transitions and crime', *British Journal of Criminology*, 43, pp. 169–195.

Smith P. M. (1986) 'Evaluation of Kent placements', *Adoption & Fostering,* 10:1, pp. 29–33.

Social Exclusion Unit (2002) *Reducing Re-offending by Ex-prisoners,* London: Office of the Deputy Prime Minister.

Stein M. and Carey K. (1986) *Leaving Care,* Oxford: Basil Blackwell.

Stewart A., Dennison S. and Waterson E. (2002) 'Pathways from child maltreatment to juvenile offending', *Trends and Issues in Crime and Criminal Justice No. 241,* Australian Institute of Criminology, www.aic.gov.au

Stone J. (1995) *Making Positive Moves: Developing short-term fostering services,* London: BAAF.

Sutherland E. H. and Cressey D. R. (1960) *Principles of Criminology,* Chicago: J. B. Lippincott.

Thomas S. (1998) 'Dealing with diversity – the Welsh perspective', www.scotland.gov.uk/cru/kd01/crime-12.htm

Thorpe D. (1983) 'Deinstitutionalization and justice', in Morris A. and Giller H. (eds) *Providing Criminal Justice for Children,* London: Edward Arnold.

Thorpe D. H., Smith D., Green C. J. and Paley J. H. (1980) *Out of Care: The community support of juvenile offenders,* London: Allen & Unwin.

Tonry M. (1994) 'Racial politics, racial disparities, and the war on crime', *Crime and Delinquency,* 40:4, pp. 475–494.

Tonry M. (2001) 'Unthought thoughts: the influence of changing sensibilities on penal policies', *Punishment and Society,* 3:1, pp. 167–181.

Triseliotis J. (1989) 'Foster care outcomes: a review of key research findings', *Adoption & Fostering,* 13, pp. 5–17.

Triseliotis J., Borland M., Hill M. and Lambert L. (1995a) *Teenagers and the Social Work Services,* London: HMSO.

Triseliotis J., Sellick C. and Short R. (1995b) *Foster Care: Theory and practice,* London: Batsford.

Tutt N. and Giller H. (1987) 'Manifesto for management – the elimination of custody', *Justice of the Peace,* 151, pp. 200–202.

United Nations (1989) *United Nations Convention on the Rights of the Child,* Geneva: United Nations.

Utting D. and Vennard J. (2000) *What Works with Young Offenders in the Community?,* Ilford: Barnardo's.

Vernon S. (2000) 'Magistrates in the youth court: teaching old "beaks" new tricks', in Pickford J (ed) *Youth Justice: Theory and practice*, London: Cavendish, pp. 75–97.

Wade J., Biehal N., Clayden J. and Stein M. (1998) *Going Missing: Young people absent from care*, Chichester: Wiley.

Walker M., Hill M. and Triseliotis J. (2002) *Testing the Limits of Foster Care*, London: BAAF.

Wates J. (2003) 'The view from the Bench', *Prison Report*, 60, 22.

Wells K. and D'Angelo L. (1994) 'Specialised foster care: voices from the field', *Social Services Review*, 68:1, pp. 127–144.

West D. and Farrington D. P. (1973) *Who Becomes Delinquent*, London: Heinemann.

West D. and Farrington D. P. (1977) *The Delinquent Way of Life*, London: Heinemann.

Weijers I. (1999) 'The double paradox of juvenile justice', *European Journal on Criminal Policy and Research*, 7, pp. 329–351.

Whitaker D., Cook J., Dunn C. and Rockcliffe S. (1985) *The Experience of Residential Care from the Perspectives of Children, Parents and Care Givers*, Final Report to the ESRC, York: University of York.

Winfield M. (1984) *Lacking Conviction – The remand system in England and Wales*, London: Prison Reform Trust.

Wright M. (2000) 'Repairing the harm of crime', *Howard League Magazine*, 18:2, p. 6.

Yelloly M. (1979) *Independent Evaluation of Twenty-Five Placements in the Kent Family Project*, Maidstone: Kent County Council.

Young J. (1971) 'The role of the police as amplifiers of deviancy, negotiators of reality and translators of fantasy', in Cohen S (ed) *Images of Deviance*, Harmondsworth: Penguin, pp. 27–61.

Youth Justice and Criminal Evidence Act 1999, London: The Stationery Office.

Youth Justice Board (2001a) 'Mental health concerns', *Youth Justice Board News*, *October*, p. 1.

Youth Justice Board (2001b) 'T Forms Guide: Guidance for completion', www.youth-justice-board.gov.uk/PractitionersPortal/Custody/

Youth Justice Board (2002) *Building on Success*, Youth Justice Board Review 2001/2002, London: Youth Justice Board.

Youth Justice Board (2005) *National Evaluation of the Bail Supervision and Support Schemes*, London: Youth Justice Board.

Zimring F. (1978) *Confronting Youth Crime*, New York: Holmes & Meier.

Zimring F. (2001) 'Imprisonment rates and the new politics of criminal punishment', *Punishment and Society*, 3:1, pp. 161–166.

Index

absconding
  likelihood 26, 214
  from remand foster care 75, 77–8,
    164–5
  placement disruption due to
    83, 224
  to rejoin friends 145
  from residential care 7
accommodation
  after care *see* move-on
    accommodation
  pre-fostering 73, 74
activities
  lack of
    custodial remand 2
    residential care 7
    in YOIs 128–9
  in placement 190–3
additional needs of young people
  197–8
adolescent behaviour 18–20, 228
  views of carers 189
adult courts, juveniles in 28, 105–6,
  213
adversities
  adolescent behaviours and 19–20
  in fostering referrals 62–3
  of girls 196
after-care 40, 206–7
  see also move-on accommodation
age
  at referral 68–9
  relevance in bail decisions 100
aggressive behaviour 185–6
agreements, written 34, 47
alcohol misuse
  bail support 32
  parental 115–16
  in placement 185
    placement breakdown 165–6
    re-offending 79
  prior to placement 120–3
alcohol use, in remand foster care
  154–5

anti-social behaviour 74
anxiety
  leaving placement 167–9
  placement commencement 132–4,
    219
Ashford Remand Centre 24
attitude of young people, in court 102
availability, remand foster care 41–3

bail
  decisions 27–8
    public protection 4–5
  failure to surrender to 5, 92
  presumption in favour of 24–5
  right to 215
    exceptions 69
Bail Act 1976 25, 69, 77
Bail (Amendment) Act 1993 25
"bail bandits" 17
bail conditions 76–7, 91–2, 148–50,
  187
  breaches of 76, 148–50, 229
  see also curfews; non-
    association conditions
bail support 8, 31–3
  availability 92, 219
  on drug misuse 154
  see also Youth Offending
    Teams (YOTs)
bail to family home 159–60
behaviour
  in placement 79–80
    changed by 211
    deterioration before sentence
      167
  at placement end 225
  post-placement 170–2
Bench Book 89, 90
birth parents, relationship with foster
  carers 199–200
black and minority ethnic children
  40, 63–4
breaches of bail conditions 76,
  148–50, 229

breakdown of placements *see*
  placement breakdowns
bullying
  in custody 2–3
  in residential care 6
  at school 117
  in secure accommodation 128, 157
  vulnerability to 197

care and control dilemma 10–11,
  145–6, 221–2
  re-offending in placement 188–9
case-file analysis 47–8
challenging behaviour
  carers' response to 181–7
  end of placement 75
  in interview 54
charges faced 64, 65, 84
  seriousness 67, 69, 127
  see also sex-related offences;
    violent offences
Child and Adolescent Mental Health
  Services (CAMHS) 72
child welfare, duty of foster carers
  222
child welfare training, foster carers
  178
children, remand provision 25–6
Children Act 1989
  extension of foster care 9
  on family life 215
  right to be consulted 44, 132
  secure accommodation orders 4,
    26
  welfare of the child 39
children in study *see* young people
Children (Leaving Care) Act 2000
  225
children of carers 165, 173, 202
  with fostered young people 165,
    184–5
children's homes
  experiences of 127, 156–7
  re-offending in 93, 156–7, 210
children's rights movement 43–4
Community Alternative Placement
  Scheme (CAPS) 10, 36–7
community-based remand 8–9, 27–8,
  30–42

advantages 14–15
life skills development 21
community links
  in bail decisions 67, 69
  damaged in custody 3–4
  effect on offending 32
  in remand foster care 38
conditions of bail *see* bail conditions
confidentiality
  in interviews 55
  in remand foster care 157–8
consent
  for remand foster care 132–4
  for research 49–50
court culture 104
court-ordered remand conditions *see*
  bail conditions
Crime and Disorder Act 1998 17, 25
Criminal Justice Act 1988 25
Criminal Justice Act 1991 1, 25, 41,
  108
Criminal Justice Act 1993 17, 25
Criminal Justice and Police Act 2001
  1, 17, 25
Criminal Justice and Public Order
  Act 1994 1, 17, 25
criminal justice system
  children's views 44–5
  foster care in 10–11, 222
  policy decisions 14–15
  previous experience 123–4
criminality, family members 116
Crown Prosecution Service (CPS)
  24–5, 103–5
curfews
  bail conditions 91, 148–50, 187
  re-offending on 78
  set by foster carers 148
custody
  consequences of 19, 21
  expansion of 13–16
  in history 24–5
  reductionist agenda 229
  remands in 1, 2–6, 97–8
  sentences 4–5, 23

data, analysis 59
decarceration 229–31
defence solicitors 101, 103–5, 187, 215

Detention and Training Order (DTO)
218
developmental approach to youth
crime 18–20
deviant behaviour
family culture 116
status in 39, 119–20
deviant identity 123–4
differential association
risks in custody 19
risks in residential care 6–7
difficult behaviour
carers' response to 181–7
end of placement 75
difficulties, at referral 62–3
disadvantaged young people, remand
decisions 212
disclosure, in interview 55
disruption of placements *see*
placement breakdowns
district judges 86n
domestic violence 67, 114–15
drug misuse 120–3
bail support 32
in remand foster care 153–5
re-offending 79
of remand prisoners 3

East Sussex Remand and Intensive
Lodging Scheme (RAILS) 38
education
bail decisions 30–1, 69
in placement 81–2, 151, 190–3,
223
pre-fostering 74–5, 116–18
for remand prisoners 2
in residential care 7
emotional abuse 68, 73, 112–14
emotional age 194–5
emotional distress, at placement end
167–9, 204–5
emotional support, need for 199
employment
bail decisions 30–1, 69
in placement 81–2, 151, 190–3
pre-fostering 20, 74–5
ethnicity
bail decisions 101
criminal justice system 20

issues in fostering 174n
in placements 40, 73
see also black and minority
ethnic children
excitement, motivation for crime
123–4
exclusion zones, bail conditions 91
exercise, lack of on remand 2
expectations, written agreements 34,
47

failure to surrender to bail 5, 92
familial deprivation 20
family characteristics
criminality 32, 116
offending behaviour 112–14
family home
bail to 159–60
return to by LA 26
family life, in remand foster care 39
family relationships
alcohol misuse 122
background 112–14
damaged in custody 3–4
difficulties 32
management of 198–200
in placement 82
pressure to offend 143, 166
at referral 63
during remand 146–8
support in foster care 220
female young people *see* girls
financial issues for foster carers
176–7, 218
foster care, extension of 9
foster carers
boundary setting 229
caring strategies 137–40, 179–82
characteristics 137–40, 141–2
demographic profile 174–5
holistic care 228–9
interviews with 46, 56–7
matching to young people 216–17
motivation 175–6
parenting styles 179–82, 221
potential risk to 71–2
pre-placement information 203–4
relationship with birth parents
199–200

relationship with young people
80–1, 137–40
reports in sentencing 109, 150
sensitivity at settling in 135–7
shortage of 214, 216–19
support for 34, 47, 201–3
by RFOs 163–4
training 41, 177–9, 201–2
fostering service regulations 158, 160
friends, removal from 144–5

gender
juvenile offending 21–2
magistrates' bail decisions 101
in placement success 57
and referral 68–9
remand provision 25–6
girls
health care needs 198
offending by 21
in placements 195–7, 216–17
difficulties 57
referred to scheme 63
remand provision 25–6
in residential care 7
guilty knowledge, of interviewer 55

health care, in remand foster care
158–9, 198
homelessness
after placement 169
pre-arrest 70
pre-fostering 73, 74
Homelessness Act 2002 225

identity
creation in interview 55
deviant 123–4
individualised care 38–9, 158, 180,
220–1
intensive supervision and
surveillance programme (ISSP)
218–19
inter-agency working 160–3, 200–1
background information 203–4
review meetings 161–3, 201, 223
interview format 50–3
interview records 54–6, 56
interviewer, implicit power of 54–5

interviews 48–58
with foster carers 56–7
with magistrates 57–8
qualitative 56–7
with young people 53–6
introductions, carers/young people
40, 132–5, 204, 215

juvenile offending
developmental approach 18–20
gender 21–2
public perception 17–18
race and ethnicity 20

Kent Family Placement Project 34–5,
142

leisure activities see activities
life skills 21
development 32, 39, 191
listening skills 142, 178, 182–3
local authority residential care see
residential care
location, foster placement 141, 143
looked after children 112–13
absconding 77–8
adolescent offending 63
educational provision 152
gender in 68
placement disruption 83
in residential care 6

magistrates 86–7
bail decisions 27–8, 212–14
factors in 67, 91–105
interviews with 57–8
political pressures on 106–7
training 88–90
views on children's homes 211
media, on juvenile crime 17
meetings, professional agencies see
inter-agency working
mental health problems
in custodial remand 3
fostering decisions 71–2, 73
lack of support for 160
in residential care 7
mental health services, lack of 223,
228

minority ethnic origin *see* black and minority ethnic children
mitigation, in sentencing 108–9
motivation for crime 123–4
money 120, 122, 123
move-on accommodation 40, 206–7
lack of 167–9, 224, 225–7

narrative interviews 50–3
National Minimum Standards and Fostering Services Regulations 2002 158, 160
National Remand Review Initiative (NRRI) 28
neighbours of carers 202
non-association conditions 76, 145, 147
non-secure accommodation 6–8, 93, 156–7
normalisation 142, 221
nurturing carers 180–3, 221
on re-offending 188–9

offence, seriousness of 5, 99
offending behaviour
  drug misuse and 120, 122
  educational status 81
  family characteristics 112–14
  patterns 127
  peer relationships 118–20
  rationalisation 124–5
  school exclusion and 116–18
  see also re-offending
offending on bail
  bail support 31–2
  remand foster care 35, 78–9
  end of placement 75–6
  placement disruption 83
  placement evaluation 210
  in residential care 7
  risk 5
Oregon Social Learning Center 35–6, 37
outcomes
  bail decisions 64–7
  CAPS project 37
  custodial sentence 4–5, 23
  evaluation of 209–12
  remand foster care 170–2

  see also placement breakdowns
  treatment foster care 36

parenting styles, foster carers 179–82
parents
  alcohol abuse 115–16
  consent for research 49–50
  payment, study participation 59
peer groups 78–9, 190
  drug misuse 121–2
  offending behaviour 118–20
  removal from 144–5, 190
peer relationships 118–20
  problems in 117, 118, 157
penal reform, needs for 13–16
persistent young offenders 17, 64
personal identity 55
  deviant 123–4
physical abuse 68, 73, 114–15
placement agreements *see* written agreements
placement breakdowns 40, 75, 164–9
  evaluation of 209–10
  factors in 82–4, 224
  perception in bail decisions 95–6
placement endings 164–9, 204–6, 224–5
  see also time-limited placements
placements 46–7, 75–6
  absconding from 77–8
  matching carers/young people 216–17
  outcomes 77, 209–12
  pre-placement information 203–4
  settling in 135–7
police, contact with 125
Police and Criminal Evidence Act 1984 (PACE) 25, 135
police bail 23
political agenda
  background 13–22
  impact on judiciary 106–7
  reductionist agenda needed 230–1
  in research 12
  status of offenders 44
political attitudes, towards young offenders 16–18

post-conviction remands 23
post-sentence difficulties 10
pre-sentence reports 150–1
prevention of reoffending, failure of custody 2
Prisons Act 1865 24
Prisons Act 1877 24
privacy
  in foster care 137
  lack of in secure units 157
professional agencies *see* inter-agency working
prosecution 24–5, 103–5
public attitudes, to young offenders 16–18, 106
public protection
  bail decisions 4–5, 27–8
  care and control dilemma 145–6
  crime control policy 17–18
  custodial remands 98
  re-offending in placement 189
  remand foster care 210
Pupil Referral Units 117, 118

qualitative/quantitative data 59

racism 20
RAILS (East Sussex Remand and Intensive Lodging Scheme) 38
rationalisation of crime 124–5
re-offending
  post-placement 170
  prevention 151
  in remand foster care 143–4, 166, 188–90
recidivism 14, 125n
reductionist agenda 11–12, 13–16, 229–31
referrals 62–7
regulatory carers 180–3, 221
rehabilitation 230
  community-based remand 30–1
  in foster care 228–9
rejection, feelings of 112, 113, 166, 200
relationships
  foster carers/birth parents 199–200
  foster carers/young people 80–1, 137–40

difficulties 164–5
  see also family relationships
remand
  community-based 30–42
  compliance with previous orders 100
  conditions *see* bail conditions
  to custody *see* custodial remands
remand decisions 23–4
  criteria 99–102
  difficulties 87–8
  disadvantaged young people 212
  young people's involvement in 132–5
  see also bail conditions
remand foster care 8–9, 172–3
  availability 41–3
  benefits 38–40, 79–82, 172–3, 212, 220–1, 227–8, 230
  breakdowns *see* placement breakdowns
  establishment of 9–11
  history of 33–7
  management 42
  outcomes 209–12
  preparation for 132–5
  problems 39–40
  reception in 220
  refused by young person 66
  as residence condition 94
  schemes 28
  young people's initial experiences 131–42
  young person refused by scheme 71
remand foster care placements *see* placements
remand foster carers *see* foster carers
remand fostering officers (RFOs) 47, 59, 163–4, 202
  needed at placement end 225
remand legislation 24–5
remand period, length of 23–4
remand prisoners, in history 24
remand provision
  children and young people 25–6
  knowledge of 90–1
remand to local authority accommodation (RLAA) 25–6, 92–7

remorse for crime 124–5
reparation, by adolescents 21
research
  aims 11–12, 45–6
  analysis 59–60
  bias potential 58, 60
  case-file analysis 47–8
  interviews 48–58, 50–3
  involvement of children 44–5
  methodology 46–7
  parameters 60
  participant selection 48–9
  sample size 60
  theoretical perspective 43–5
research summary 209–31
residence, pre-arrest 70
residence conditions 91, 94
residential care 156–9
  bail decision 6–8, 25–6, 64–7
  compared to remand foster care
    156–9
  disadvantages 39
review meetings see inter-agency
  working
RFOs see remand fostering officers
  (RFOs)
RLAA (remand to local authority
  accommodation) 25–6, 92–7
running away see absconding

Saturday courts 105–6
school exclusion 116–18
  anti-social behaviour and 74
  offending peer groups 118–20
Scottish Community Alternative
  Placement Scheme (CAPS) 36–7
secure accommodation 6–8, 157
  bail decisions 25–6, 64–7
  experience of 127–8
  girls in 57
  magistrates' powers 97
  reception in 219–20
  reductionist agenda 229
  YJB statistics 1
security requirement, on RLAA 26
self-esteem, boosted 137–8, 181,
  183–4, 191, 193, 227–8
self-harm 68
  pre-arrest 71, 73

reduced in foster care 197, 220
  in residential care 7
  risk of 26
  in secure units 2–3, 127
sentences
  effect of 125
  effect of remand decisions 107–9
  impact of foster care 226–7
  pre-sentence reports 150–1
seriousness of the offence 5, 99
sex-related offences
  attitude of carers 139
  remand foster care 95, 100, 197,
    216
  suitability for 71–2
  vulnerability on remand 6
social deprivation 20
social research, aims of 12
social services
  at moving-on 168–9
  in remand fostering 42, 47
social workers 160–1
  shortage 200–1
special needs of young people
  197–8
specialist foster care 35–7
status, in deviant behaviour 39,
  119–20
statutory agencies 125–6
stigmatisation
  custodial remand 2
  in residential care 6
street age 194–5
suicide attempts
  at moving-on 207
  pre-arrest 71, 73
support
  for foster carers 34, 201–3, 217
  at placement end 204–6, 225
  for young people 220–1, 226
Sweden, foster care programme 34, 142
systems management approach 16n

theft, placement disruption 83
time-limited placements 34, 37, 39,
  46–7, 95, 164
  endings 167–9, 206–7
training
  remand foster carers 33

youth magistrates 28
treatment foster care 35–7
truanting 117, 118

United Nations Convention on the
    Rights of the Child (UNCRC) 1989
    on community remand schemes 8
    on custodial remands 4
    promotion of self-worth 138
    on removal of child from family
        home 215
    right to be consulted 44, 132
    right to good health care 160
    on welfare of the child 39
USA
    treatment foster care 35–6
    youth justice reforms 15

violence, in secure units 127–8
violent behaviour 185
    in placement 165–6, 203
violent offences
    alcohol and 122–3
    placements 216
    remand foster care 95, 100
violent offenders, unsuitability for
    fostering 71–2
vulnerability
    in alcohol misuse 122
    in bail decisions 70–1, 73, 100–1,
        212
    benefits of foster care 197–8
    care and control dilemma 145–6
    remand provision 25–6, 27
    in residential care 39
    in sentencing 108

welfare of the child principle 39, 70
welfare system, foster care in 10–11
written agreements 34, 47
written reports
    inter-agency meetings 163
    pre-sentence 150–1

Young Offender Institutions (YOIs)
    reception in 136, 219

remand provision 2–3, 25–6
violence in 128–9
young offenders
    cultural status 44
    public and political attitudes
        towards 16–18
young people
    agency support 47
    attitude in court 102
    background information 48, 203–4
    childhood 111–16
    offending history 123–4
    characteristics of 62–85
    coping strategies needed 224–5
    at inter-agency meetings 161–3
    moving-on 206–7
    placement
        behaviour in 79–80
        commitment to 186–7
        rejection of 66
        relationship with carers 80–1
    post-placement 170–2
    remand provision 25–6
    in research 44–6
        consent 49–50
        interviews with 53–6
        selection for study 48–9
    unsuitable for fostering 71–3
    see also girls
youth courts
    bail decisions 28
    bench guidelines 89–90, 99
youth crime see juvenile crime
Youth Justice and Criminal Evidence
    Act 1999 25
Youth Justice Board (YJB) 1, 218
Youth Offending Teams (YOTs)
    bail support 26, 31–2, 47, 160–1
    failures in 163
    in court 94, 101, 103–5, 213–14
    education officer 192
    needed at placement end 225
    remand management 8–9, 42
    reports in sentencing 109
    staff shortage 200–1
    in study 59